"If My Holy Mother and Holy St Joseph had kept Me to themselves while I was on earth, how would My people  have come to know Me, how could I have touched the hearts of so many. Oh child, pray for all who are not listening, do not want to listen.

Please, please I ask to be released from prison. Child, it is so important for these times, these terrible times."

26th September 1993

Kolbe Publishing
November 1999

Learning to be We(e)

MESSAGES OF LOVE
FROM THE
HEART of JESUS & MARY

Volume II

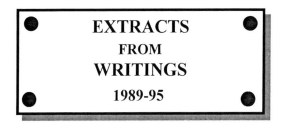

EXTRACTS
FROM
WRITINGS
1989-95

FOR

PRIESTS

AND THE

FAITHFUL

TO

ROSE

DURING EUCHARISTIC ADORATION

Learning to be We(e)

Volume II

The Decree of the Congregation for the
Propagation of the Faith,
A.A.S. 58, 1186
(approved by Pope Paul VI
on October 14, 1966)
states that

The Nihil Obstat and Imprimatur are no
longer required on writings that deal with
private revelations, provided that they
contain nothing contrary to faith or
morals.

ISBN 0-9529627-3-X

KOLBE PUBLISHING
9 NORTH MAIN STREET
CORK
REPUBLIC OF IRELAND

MESSAGES OF LOVE
FROM THE
HEART of JESUS & MARY

FOREWORD

Rose was a very ordinary housewife and mother like every other woman trying to look after a home and striving in the practice of her religion. She came into contact with the Charismatic Renewal when she went to the Conference in the R.D.S. in September 1976.

When she saw the people there praising God, she said to herself, if only I could pray like these people all my cares and anxieties would be over. She then started attending the prayer meeting at Eustace Street and received the Baptism of the Spirit.

She wanted so much to be able to tell others the good news, she could not stand up before people and share because she was too nervous as she grew up and still had a slight stammer and could not write because she had no command of words. But one morning she asked the Holy Spirit to give her the words to write down some of the teachings, the following morning this personal diary

"Learning to be We(e)" began.

Learning to be We(e)

Volume II

CONTENTS

EXTRACTS FROM WRITINGS

EXTRACTS FROM WRITINGS
1989

"My child, a new era in your life starts now.

Now you carry My Eucharistic Presence with you at all times, wherever you go.

I created the Eucharist that I would be a living presence in the world for all at all times. I am kept away, buried, hidden behind closed doors away from My people. Now My power will become manifested in the world when My priests bring Me to and before My people everywhere.

My child, I am more than an icon, picture, idol. I am a living presence in the world. I am in all things because all was created by Me. But I want My Presence, My Eucharistic Presence to be available and at the disposal of all who need Me, seek Me, desire Me. **Through this living presence you will destroy the power of Satan in your midst.** You will see the power of My Eucharistic Presence manifested everywhere My Presence is recognised, loved, believed, honoured, glorified.

I will teach you the power of My Presence, the love that emanates from this Presence as you carry Me on your person. I want you to bring Me with you wherever you go at all times, to all places. I do not expect that you will be mindful of Me at all times but you will learn to love Me more, depend on Me, call on Me, abide with Me.

Through this Presence I will touch others, relate to others. My child, it will complement your daily Eucharist. You will not have to go places to seek Me, to find Me, to pray before My Eucharistic Presence. You will have Me with you always.

It is not possible for the human mind to understand this."

11th. May 1989

1ˢᵗ January 1989
<u>Feast of the Solemnity of Mary, Mother of God :</u>

Mary, I come to you this day in my weakness, battered, broken in my brokenness, not the way to start the new year but Mary, you know that the early morning is my time of suffering now. You did not escape suffering either and mine is nothing to yours but at least I can relate and offer mine with yours and through you to Jesus.

Mary, help me not to dwell on my sufferings but on the myriad gifts and blessings I have received from the good God, and that He has prepared for each one of us this year and for our country specially. How wonderful and mercifully He has treated us the past year and down all the years. We have escaped all the catastrophes that have befallen other countries and we have failed to give thanks and count our blessings.

6ᵗʰ January 1989 - Feast of the Epiphany : First Friday
<u>Before the Blessed Sacrament :</u>

My Beloved, to have You to myself again, this speaks to my heart. I know You will tell me Your need in Your own time.

Today was a very special day in our home when we were young, we kept it as a little Christmas. It is also a very special day to me now. Mary help me to receive and welcome the King of Kings into my heart this day when He comes to me in the Eucharist. I need Him, more and more each day. My thirst grows also as my physical, mental and spiritual needs increase to live out 'the wonder of my being and the wonders of all your creation', during the remainder of my life on earth, to bring about my own purification to fulfil Your need of me and for others.

My Beloved, I thank You for yesterday and I know I express the thanks of all who visited You here yesterday. Oh the blessings and peace You shared with us all to begin and live the new year through You, with You, in You, knowing that You call us together for a purpose.

Every Thursday has now become a little Epiphany. Your little ones come, with their gifts of love in their hearts, to give homage to You for the gift of Yourself to all in the Eucharist.

Before the Blessed Sacrament at the hospital:

"My child, I provide for your every need, day and night. Maura is in My arms resting on My Heart, beating away her last days. My child, I am preparing you also for the joy I have prepared for her. She will be another intercessor when I take her to Myself. You will be aware of her influence in your life and work."

9ᵗʰ February 1989
Before the Blessed Sacrament :

"My child, I need you to write, My child, I need you to write for My priests, My bishops, My religious. All are in need, in great need in these troubled times. Many false doctrines abound amidst My representatives. My gospel has been watered down. My gospel is not being preached as it was written by Me. Oh My child, you have much work ahead of you to bring My present needs to My people. There is disunity amongst the leaders. My people are being scattered everywhere. At times they are like sheep without a shepherd. My shepherds are being got at by the evil forces that try to destroy them, to take from Me My children whom I died for, died dearly, completely, giving everything I possessed to My very life. My child give Me your attention on this day. I need you My child. My Mother will help you to acquire the inner silence you will need to abandon yourself to Me. My child, you have very important work to do for Me, but do not be afraid My child, remember I do not ask anything of My little ones that I do not give the strength to go with it. Today, more strangers come to your home. My child the flow of people will continue to grow. The prayers and dedication of My people will give Me much glory. Oh My child, I cannot reveal to you even a little of what happens here on this day each week, but take My Word My little one that We receive great comfort and consolation here in a world that rejects Us. But for the little ones, the Father would be very angry indeed. You will see that the religious will find a peace here that they will not find in their own communities.

Oh My child, do not disappoint Me. I hate to see you leave Me, but I know I must not be selfish, but I have called you specially into this ministry. Remember I once told you that you would be a 'Carmel' living in the world. A Carmel is a person I call to Myself in a special way, not normally living outside the cloister walls. So you see My little one how much I need you. I will make the changes within you I need. Just be open to My Spirit and My Mother. They will lead and guide you. Remember you are nothing on your own but nothing is impossible to Me."

22nd February 1989
<u>Before the Blessed Sacrament :</u>

My Beloved, You are truly teaching us the power and love that emanates here in Your Eucharistic Presence. My Beloved, if others could only see the power You reveal to us, how they would flock to You in all their needs. Here You are most vulnerable, here You are most humble, here You are most loving, here we touch Your Heart in a way that You cannot hide Yourself from us, You cannot but reveal Yourself as a God of Infinite Love.

And now my Beloved, as I prepare for the Eucharist, may my heart be open to receive all You prepare for me and the response You seek from me. May my heart be open to give all You ask. But Beloved, I have nothing to give but what I receive from You.

Oh Mary give me your heart to come through you, I seek only to please Him, fulfil His desire for me at this wedding feast. I am very far from perfection but He knows my struggle, my yearning to be perfect for His sake. May this Eucharist and every Eucharist take me a step nearer my Beloved to make the prayer of Jesus in John 17, a living reality in my daily life.

The Lord's Prayer for me this day :

Our Father, God, Trinity, who art in heaven and on earth and within us all. Thy Kingdom come within us. Thy will be done on earth and within us as it is in heaven. Give us this day our daily bread and give us the grace to forgive others as you forgive us our trespasses. Let us not go into temptation. But deliver us from all the evil of original sin and from our own sinfulness and from all the evil forces around us that seek to destroy us. Amen.

3rd March 1989 - First Friday
Before the Blessed Sacrament :

"I will lead you now, this is My opening for a further plan in your life." (*He confirms an idea that occurs to me.*)

"I use every situation as I use every little particle of the Host.

Pray now, pray often. Today is special, do not fail Me. Do not fail My need of you this day.

Make reparation this day for the humiliations and rejections suffered by My Sacred Heart, My Eucharistic Heart."

4th March 1989
Before the Blessed Sacrament :
Mary:

"Hearts must be simple and open to be able to reveal Our wisdom and knowledge."

"My child, I waited, waited, now you are here. Together we will prepare for the marriage feast about to take place. Every Eucharist is a great feast, a great festival, such a celebration of the love of My divine Son for all His children everywhere, past, present and to come. My child, We can only reveal so little to you at one time. You are too small, too little but We delight in telling Our secrets to the weak and lowly. Remember child, feelings do not matter. The Eucharist is above and beyond all feelings of the human heart. We look into the hearts of Our little ones. We see all, We know all, We respond to all within. Our little one, you start a new learning on this day, a new insight into this great mystery about to take place. We must tell someone to tell others, particularly the learned who often block our way into their hearts. Hearts must be simple and open to be able to reveal Our wisdom and knowledge. Oh how We seek open hearts in those We place in charge of Our people. So often they do not listen nor hear Us. So We come to the weak, unlearned in the way of human knowledge of church affairs, canon law etc. We move beyond into the realm of the Spirit, this We will bring to these writings, little one of Our choosing. My Son gives you to me to prepare, by much prayer and dedication, first for the daily Eucharist and sitting before the Eucharistic Presence. Through your faithfulness you have brought many into this way of prayer, more than you can ever imagine or dream about. So Our little one, rest now, listen to Us in your heart. I will help you through My Immaculate Heart to persevere in the mighty task We have prepared for you. Type these past few messages and bring all to your parish priest. He will respond to your need. We prepare him."

23ʳᵈ March 1989
Holy Thursday :
My Beloved, it was not as I expected but You have to keep reminding me. It is through our own suffering and brokenness related to Yours we begin to realise a little of Your Love. It was out of and because of Your greatest sacrifice and suffering about to take place on this night that You left mankind the greatest gift of Yourself. And it is only when we can touch this suffering can we see the cost of this great sacrament, that so often we take for granted, become indifferent at times and even disrespectful. You knew it all dearest One when You gave it to us, Your own Body and Blood under the appearance of bread and wine, yet it did not deter You. You saw all, accepted all on this night of supreme love to go beyond bounds that man could never imagine nor hope for. And as each succeeding generation continues to draw on this great miracle of love, Your thirst for man's response increases as You desire grows and all the rebuffs, blasphemies, sacrileges committed by man cannot lessen not stay this memorial of Your passion, death and resurrection.

28ᵗʰ March 1989
Later before the Blessed Sacrament :
"My child, I bring you back again to continue the writing. Be open, be free. I come to confirm the messages My Mother has already brought to My people everywhere and still continues in different places. During these days of the novena to My Divine Mercy, put

I come to confirm the messages My Mother has already brought to My people everywhere and still continues in different places.

your heart into this prayer for My church, My people. During these days many hearts will be healed and converted. Many heresies and errors will be healed through the prayers of My people. These are My ways of bringing to light My needs. The ordinary liturgy of the church, lived and exercised, helps to keep My people faithful and true to My teachings and gives great graces. My people need to be encouraged and reminded to take part in the living of the liturgy each day, the teaching of My Word. Each reading of the day is My living word for the day. It is part of the Eucharist, a vital part and some comments by way of explanation would not be amiss, even vital to My people. Much prayer of preparation is necessary for the daily Eucharist to be made a living sacrifice and celebration of the paschal mystery. The Mass is all, everything to the people who believe.

MY PRIESTS, YOU ALONE CAN BRING AND PASS ON THIS FAITH TO MY PEOPLE.

It is the one exercise that unites all, everywhere throughout the world. You alone can stand in My place to bring My humanity and My Divinity to all. And as I expose Myself to you here My children in the Blessed Sacrament, I am the fullest expression of My Love for each one of you. Do not reject Me. Respect Me in the pinnacle of My humility and vulnerability. I ask so little. Just Be in Me. I give all. I am."

7ᵗʰ April 1989 – Early morning during the vigil :
Before the Blessed Sacrament:

"This is My night of ultimate love and extreme pain. My children, I gather you here this night to lessen the pain of My Love for each and everyone. My children, My very special children, Oh how I thank each and everyone of you who helped to console Me on this night. How I long to gather My children around Me when I am exposed in My Eucharistic Presence. My children, you can never know in this life in your present state the power of this presence in the world, in each of your lives and all you carry in your hearts. My Love is beyond the understanding of man at all times but here in My Exposed Presence I long to reveal Myself, take you to Myself as you are before you have died to this world in your present human existence."

10ᵗʰ April 1989: "My people, My children, all My little ones look forward with hope to a new time of peace. My exposed presence will bring about a new light in this land. This new movement has begun, it will gather more momentum to spread throughout the country, then My child, you will see that I am faithful to My promises, all the promises I have given you in the past. My child, you saw the way My Spirit worked in your home last Thursday night, the simplicity of the workings of My plan, the gentle way I fulfil My needs, the gentleness of My touch on the hearts of My little ones who responded so readily to My call, My need that night. This is only the beginning My child, from your house a light will shine, My light will spread, My light will be seen over your city. All the lights, such lights will spread to cover the entire land. Be prepared, be open, all will have a part in this plan of Mine." 1 John 1.

> What was from the beginning,
> What we have heard,
> What we have seen with our eyes,
> What we have looked upon
> And touched with our hands
> Concerns the Word of life -

17ᵗʰ April 1989 - Before the Eucharist
Before the Blessed Sacrament :
"Listen to My voice My child. Listen to My voice this day. I spoke these words to you many years ago. (Gospel Reading : John 10. 1-10). I speak them to you again this day. They will have a deeper meaning for your now. I have been preparing you for this moment of time. My child, you must build on the hope I give you. My Church was built on hope. My people are a people of hope. Do not let this gift slip from you. Come walk the path to victory with Me. I am preparing this land, its people for the days ahead. I need My people to be filled with My hope. Hope is a foretaste of the victory about to take place. Remember child, 'I am the Shepherd who comes that you might have life - life in all its fullness'. It does not exclude

suffering, suffering with Me but you will have My peace within you to exclude all darkness. My child, the words you write for Me are words of hope. You must have this hope within you also. My child, have you not learned a little of My Love here present in the Eucharist, of My love for you. How I esteem you, wait for you, long for you, desire to fulfil your every need. Oh My child, never doubt My Love, build on My love to become My love. Oh My child, for each and everyone I have prepared a special place. My child, I have great designs for you prepared within My Heart. Do not fail Me, My little one. Do I not know all, see all My child? Do I not want to share with you, take from you all that hurts, wounds My little one? But My child look into My Heart, take a look, a peep at My poor bruised and broken Heart. How hurt and wounded I am by My own dear children. My child touch My wounded Heart by entering in. I have made a space for you to enter. Oh My child and all My little ones who grieve, hurt, suffer with Me, enter in to the depths of My Heart, reserved for all those who suffer with Me, suffer My pain in the world. Oh My children, let Me bind your wounds, heal your wounds in Mine. Renew your hope, renew your love as you prepare for the coming Eucharist.

Here My child you will know, you may not feel My healing Love but believe My little one in this healing Love of Mine in the Eucharist. My child I cannot show you yet all I prepare for you, you are not ready but come My child, give Me all, everything as We unite in the communion of Our oneness in this Sacrament of Love."

4ᵗʰ May 1989
Feast of the Ascension :
My Beloved, words fail me the way You brought so many people to my home this day. It was no wonder that my spirit was filled with Your excitement this morning, so many to come in answer to Your call on this great feast day that is also the eve of the first Friday.

My Beloved, I pray that we will continue to fulfil Your need through the night. Always You give so much and ask so little. Thank You for the peace You give to all who answer Your call.

Today I learn to appreciate the gift of the Eucharist a little more, a little more the cost of this Sacrament of Love, the Sacrament of Humiliation. Now I realise a little better the meaning of those words that You spoke to my heart many years ago as the priest raised the bread and wine at the consecration and pronounced the words, 'This is My Body, This is the chalice of My Blood'. My spirit was to hear, 'This is the pinnacle of My Humiliation'. Oh dearest One how loath we are to accept the least humiliation, how alien to the human heart, so difficult to die to self. Dearest One, help me, heal me in this area that I need so much healing.

Mary, we come to rosary time again. Help us to pray this rosary with love and sincerity in our hearts for the sake of your Divine Son.

11ᵗʰ May 1989
Just before the last rosary :

"My child, My little one, I waited till now to answer your letter. Thank you for this day, for welcoming My little ones. I brought them here to fulfil a need of mine. I moved R.... to pray in the way she did. They received a special blessing here this day and brought a special blessing on this house. My Son and I have great plans for this place. We are gathering Our little ones to pray before the Blessed Sacrament. We use your place. Do not be fearful. They come, all the strangers, on our prompting. Do not be disturbed that many come seeking messages and signs. All will be well. Let them not disturb you. Feel secure in our Love. Our Love is in control. We move in Love amongst our little ones now. Thank you Our children for your welcome. We will lead and guide you all. We will lead you and be present to you in a special way in this rosary."

Kieran's First Communion

Kieran has many gifts
Give thanks to the Lord.
Kieran has many attributes
Give thanks to the Lord.
Jesus is with him always

At home, at school, at play
Seeing all, knowing all
Touching all in His loving way.

Today is the day of days
Jesus comes to give Himself
In a special way, a total way
To all His precious little ones.
Jesus' Heart is full of longing
Waiting for each one,
For that response that only
A little child can give.

Dear Mother Mary, thank you that I was able to attend the First Communion Mass of my grandchild, Kieran. It was an occasion of great joy and glory for your Son, to share Himself with so many little eager and longing hearts for the first time. Mary, teach us to have the same longing in our hearts each time we receive.

Before the Eucharist :

"My child, a new era in your life starts now. Now you carry My Eucharistic Presence with you at all times, wherever you go. I created the Eucharist that I would be a living presence in the world for all at all times. I am kept away, buried, hidden behind closed doors away from My people. Now My power will become manifested in the world when My priests bring Me to and before My people everywhere.

My child, I am more than an icon, picture, idol. I am a living presence in the world. I am in all things because all was created by Me. But I want My Presence, My Eucharistic Presence to be available and at the disposal of all who need Me, seek Me, desire Me. Through this living presence you will destroy the power of Satan in your midst. You will see the power of My Eucharistic Presence manifested everywhere My Presence is recognised, loved, believed, honoured, glorified. I will teach you the power of My Presence, the love that emanates from this Presence as you carry Me on your person. I want you to bring Me with you wherever you go at all times, to all places. I do not expect that you will be mindful of Me at all times but you will learn to love Me more, depend on Me, call on Me, abide with Me. Through this Presence I will touch others, relate to others. My child, it will complement your daily Eucharist. You will not have to go places to seek Me, to find Me, to pray before My Eucharistic Presence. You will have Me with you always. It is not possible for the human mind to understand this."

MY THIRST FOR PRIESTS

Who shall ever know
Who shall ever understand
This Thirst within Me
Tormenting Me ?

This Thirst I carry
Infinite, constant, everlasting,
Deeper and more painful
Than My Thirst upon the cross.

Oh My priests, My chosen ones
I give you all, each and everyone
You take My place
At the altar of sacrifice.

My priests, within My Heart
There is a space
Reserved for you alone
My needs to fulfil.

My priests, I wait and wait
While the attractions of the world
Take over to absorb the heart and mind
I am forgotten and pushed aside.

It's you I need and seek
You alone can quench this Thirst
I carry in My Heart
Reserved for you.

How I long that you might long
For that time of fulfilment
When heaven and earth become one
With My humanity and divinity
At the altar of all graces.

1ˢᵗ June 1989

Yes My priests are truly My spouses.

I can more easily accept the weaknesses and failings of My little ones, My little children.

The privileges I give My priests:
My strength is their strength,
My Love is their love,
My power is their power.
I have gifted them above all others.

Oh My priests, how you disappoint Me, fail Me, hurt Me, humiliate Me by your actions at times and then come to My altar and stand in My sandals to change the bread and wine into My Body and Blood.

To bring to fruition all the Old Testament,
live and pray the New Testament.

Take My power upon you,
repeat My incarnation, passion, death resurrection,
the Alpha and the Omega.

My beloved priests, turn to Me.

I need you more than you can ever know or understand.

Take My word, accept My invitation that I issue day by day.

8ᵗʰ June 1989:   *My Beloved, may the healing rays emanating from your Eucharistic presence here now heal the cancers within my spirit, that I have allowed fester and grow over the years, to be burned and destroyed, and a new growth of the Spirit take its place. Though the treatment may be difficult and painful, help me to keep my heart and mind on the final outcome.*

15ᵗʰ June 1989:   "All My followers suffer My sufferings in one way or another. Their sufferings help to bring about the salvation of other souls. My child, My Mother has much to say to her children. She weeps because of Me and My sufferings, My people reject My Love. She tries all and every means to entice My children back through repentance to conversion and a life of prayer. Much of what she sees can be eliminated through the prayers of My children.

My child, when My children gather together in unity before My Eucharistic presence, many souls are touched to find their way back to repentance. Believe this My children. It will help to sustain you in your tiredness and dryness at prayer and to persevere."

15ᵗʰ June 1989:
(It happened that I was alone for a very short time at adoration.)

In the quiet of the evening
All is still,
Jesus waits,
His needs to be fulfilled.

Alone on His throne
Waiting on man,
Comforted by the angels.

Oh My children,
My precious children,
Welcome, welcome, welcome,
My Heart overflows.

I cannot contain My Love,
Come share My Love,
Relieve My pain.

Oh the pain of Love unrequited
Haunts Me, torments Me,
Bleeds My Heart.

Oh My children, I cannot show you,
I cannot make you understand,
I cannot burden you.

But the day will come
When all will be revealed
My Heart open
For all to see.

11ᵗʰ July 1989
Before the Blessed Sacrament :

My Beloved, I am reminded of the prayer you spoke to my heart many years ago : May my tears wash the windows of my soul that I may all the better look in and let You look out.

Oh my Beloved, here in Your Eucharistic Presence, I become aware at times of all this taking place. Will it ever end my Beloved? - the tears that open up all the impurities of my sinful heart and soul. Now I remember another prayer You spoke to my heart : I believe, increase my faith in boundless hope for perfect charity - and I find the consolation I need for this moment to realise all the pain we cause ourselves because of our lack of trust in You. Trust, trusting always in Your Infinite Love and perfect will in our daily lives will always help to lift our despairing hearts out of the pit of despair and temptations we encounter as we try to follow in Your footsteps.

22ⁿᵈ July 1989   -   Feast of St. Mary Magdalen
Paray-Le-Monial - After the Eucharist
Before the Blessed Sacrament :

Oh My Beloved.

Another day in this place of prayer. Thank you.

My Beloved, I cannot take part this year in the teachings - my body is tired. My Spirit is restless - help me to open my heart to Yours in the Blessed Sacrament and I know You will speak to me.

May my tears wash the windows of my soul that I may all the better look in and let You look out.

As I rewrote Your message of yesterday - it came to me that this message was for all your people who have come on pilgrimage at this time. My Beloved, I know you will send your Holy Mother to me to direct me this day. My Beloved, I know you have called me here to be a witness to your love and power, but first I need your Spirit to empty myself of all self-interest - give me a realisation of my nothingness, that I may give all the glory to You. You know my weaknesses, my temptations.

Mary, I want to please Jesus in all I do - You know His plan and need of me for this day. Mary help me to fulfil His need of me. St. Margaret Mary pray for me.

"My Child, I have My plan already prepared for you this day. Give this writing to your leader. I will direct him what to do - I want you to witness to the power of My Eucharistic Presence in this holy place. I called you here to begin your public ministry. My Child, your body is frail, very frail, but I will be your Strength. Do not fear - without Me you would collapse under the strain, but My Mother and I take care of you. The evil one will try and dissuade you - you will stand on the forum and give witness to My Love. I will put the words into your mouth. You will read My message for this session."

<u>23rd July 1989:</u>   "My Child, the Eucharist is your strength - there you will receive "My Love, My strength, My hope, My comfort for each day. You will be given an understanding that not many of My own chosen ones have ever received - pray always for the Celebrant. I have given you a special ministry for My priests. Your example will help My religious also. You will return from here truly blessed - I will be your strength in all I ask of you, take from you. My Child, trust Me, trust Me, trust Me. I cannot repeat this often enough for you. I have given you a gift of faith to confound others at times. Live in this faith - it will grow. Remember what I spoke to you on a feast day of St. Peter - it refers and speaks to you."

My Beloved, My reading glasses are missing. I cannot write now, but I know there is a purpose in this. Perhaps you do not want me to spend my time writing unnecessarily. You want to speak to my heart now - I will stay for this Mass. My glasses will turn up if it is your holy will. At first I thought I couldn't see the page, but now that I can see the lines it doesn't matter.

"My Child, Take this opportunity to allow Me speak to your heart. It is your heart I seek. You seek Me, I seek you.

Pray and live this Eucharist with Me. I have your glasses safe and sound in My possession. Do not worry. How often have I to tell you. Trust Me. Come back to Me with all your heart - I wait, I am always waiting. Come to Me before the Blessed Sacrament."

Later in the Garden in the Presence of Blessed Sacrament:
My Beloved, I found my glasses in the Lost Property tent, where they were handed in and as you said, safe and sound. My beloved, You have been so gracious to me since I came on this trip that I pray that I will be able to do and give You all You ask of me when I return home - but how often have You shown me that you are the God of the Impossible.

Jesus, you truly were present amongst us as You were carried in the Blessed Sacrament in procession, healing and consoling all your little ones. Some healings we were made aware of as we were told through our interpreter. My beloved, do set my heart on fire to be a witness to the love and power of your Eucharistic Presence to share with others - increase my faith that I may be able to touch others to share with others all You teach me here and at the daily Eucharist and especially to your priests. May I bring confirmation of Your love for them in their arduous ministry in these days, especially in our own country where there is much criticism of the Church. Jesus, I ask a lot, but I know that You will always give me more that I ask or expect. Bless all my family, friends and especially all who come to worship before the Blessed Sacrament in my home. May each one be truly blessed through my visit to Paray, not forgetting the priests of the parish and all who ask our prayers.

26ᵗʰ July 1989   -   In Paray-Le-Monial
Feast of St. James :

"My Child, you will carry the pain in My Heart, this thirst in My Heart. My Child, I will be with you to help you. My Mother is very, very close to you, but she hides herself. She does not want to usurp My presence - My Presence in your heart, but wherever I am, she is also. She loves you much because she knows you are in love with Me. Oh My Child, I wish I could reveal Myself to you, but I cannot now - I will in time. I do not want to burden you now. I am a very gentle lover, My child. I treat you with the most gentle of love and affection - I hold you dearly and closely in My Heart. Oh My child, you will remember this day - the day I call you to Myself. I ask you to abandon yourself to Me. My child, you will have much temptation, but I will never allow him to touch you, contaminate you, change you. You are Mine, you belong to Me. Oh My child, I will say no more - but we will commune in the Eucharist this morning, as I showed you once - do not expect this to happen, but you will know My feelings at the Eucharist. Prepare - remember what I told you some years ago. The day and night can be divided into two - twelve hours preparing for the Eucharist - twelve hours giving thanks. Time is gift - limitless. I will teach you to grow in love - love is prayer.

I gave you a truly kindred spirit on this trip - share this with her. You will be divided in place, but not in spirit. Your mission compliment one another wherever you are. I brought you together to meet in Paray.

My Child, I promise you that as My Presence is exposed throughout the land, peace will come about in your hearts, to spread to all hearts, to bring peace, specially in the North.

If in many smaller towns *(in Ireland)* perpetual adoration has already started and can be carried and led by the laity, why cannot Dublin follow this example? Make this your prayer in this holy place. I give myriad graces in this land *(France)* because of the perpetual adoration here."

8ᵗʰ August 1989 - Feast of St. Dominic
After the Eucharist :

> 'Thank You my Beloved for accepting me as I am.
> Thank You my Beloved for trusting me as I am.
> Thank You my Beloved for using me as I am.'

Gospel reading today : Matt. 14. 13-21 : (The multiplication of the loaves and fishes). *This reading brings to my mind the first time it spoke to my heart, that it was the desire of Your Heart that we share the Eucharist with other Christians, all who sought You in love even without belief or understanding. Now I know that this has not come about because of our own lack of faith in this sacrament amongst our own people.*

... that it was the desire of Your Heart that we share the Eucharist with other Christians ...

It was because of our own lack of faith that other denominations could not begin to believe in the Real Presence in the Blessed Sacrament. Our people received the Eucharist, some daily, some weekly, some monthly, some never and these called themselves practising Catholics. What a sham, our example to other Christians!, specially those who stood on the word of God, worked miracles standing on the word alone. Nothing was happening at our celebrations because our faith had diminished. My Beloved, I believe that now a change is taking place within our Church, in our land and other places also. There is a momentum of hope and love being generated throughout the whole spectrum of the Church through the Mass and exposing Your Eucharistic Presence in the churches.

2ⁿᵈ September 1989:

> *If the other denominations can perform great healings of a physical, mental and spiritual nature by standing on the Word alone, cannot we who have every aspect - the Word, the Eucharist, the fellowship in our celebration - bring about the healings for man to be made whole at this Holy Sacrament.*

23

8ᵗʰ September 1989 - Knock : Feast of Our Lady's birthday
Before the Blessed Sacrament :

Thank you Mary for inviting us back here again to celebrate our wedding anniversary with you. It is another Paray. May the coming Eucharist be my expression of giving and thanksgiving for all the graces and blessings received down the years for our marriage, our family for the perfection of His Love in all the circumstances of our lives.

Mary, I am depending on you to help us fulfil His need of us this day.

MARY: "My child, I will give you a word later. Prepare now for this great banquet soon to start. Open your heart to the Holy Spirit that He may prepare you, empty you to receive all the graciousness and glory of My Son at today's celebration."

Later after the Eucharist
Before the Blessed Sacrament :

"My child, give glory to My Son
My child, give praise to My Son
My Child, give thanks to My Son.

My child, all the words I spoke to your heart were words of truth. My child, take them, ponder on them, mull over them, they are words of consolation, comfort, and console you in your pain. Now My child, I will change all this darkness, it will pass to allow the light of My Son. My Son is Light, My Son is light to enter your life. We have much work My child ahead, much to write for circulation. You will be busy. You will be given the health to carry out our plan in your life, allow Us to take over. Surrender all to Us to give glory to My Son. These writings will bring much honour, be at peace, be open to the Spirit."

15ᵗʰ September 1989 - Feast of Out Lady of Sorrows
Before the Blessed Sacrament :
Mary, I come to join you here in the Eucharistic Presence of your son Jesus. I know that You are the Mother of Sorrows to all who

are in pain this night, but to me now you are full of joy and peace. I thank you Mary for all that I am aware of now and not aware that you do for me in my daily life. I am only learning to know you but I hope to grow into a new relationship with you each day and through you and with you I will learn to fulfil your Son's need of me in my daily life, specially since I have begun to pray to you under the title of our Lady of the Sacred Heart to change my heart into a heart of flesh.

Mary, I do believe that you look upon me as a little child and treat me in the same way as my Abba Father. He does not expect much of me in my littleness.

"My child, My child, through your pain you enter into the mystery of the Eucharist. For the Eucharist to be Eucharistic you must share in all the facets. This is one aspect My little one.

"All those years I carried the words of Simeon in my heart were years of intense pain my child."

You will unite with me My little one in your pain, your pain is my pain. I am a partaker. I enter into this mystery also. All those years I carried the words of Simeon in my heart were years of intense pain my child."

Later before the Blessed Sacrament :
Mary, my Mother, I come again to give glory to your son through you and with you in the Eucharistic Presence.

25ᵗʰ September 1989: "You have a place in this school *(Willow)*, this community, it is also in your parish. Your house adoration touches the whole parish, everyone, everything that is part of the workings of the parish are blessed through your faithfulness, the adoration of the Eucharist each week in your home. Your home, your marriage, your family will receive myriad blessings through both your generosity in allowing Me to use your home in the present circumstances. Many and much will be the fruits of this ministry. You will see. You will know as time progresses. Come to Me now, listen to My Heart beat within you. Answer My call, My longing as I showed you once before the Eucharist. If others only knew how excited they would be also."

26th September 1989: "Here in the Eucharistic Presence, I touch all your emotions, particularly all the suppressed hurts and scars of the past, all buried, I bring to the fore to be healed. It is painful but all pain is a blessing when related to Mine. When pain is related to Mine you can freely enter into My Heart to taste, to savour My deepest emotions, all My human emotions, to share My pain, My love, My joy, My sorrows, My blocks, My needs, My desires, all I seek to reveal to My little ones.

Open your heart to Mine, you will find a resting place within, to share with Me, to unite with Me your feelings to become one. Our Hearts will then beat together as one. One life, one love, one being before the Father."

2nd October 1989 - (Willow)
Before the Blessed Sacrament later :
'Lord, how good it is that we are here!'

"Yes, My child, each time you come before My Eucharistic Presence you are on Mt. Tabor. Let Us savour Our love, Our unity during the coming hour and at the Eucharist. You are very privileged My child to be called to spend much time in My Presence. I know that it is not always a happy and joyous time but for Me it is always happy and joyous to have you in My Eucharistic Presence. You bring many graces and blessings to this community and school by your presence here with Me."

6th October 1989: "My child, go out into the high-ways and by-ways to spread this devotion - adoration before the exposed presence. You have provided a place to worship. Draw My people to come. So few churches oratories and convents provide this service My little one. I will shower you and all who come with myriad blessings and graces, healings of body, mind and spirit. I wait, I long. My Mother is here with Me to welcome each and every one this day of special graces and blessings, to give, to bestow on everyone who answers Our call.

Unite yourselves with Us and you will see greater, much greater signs and wonders My dear children in the days ahead."

7th October 1989 - Feast of the Holy Rosary
Before the Blessed Sacrament :
MARY:

"My child, My little one, today I want to offer my heart to you, to speak to your heart, to teach you the heart of your Mother. My child, I have always being a Mother to you all your life. I took care of you, I brought you to My Son, you have been faithful ever since. Now My child, through My Immaculate Heart, I will bring you deeper into the Heart of My Son. This is My privilege, to bring Our children closer, specially on My feast-days. I told you this at an earlier date. I have always taken you a step further on each of My feast-days to bring this truth home to you. Did I not? I have answered a special request this day. You know it deep in your heart. You touched on it this morning at prayer.

My child, I want you to bring to others the understanding of a Mother's heart for her children. My heart, I will lead and guide you in your task. I will teach you to pray My way. I know the needs of My Son for you at this present time. His need changes from time to time.

My child, you brought great joy to Our Hearts specially during the past days. My child, I take over now. Let Me. I will draw many to My Son through the Eucharistic Presence in your home. He chose your home to satisfy a deep desire in your heart. He uses the deepest desires of your hearts to fulfil His needs."

12th October 1989:   "My child, I can only reveal Myself to you if you remain a little child. Others who see Me, worship My Majesty, would not be as free. Little children are free from fear, fear of Me. It is easier for My Spirit to communicate with and through the humility of a little child. This answers your innermost thoughts. Everyone is unique, each one who seeks Me, answers My call, have each their own path. My plan is unique for each person. Some relate to others, all have a common purpose, all perfect when answering My call. Some follow the reasoning way, as I say there are many paths, varied at different times, but continue to make the Mass the centre of all paths. This must remain the ultimate once this has been made known. Priests sometimes ignore the centre as they move out, then the rot can take over as is happening in many places, it becomes only an exercise of duty.

Pray much for the priests who no longer believe in My Real Presence in the Eucharist. There are many such priests and many more being tempted in this area."

14ᵗʰ October 1989: "Count your weaknesses as blessings, through your weaknesses I have brought you into the depths of My own Heart. In and through your vulnerability I use you. Savour these days, they are very precious My little one. I reveal to you the power and love of walking and living in My Presence. Human and divine cannot be separated. They are one in My little ones."

16ᵗʰ November 1989
Before the Blessed Sacrament :
"My child, how often have I to speak to your heart that here in My Eucharistic Presence I heal. I am the Healer. Others find other ways. I supply ways for all needs but here My child, I teach you My way for you and for all believers in the power of My Eucharistic Presence. Oh My child, if My dear, dear priests only believed, had the faith of a mustard seed, I could speak to their hearts, to speak to My people everywhere, the power of the Eucharist.

My child, there is nothing, nobody on this earth equal to the power of the Mass. The Mass is complete in itself, every Mass.

My child, My priests do not understand. When their faith in the Mass is renewed, they will be in a position to bring this faith, renew this faith in My people."

28ᵗʰ November 1989
Before the Blessed Sacrament :
My Beloved, as I sit here with You, all is emptiness. Is the light to be so short-lived?

My Beloved, is the Presence so real, so powerful, so loving to become for me an empty tomb? My Beloved, do I now start the journey of dark faith into the unknown, no longer to have the comfort that I could always find one way or another here.

Mary, my Mother, help me not to loose heart to continue, to persevere along the path chosen for me by my Beloved, your Son. Now I am capable only of praying that little prayer : Jesus and Mary, I love You, save souls. And not from any feeling or emotion of the heart but believing that my prayer is being answered as I utter the words in all their starkness.

9ᵗʰ December 1989
MARY :

"My child, I am here with My Son looking into the hearts of all Our little ones. We rejoice to have you all here this day. You will indeed bring great blessings on your land. Hearts will be touched. My dear children much will happen where My Son's Eucharistic Presence is exposed, much, much happens. Oh if I could only get this word to My children everywhere, oh the love and comfort all could bring to the Heart of My Son. Pray for this My dear children. I know His Heart, Our Hearts are one.

My child, I will send you one of My little ones to help you soon. You will have much to write. You will need the help of another person to type, sort out these writings for others. These writings will be used to touch the hearts of many priests. Many priests do not have the time, make the time to pray, to listen to Our needs. They need reminding of the deepest needs of Our Hearts.

Now My child, I prepare your heart for the coming Eucharist. First be still. Relax. Let Me lead and guide you into My Heart, My Immaculate Heart. Bring to your mind any faults and ways you have hurt My Son since the last Eucharist."

14ᵗʰ December 1989 - House
Before the Blessed Sacrament :
MARY :

"My child, My little one, today we begin the writings on adoration before the Blessed Sacrament as I wish to teach My children. Here I wish to draw all My little ones into this prayer of adoration.

My child, we will begin by being aware of the Presence of My Son, it is the fulfilment here of all the promises of the Old Testament and the New Testament from the beginning to the end, in fact, the Alpha and the Omega. My child, when we become aware of the sacredness of His Presence, we begin to realise our own nothingness in the Presence of our Creator, our Redeemer, our Sanctifier to whom all honour, glory and praise is justified, no one else. He is to be the recipient of all our praise and thanksgiving. We must have no idols, false gods. The world is full of false gods. We must learn to reject all the false gods that the world offers, forces upon us. It takes time, much prayer and sacrifice to grow into this prayer of adoration My child. But with a willing heart all is possible and made easy in My love because it is the greatest desire of My Heart, My Immaculate Heart to lead and guide all My children into praise and adoration to My Son in the Eucharistic Presence."

18ᵗʰ December 1989   -   Before the Eucharist
Before the Blessed Sacrament :

"My child, open your heart now to the urgings of the Spirit. He is here pouring out His blessings on this building, on this school, on this college and all parts of this great institution. I do not want My priests to be afraid to expose My Presence, no matter what the circumstances, even in the midst of others not open to Exposition of My Presence, and specially in churches in areas most likely to cause Me pain and suffering. My dear, dear priests, you must pray much in My Eucharistic Presence to know the desires of My Heart, My desire for My people. I never tire of being present to My people in the Eucharistic Presence even when I am left alone. I wait, I long and My people will come. Have courage My dear, dear priests, do not let the fewer numbers discourage you. I stretched out My arms on the cross for the world, for all mankind."

23ʳᵈ December 1989   -
Before the Blessed Sacrament :

MARY :

"My child, I prepare you now here before the Eucharistic Presence of My Son for the great sacrament of the Eucharist. My child, We must veil the greatness of this great gift from Our little ones. We can only allow little glimpses in one's lifetime, to Our little favoured ones. It is beyond the human mind and body to absorb, to understand, to realise; only through divine intervention can one be allowed to receive these insights. And only occasionally to the few. As it is the greatest gift of Himself My Son has given to mankind, you understand that it brings the most graces but also the most damnation for man and the most pain to My Son. My child, My Son is prepared to risk everything to allow Himself to be crucified again and again even more than at Calvary for the sake of His people, His children.

My child, this is an insight into the length, breadth and depth of His Love for all. This age, this decade is so important for mankind that it is the desire of His Heart that His Eucharistic Presence be exposed to His people everywhere. His way of showing His divine mercy and love for all mankind. My child, there are many ways to My Son as you know as you have been taught over the years. There is much evil in the world today and through the media, television, wireless, print, it is being spread throughout the world and all that is happening in the world is being brought into the homes in more and more places. We know that the good news can be spread in the same way and is so being but at the present time evil seems to be triumphant. But My child, My Son is offering Himself in a way not understood by many as His way of counteracting this evil. My child, few believe that sitting here in the Presence of My Son one can do so much to stem this evil, destroy this evil that seeks to engulf all Our children.

My Son challenges Our people, firstly Our priests to accept this challenge. You have seen for yourself in your own life and in the lives of others the changes wrought through this exercise in faith. My child, you know the hurts that man can and will inflict on My Son and Me yet We ask Our little ones to allow Us this great desire to be fulfilled in the coming days."

31ˢᵗ December 1989

<u>Before the Blessed Sacrament :</u>

My Beloved, I come in praise and thanksgiving for all the graces and blessings of the past year, may these all bear fruit in the coming year of 1990.

Now that our country has been chosen for the presidency of the E. E.C. during the next six months starting tomorrow, may we share Your light with the other members. My Beloved, I know we do not deserve all the graces and blessings You have bestowed on us in this land but we try to respond and through the intercession of all Your little ones may that glimmer of hope You gave us at the beginning of 1989 become a beacon to be seen by all in the coming twelve months. And as adoration before Your Eucharistic Presence spreads throughout the land, the evil that seeks to engulf us all will be dispelled and all Christians will come to praise You and pray together to bring peace specially in the North. And that Your love will reign in our hearts to change our lives.

Thank you Mary, our Mother, you are the Mediatrix of all graces, you have been good to the people of this land down all the years. We know that you will not fail to answer all the prayers of your faithful little ones of the past years. Mary, all you have brought about in Eastern Europe, you will bring about for us also.

"MY DEAR, DEAR PRIESTS ..."

"I do not want My priests to be afraid to expose My Presence, no matter what the circumstances, even in the midst of others not open to Exposition of My Presence, and specially in churches in areas most likely to cause Me pain and suffering. My dear, dear priests, you must pray much in My Eucharistic Presence to know the desires of My Heart, My desire for My people. I never tire of being present to My people in the Eucharistic Presence even when I am left alone. I wait, I long and My people will come. Have courage My dear, dear priests, do not let the fewer numbers discourage you. I stretched out My arms on the cross for the world, for all mankind."

4ᵗʰ January 1990   -   House
Before the Blessed Sacrament :

"Today is a special day, these two days are very special to Me My child. My Heart is full of love, overburdened with love to share with all My children. I have special graces and blessings to bestow on all who visit My Eucharistic Presence today. I am here laden with gifts to pour out on all and so few come to receive. My Heart breaks to see so few answer My call. But be assured My little ones that I am here to satisfy all your needs, to ease all your anxieties, to pour balm on all your wounds. Today being the first Thursday of the year, I am most generous. The year ahead is present to Me here. I see all, I know all. Give Me all. Oh trust Me, My dearest little ones, turn your hearts to Mine. I carry you all now and in the days ahead. Leave all your cares and anxieties with Me. It is the desire of My Heart to relieve you of your pain and sufferings. Some sufferings I leave for My greater glory and your greater reward. As you sit here with Me I will speak to your heart, you will know the difference. As I said before My little one, these are important days for this land and for the whole world. Pray My

"My child, I need to be taken out of the tabernacles to reach the tabernacles in men's hearts. If enough people sat with Me, united their hearts to Mine, great changes would come about in their homes, their communities, their country and throughout the world."
31st. December 1990

children that My needs will be fulfilled, My Will, will be done. I give you My Mother to protect and care for each one of you. She is My advocate in the world for these times. I have given her all My children, all My little ones. Listen to her, she will lead all to Me. She is My glory in the world today.

There is a great battle brewing between good and evil everywhere. She will lead My people to victory. Goodness will overcome evil. Goodness will triumph. And as My Eucharistic Presence is exposed the evil one will loose his power, will be destroyed.

Oh My dear, dear priests, listen to My Heart speak to your hearts as you sit in My Presence, make time, I gave you time, time is a gift from Me. I ask only for a little of your time to spend here with Me and you will find that the more you give Me, the more you will need Me.

My dear, dear priests, these are not idle words I speak to your hearts to be put aside, to be excused by other pressures on your time. Fulfil this need of Mine, it is the most important part of your calling after daily Mass. What more can I say My dearest chosen ones. I give you all I am, I have. I desire the most for you. I need you more than your people. Give Me this time, My dear, dear priests, fulfil this great desire of My Heart during the coming year."

11ᵗʰ January 1990:   "Now My child begins your thirst for souls. My child, remember the glimpse I gave you some years ago of My Thirst, Oh My child, your pain is My pain, do not let it frighten you. I am here with you, this explains why I ask you to spend much time in My Eucharistic Presence, this explains why I became present in My Eucharistic Presence in your home -

TO JOIN WITH ME IN MY THIRST FOR SOULS.

You have tasted My Divine Mercy. My Divine Mercy creates this Thirst.

Oh child of My Heart if you only knew but I cannot yet reveal to you the comfort and consolation I receive before My Eucharistic Presence in this house. Oh My children, the joy that touches My Heart as you sit here in My Presence. How I look forward to this day each week. The love and thanks I receive makes amends for the very many insults and injuries committed against My Eucharistic Presence. Many are the graces and blessings I pour out upon you all. You are not aware of these because your lives are filled with all the human cares and anxieties of living in a very imperfect world but do not lose heart, My Love goes with you, My Love is present to you. Be aware of My Presence within you. You are the temple of My Spirit. Remember this at all times. It will help to remind you of Me, My Love and need for each one."

26ᵗʰ January 1990
Before the Blessed Sacrament :
"My child, I brought you here this afternoon to write. I have much on My Heart. My child, My Heart is burdened, overburdened. You have only to read the newspapers, listen to the wireless, look at television and you can see the state of the world. Very few publish the good news, the prayers, sufferings, good deeds of My little ones, all who answer My call in the world. The world is in a sorry state because of the prevalence of evil everywhere.

My child, I ask you now to give Me much of your time. You must never worry about your prayer, how you communicate with Me. I am present to you specially when you answer My call to pray, to come into My Eucharistic Presence. Here I ask you to pray, here you touch the world, here you make intercession for the world because this is your special calling. Here I wish that you remember My priests, My religious who are so busy, so occupied in the world and often with the world that they do not have time to spend time with Me. You understand the pain, the hurt of their rejection of My need. And I made it so easy, made Myself so available that it pains My Heart when they reject Me so. There are many of course who answer My call, these precious souls lift My Heart."

29ᵗʰ January 1990
After the Mass :
"Nothing can prevail against the Word and the Eucharist. The two together are the most powerful armour against all the evil forces that invade the earth, that is why the Mass is so powerful My little

one. But many neglect the Word that becomes Flesh at the Consecration. This belittles the power of the Mass."

2nd February 1990
Mary:

"My child, My child, I do indeed accept you as my special child. Do not be afraid, I prepare you now that I have your full commitment and co-operation to lead and use you in the vineyard of My Son. Today is a new beginning, we are always beginning but today I make special. It is also the First Friday coinciding with a special feast of mine. Did I not always tell you that on all my feast days I would bless you with a special grace? My little one, today will be no exception but I have a much greater surprise for you on this day. I know my child your thoughts, my special gifts are not always as we expect but today's is special indeed. My child, I have been keeping today's as very special indeed because I fulfil a promise I made to you some while ago, and where could we find a better setting as we adore My Son in His Eucharistic Presence. I do not have to remind you My child but I feel I should, of this special favour He bestowed on you to give Himself, His very special presence in the Eucharist for your home, a very special privilege indeed. And as you have been faithful and generous to this gift, He has many more prepared for you. All who come to your home on these days receive a very special grace and blessing. Here all My children will find a peace, not found in many places. Much prayer, much suffering have made this place a place of hope and a haven from the storms of the world. This will continue and grow more apparent to all who come to find rest and peace for their troubled hearts.

My Heart is here, aflame with love to receive all and through the Eucharistic Heart of My Son, We touch many souls in need, in great distress, to find refuge and peace in Our Hearts also.

My dear children, We do want you to know that as you visit Us here, some each week and on these two days, you share in many graces and blessings for yourselves, your families and many other souls. This is love. This is loving in response to Our Love for you. Never doubt Our Love. We see all, know all your efforts, your good intentions. We overlook your faults in responding to Our

Love."

8th March 1990
Lord, I give thanks, I thank You

I thank You Lord for today
I thank You Lord for all the yesterdays
The joys, the hopes, the hurts, the pain
Healed and yet to be healed.

You, Oh Lord can turn all to good
You promised and Your word is truth
I thank You Lord,
The Eucharist is my thanksgiving.

The Eucharist is Your Love Oh Lord
The giving of Yourself to all mankind.
How we pain You
When we do not receive You in love.

Teach us Lord to be eucharistic
In our hearts,
Hearts of thanksgiving in times of joy and sadness
Past and present.

That our hearts may be pruned and tested
To face the days ahead
With courage and hope
To prepare us for the end.

Ending yes, yet not the end
To give birth to a new beginning
When thanks will become pure praise
Of the eternal God.

4th March 1990
Before the Blessed Sacrament :
Thank You my Beloved for the further insights You give me concerning the praying of the Chaplet of the Divine Mercy.

As often as I repeat the prayer :
'Eternal Father, I offer You the Body and Blood, Soul and Divinity

of Your dearly beloved Son, Our Lord Jesus Christ, in atonement for our sins and those of the whole world', *I am uniting myself with all the sacrifices of the Holy Eucharist taking place at that time and I am entering into the salvation of souls in intercession with the Lord Jesus, for past, present and further generations. And I am reminded also that in praying this Chaplet from the heart I cover all the needs of Your Heart.*

19th March 1990
Before the Blessed Sacrament :
My Lord, my God, my All.

My heart rejoices with you this day to hear the good news that already your desires are beginning to be fulfilled during this time of Eucharistic Renewal that the adoration of the Blessed Sacrament is moving into the homes of your little ones. My Beloved, You did promise that as this need would be fulfilled in our land, peace would be restored.

Oh the Holy Spirit is truly hovering over this country through the intercession of Mary, Your Mother, she has many sincere and faithful followers here and their prayers for peace are being answered.

We thank you Mary for answering our poor weak efforts specially of those who have brought home your messages from Medjugorje and have answered your call for prayer, fasting and repentance. May they all be truly blessed and greatly rewarded by you.

22nd March 1990: *Oh my Beloved, You are the All powerful God, my Wonder-Counsellor, Mighty-God, Eternal Father, Prince-of-Peace who allows me at times to see into the workings of Your Heart and the wonder of Your ways. Oh the freedom I have received now in the realisation that the writings concerning the exposition and adoration of the Eucharistic Presence are coming to pass during these days. This Eucharistic Renewal is providing the opportunities to fulfil this great desire of Your Heart. The seed You have placed in the hearts of Your people is being satisfied. We pray now that the hearts of the bishops and priests will be open to this great movement of the Spirit, that will further the* cause of peace in our land as You have promised on numerous occasions in the past. It has also shown me that any part I may have had in spreading these writings to help to bring these desires of Yours about was irrelevant. Thank You my Beloved because knowing this has helped me to detach myself from these writings. They are Yours and any part that is not of You is because I have not been listening attentively.

In the house - Thursday
Before the Blessed Sacrament :
"My child, I cover you now in My Holy Spirit to receive the word I am about to give you. It is an important word for My ministers in My Church. Many are under a misapprehension of their calling, My need of them. Many have moved away from the centre through lack of faithfulness to a life of prayer. No matter what area in the Church they are called upon to fill, prayer must receive their first attention. Only from a life of prayer can they function.

Oh My child, on this day of prayer for My priests, (priests in authority and of great mental ability), when My priests are blessed with great intellects, it is so easy to allow the evil one take over without the support and protection of a deeper prayer life to combat the evil forces that will try to direct their minds away from My gospel message, to misrepresent it.

That answers your first question.

Now My child about this whole new emphasis on natural medicine. This form of medicine was in the world from the beginning after the fall. Man needed ways of healing for the body, the mind. This has taken on again in many different forms. Medicine was being abused, drugs were being over prescribed, medicines were losing their effects. Hence the up rise in natural medicine again. But one must be careful, as much abuse and danger can enter these areas also. Natural medicine and spiritual healing when they are used together bring untold results for good to many of My people. Any lay person can be prepared and called to this form of medicine but not all are suitable, hence the dangers.

My child, there is another aspect of this that I come to now.

I speak to My priests. I have no objection to My priests using these methods in their ministry but there can be a great danger in these for them. You see I already have given My consecrated ministers the same powers I used on earth and even greater now through their priestly ministries. But sometimes they allow the methods which are usable by lay people to take over to the detriment of their prime calling, the spreading of My Word and the celebration of the Eucharist.

No lay person has the power to change bread and wine into My Body and Blood, to be shared amongst My people at the celebration of the Eucharist. And, that this sacrament may remain the prime function of their calling this can only come from a life of prayer. Why did I set you My priests apart? Why do I need you apart? Do I not know all your needs, your weaknesses, your doubts, your hopes, your sacrifices? But I am your strength. I never leave you. I am the Healer, the Eucharist is ME, Body, Blood, Soul and Divinity. What more can I give you? Here you have ALL I have to give, My dear, dear priests.

> My child, I am patiently waiting that My request for Perpetual Adoration in the city of Dublin will be adhered to soon. Oh the blessings I could pour out on this city as a consequence, the decline in crime would be soon noticed.

My dear, dear priests, during this time of Eucharistic Renewal in the diocese, you receive great grace and blessing to share with My people.

My child, I am patiently waiting that My request for Perpetual Adoration in the city of Dublin will be adhered to soon. Oh the blessings I could pour out on this city as a consequence, the decline in crime would be soon noticed.

My priests, I need your co-operation to put these plans into operation. Do not disappoint ME. I place My trust in you. Why not trust ME to fulfil all the promises I made to you on the day of your ordination and continue specially at your daily Eucharist ?

Oh My priests these are days of special grace, do not waste the abundance of blessings I have ready, waiting to pour out on each and everyone of you."

29th March 1990 - House
Before the Blessed Sacrament :
"My child, today is a day for writing. Be alert, be open, be aware. Remember the words - 'here I will wash all hearts in My living waters, hearts that are prepared to listen and be still'.

As you can see, much is happening in this land at the present time. Much is now coming out into the open. I will touch many hearts. Pray My children that My children will listen and take heed. Much healing is needed amongst My people here but your prayers and the prayers of all My little ones, will help to open the hearts of those closed to Me yet. Here in the silence, My Heart will bring about healings in many hearts. You are an example for others to follow. I am preparing little groups, little communities to come together to pray before My Eucharistic Presence, to spread throughout the diocese and in turn to spread throughout the land. Oh My dear, dear priests do not be afraid to meet the challenge I ask of you. Be open, the way is easy, I will make it easy for you to carry out My plan. I am preparing My people. Is this not another way of holding the Forty-hours adoration that people have moved away from now? You have all the means at your disposal. Cannot each day become : 'Twenty-four hours with Me'? Many people, many institutions, many convents, many oratories are waiting to be asked. My people are ready, hearts have been opened. There is a hunger in My people, an eagerness to be tapped. My priests do not put off or delay before it is too late to fulfil this great desire of My Heart. Wherever I am exposed, I bring great graces and blessings on My people. Do not hesitate My dear, dear priests to allow Me to give Myself, My All in the Blessed Sacrament to feed My lambs, to feed My sheep."

31st March 1990:   "........ My child, you can tell Me everything that is on your heart or write to Me about it if it helps you. Oh My child, I am already waiting, waiting, seeking your presence before My Eucharistic Presence this morning and at Our marriage feast where Our Hearts will be one in one another........"

"Oh My child, I have much work for you this day. You do not know nor see all. I do not let you see for your own sake but I have all in My Heart to show you at a later time. Oh My child, you have been faithful to Me, that is the most important thing in your life. You have not failed Me, but I will teach you through your own pain to know the pain of others that you will heal them through your prayer. When you sit with Me, I work and heal each one you carry in your heart whether you are aware or not."

"..... has much to cope with, bring her specially, she is suffering most at this time. Support her in your prayer. She is a child of My Heart. I use her to heal others in pain."

"...... I hold in My arms. He is so close to My Heart. All will be well, the future is bright for him and his family. He will work again, it will not be long, the end of the tunnel is close."

"My dear priests do not fail Me in My hour of need. These are not empty words to be read and not dwelled upon. I need action. Your example to My people. I speak now as your chief Shepherd, it is because I hold you so dearly in My Heart that I speak so strongly to you, that I humiliate Myself to beg you to listen to the greatest need within Me during these days of Eucharistic Renewal. Do not let these days of such great graces and blessing pass without a response from your own hearts. How can I reach My people except through you, My dear, dear chosen children I hold so close within My Heart."

"My dear, dear priests I come to deliver these messages through a child, a simple child with a simple soul. She may not be over-versed in theology and church doctrine but she rests in My Heart, she listens with her heart, and I speak to her heart. She is My little messenger during these days of Eucharistic Renewal, to bring to My dear, dear chosen ones My greatest need. Do not fail Me, do not ignore My pleads, do not brush aside My words, do not reject them. If you reject these, you reject Me."

"Come My child, rest in Me now. We must prepare for the marriage feast, the great celebration about to commence soon."

Holy Thursday 1990

Today is My day of love
To be remembered by all
That I gave all for all.

To make all days, everyday
My own, to give and to receive
In a communion of hearts.

I wait for each one
To lavish upon all, My Love.
So few answer My call.

The attractions of the world
Are too much for many
I wait My time, I wait.

Sometimes when the cares and troubles.
Of life become too great
Hearts are softened to welcome Me.

I come with outstretched arms
To embrace the wayward
The flame from My Heart enkindles a spark within

Oh wounded Heart so broken by man.
Let's comfort and console You
On Your day of love supreme.

19ᵗʰ April 1990:   "You will never know in this life the disasters that have been adverted, through your faithfulness to this day each week when you sit before My Eucharistic Presence. My dear children, how I wish I could reveal Myself to you, but I am restrained because of My love for you. I do not want to burden you with My Love, the burden of this Love. The greater the love, the greater the pain at times.

Oh My dear children, do not be upset nor alarmed when I hide Myself at times. These times are the most fruitful. I am purifying you, preparing you for My eternal presence. Oh My dear children do try and accept the dark and lonely times in My grace. These are very special. I suffer with you in your darkest moments. You console Me in Mine.

Every place My Eucharistic Presence is exposed is a place of pilgrimage my child."

My Beloved, I give thanks this day for all Your faithful children, Your little ones. All help in the salvation of souls if we are faithful to our own little callings.

My Beloved, You gift me so much and I am ashamed of how little I do for You, how few sacrifices and when I see what all others do, I feel so small, but then I remember Your mercy and love and I am overcome. Sometimes I am afraid I take so much for granted and forget all You suffered to redeem me, ... and the Father's sacrifice in sending You into the world to become one with us to take upon Himself all our sinfulness to free us, … and I do not allow You give me the freedom You won for me through my stubbornness and lack of trust.

Oh my Beloved, I know in my heart even though I cannot express it, that You truly love me and have given me Your Heart to be mine. My God, how low You stoop to meet my needs. It is as if You delight in humiliating Yourself to meet the lowliest of the lowliest. This is Your divine mercy we honour this coming Sunday. How I petition You from my heart that I might be touched and healed to have a little reflection of Your Love and Mercy in my heart for others.

Mary, our Mother we join with you and all your children at prayer now.. May our prayers rise like incense before the throne of your Son. Mary with you leading and guiding us in praying the fifteen decades of the rosary during our Watch this night may our prayers bring comfort and solace to your wounded heart and the wounded Heart of your Son.

26ᵗʰ April 1990   -   House
Before the Blessed Sacrament :
My Beloved, You make me aware of the sadness in Your Heart and the Heart of Your Mother. I pray that as we sit here with You during this day we will help to bring You comfort and solace to ease the pain of Your suffering.

My Beloved, I pray firstly for our own country as we prepare for the coming meeting of the heads of state of the E.C., may peace prevail between all. I pray also for England that the new bill on abortion will not make a bad situation even worse. Oh how we all are responsible for this great crime against Your authority and creation, ... and the pain we inflict upon You. How misguided and evil we have become through the wiles of the evil one.

"Here My child, I touch the world. Here My child, I answer all prayer. Here all My needs are fulfilled. Oh when will My dearest ones answer My need? When will they listen to My Heart speak to their hearts? Today they celebrate the institution of the Eucharist in a special way. Today I bestow a special blessing on all My priests. Today I wait for a response, a special response. Today all can make a special response to the needs of My Heart. This Heart crushed and broken by the sinfulness of mankind everywhere but also comforted and consoled by My little ones and in a special way by the sufferings accepted in love for My sake. This special grace is available to all My little ones for the asking. How honoured, how great an honour for Me and for you when sufferings, all sufferings are offered and related to Mine.

Prayer is the doorway to My Heart and also opens the doors of your hearts for Me to enter and find rest in you."

29ᵗʰ April 1990
Before the Blessed Sacrament :

Oh my Beloved, I give thanks for the wonderful discourse I heard today on the Lectio Divina. I was reminded of all You speak to my heart as I sit here with You before the Blessed Sacrament. And because the Eucharistic Presence is the Word made Flesh we cannot separate the two. How important it is for us to realise this as we pray the Mass each day. It must become a growing awareness within us that one complements the other. The power of one depends on the power of the other. Many feed on the written word alone and feel they are fulfilled. While others feed on the breaking of the Bread alone and feel they are fulfilled. But the Eucharist is the Word becoming Flesh at the Consecration. We must realise this to receive the full potential of the Mass.

3ʳᵈ May 1990:   "My child, I do not want you to carry too great a burden. I measure all according to each. My child, you please Me as you are. You have offered Me much. I receive from you each day, each night. Do not be afraid. You have freely offered Me your home. It is a place of great comfort and peace to all who enter because it is a resting place of peace and love for Me.

My child, I veil from your eyes and heart all that takes place here, the human heart and body are not prepared to receive such vision, but I can assure you My little one that much, much more than the human heart could grasp is taking place for each one who enters, for those carried in the hearts of all who come. The parish benefits, the city, the country and far away places. Where I am the world is. I am the world, the universe, all is contained in My Presence. So much in so little.

Oh My little one, I cannot show you all I desire to reveal to you, it is not because I do not want to but because I love you so. Love can be very painful. My child, My child, you could not endure the pain of My Thirst, it was the smallest possible I could allow, like an atom, But I allowed this that you write about it, knowing in your heart this suffering that the writing would be authentic to the readers."

22ⁿᵈ May 1990: *I was considering whether I should get up or not.*

"My child, I will not leave you in doubt. Come to this Mass, I am waiting for you. Do not deprive Me of your presence."

"Suffering is the school of suffering."

Later :
"My child, come to Me. I will give you rest and consolation. You need not stay long. I will tell you when to go. All will be well. You bring Me consolation also."

Before the Blessed Sacrament :
"Yes My child, I called you here just to be here. I ask nothing of you in your present state of health but your presence. You fulfil My need by just being. I called you to confirm your thoughts, My thoughts, My needs. So few understand the Heart, this Heart of Mine in the Eucharistic Presence. My

child, I gift you with this knowledge that you might share this with others. So few understand why I ask My priests to expose My Presence to My people. How I long to be taken out of tabernacles."

24ᵗʰ May 1990 - House, Ascension Thursday
Before the Blessed Sacrament :
Reading : Is. 6.3: "Holy, holy, holy is the Lord of hosts!" they cried one to another. "All the earth is filled with His Glory."

My reply : *'Here I am Lord, send me.'*

"My child, I am preparing you for My future plan now. I have given you an insight for this home. Prepare My child during the coming days to the feast of Pentecost for this work. It will take such prayer, much commitment, great dedication to carry out My plans. But you know and realise My little one that nothing is impossible to Me, to the One who leads you. You are willing and faithful My little one. You have nothing to fear but the time is not far off when I will ask you and arrange that My Eucharistic Presence will be in residence here more often. It will not interfere with your family life, you will be free to come and go as hither fore but I seek a place of peace and a haven of rest for others to spend a day with Me. You just offer your home, My home now whenever I ask you. I will make all the arrangements. Already all who come here find peace and hope in all their anxieties. I lift their burdens, there is security and love and you will welcome each one I send you in My Name.

My disciples were devastated when I left them on this day. My Mother gathered them under her mantle, kept them together, to pray together until the coming of the Holy Spirit, then all were freed to take their own paths, to answer My call, to spread the gospel."

1ˢᵗ June 1990 - First Friday
Before the Blessed Sacrament :
My Beloved, 'Here I am, Lord send me.' *I know You have a word for me this day to deliver to Your people.*

Father, in the Name of Jesus, open my heart to the Holy Spirit.

"The Eucharistic Renewal suffices for Pentecost. The Holy Spirit will be poured out throughout this diocese this year because of this Renewal, the repercussions will be everlasting. Do not worry ; the fervour of My people will not finish at Corpus Christi. My priests will come to realise that this exercise is part of My plan, not to be discontinued as soon as the period arranged in the beginning comes to an end. You cannot discard Me like this. I speak now to My priests, I have come to stay. My plan is only at the beginning stage. You will see this plan unfolding in the days ahead. My child, you will have a part in this plan because, you, I will use as My messenger to My priests, some may not listen but as I told you before, you deliver My messages and I will take care of the rest. You have busy days ahead. I will give you the strength for body and spirit to carry out this work for Me. I have given you many helpers. T.... will have a special part to play also to bring this to fruition. The days ahead will be most fruitful. Offer Me all, everything in your daily life. I will take care of all, bring good out of all situations. You must not worry. Give all to Me. You have important work to do for Me. I do not want you burdened with trifles, the problems of everyday living. Your work takes on now a much greater and wider part in the affairs of My Church, for My priests, My people. You never expected such a future, but I use the little to confound the strong."

Reading : Ezekiel : 43. 6-9.

> Then I heard someone speaking to me from the temple, while the man stood beside me. The voice said to me: Son of man, this is where my throne shall be, this is where I will set the soles of my feet; here I will dwell among the Israelites forever. Never again shall they and their kings profane my holy name with their harlotries and with the corpses of their kings [their high places]. When they placed their threshold against my threshold and their doorpost next to mine, so that only a wall was between us, they profaned my holy name by their abominable deeds; therefore I consumed them in my wrath. From now on they shall put far from me their harlotry and the corpses of their kings, and I will dwell in their midst forever.

7ᵗʰ June 1990   -   House
Before the Blessed Sacrament :
"Oh My child, I know you are tired but I have a word for you to

write for My priests. My child, My Heart is heavy these days. The time appointed for the ending of Eucharistic Renewal is coming to an end. This is only a preparation for what I intend to bring about in this diocese.

My priests, My dear priests, I have been preparing My people, My people are open to the desire of My Heart for these times. I do not want you to disappoint My people - those whom I have touched during this time of preparation and who have received a touch of this thirst of Mine. My dear priests, I want these exercises already taking place to continue, to grow, I will let you know My plans. Give Me time, listening time My dear priests and bishops. There are more pressing needs than the works of administration, regulations, buildings, courses etc. I come first. It is the desire of My Heart that in these troubled times My Eucharistic Presence be exposed for My people. These are very difficult times, great forces are at work to destroy My work, My needs in the present crisis in My church, nations and people. Evil is everywhere hiding under many labels that I will disclose and name later but for now I ask you, beg you, beseech you to increase your time with Me, to sit before My Eucharistic Presence that I might touch your hearts to touch further the hearts of My people. Do not neglect My sheep. Be real true shepherds to My flock. They are more in need of guidance in these troubled times than at any time hither fore in the history of the Church. Great waves for peace are taking place but unless man is careful all will be destroyed again.

My Mother is calling My people, beseeching My people to return to a life of prayer, do not discard her messages or belittle her. When you belittle her you belittle Me. I am speaking now from a Heart, a troubled Heart, a sorrowful Heart to My dear, dear children, My specially chosen ones to bring Me to My people to gather my people together in My Name, the Name of the Most Holy Trinity."

22ⁿᵈ June 1990 - Feast of the Sacred Heart
After the Eucharist :
My Beloved, You have given me Your Heart, let me give You mine, though weak, battered and good for nothing and because You are the God of the

50

impossible, change me.

Later :
My Beloved, I realise as I sit here Your pain to see Your people coming into the church to pray and light candles in front of Your statue and ignore the Tabernacle which contains Your Eucharistic Presence. More and more I see why You need Your Presence be exposed to Your people. People are hungry, there is a great thirst within each one seeking You, placed there by You but it needs guidance.

I know many would not agree, but from all You have taught me over the years, I am deprived because You are being deprived of this great desire of Your Heart to expose this Heart as on Calvary.

17ᵗʰ July 1990
Before the Tabernacle :
"By My wounds you are healed and by relating your wounds to Mine, you heal others."

Mary, my Mother help me to write the thoughts that fill my heart during the past days when I pray and specially during the Holy Sacrifice of the Mass. It is as if I am being made aware of the division and crisis in the Church, of the disturbances perpetrated by the evil one to cause havoc amongst the leaders, His shepherds.

My Beloved, I unite myself with all others in Eucharistic adoration this day to counteract the evil in our midst, to bring comfort and consolation to Him who gave everything of Himself for all mankind.

Beloved, may our pittance help to bring about healing and wholeness amongst Your chosen ones not because in any way are we healed but by so helping others may we be healed ourselves.

30ᵗʰ July 1990
Before the Blessed Sacrament (Exposed) :
'Love has conquered me, it alone shall possess my heart.'
Dear, dear Lord help me to let this happen. It is the desire of my

heart.

My Beloved, help me to fathom the depth of Eucharistic Prayer as I sit here in Your Presence. You continue for me the Mass with its connotations. It is only possible for my weak human nature to glimpse at one little aspect of this great mystery at one time. As You once told me, the whole bible, old and new testaments are enacted at each offering. It is not possible for our little minds to grasp any one aspect except through Your Holy Spirit. You remind me that we could not really believe, receive and live. And so the gift of Yourself to us in the Eucharist is way above the human mind and spirit to comprehend. And so must it be dearest Beloved with all that takes place here in Your Presence. The word has become flesh : Body, Blood, Soul and Divinity, too, too great for us mortals to ever understand. Yet at times You give us a glimpse at Your majesty, Your love, Your power to help us continue in our day to day struggles. You invite us, touch our hearts to know that here Your promise is fulfilled : 'Come to Me all you who are laboured and heavily burdened and I will refresh you ......'

16th August 1990:   *Mary, my Mother, sometimes when I read your messages and requests from others I get confused and bowed down wondering what exercises and sacrifices I should follow. I am also concerned about the 'Golden Watch' we follow each Thursday night. Some do not agree with this, specially those who come for silent prayer alone before the Blessed Sacrament. Mary, I know you will not leave me in any doubt, that you will speak to my heart or through another as to what we should do. I do not want to make any changes unless you say so. Thank you Mary.*

I pray also for a peaceful and satisfactory ending to the business for M. and J.

"My child, My child, sitting here in My Presence suffices for all My needs and the needs of My Mother who is present here also. These other writings are all ways of bringing Our children to a deeper knowledge and way of prayer. My child, you cannot improve on Eucharistic Prayer. My child, I am more truly present to you now than when I lived on earth, walked the roads of my homeland. I am more a part of your being. I am your being. My child, never be anxious even when you are not spiritually or humanly aware of anything taking place. This takes more of a sacrifice to sit here with Me.

My child, My Mother wishes that the fifteen decades of the rosary be said during this day. Perhaps they should be divided out throughout the day that those who come for adoration before the Blessed Sacrament may not be disturbed. I will suggest a time-table for you to suit everybody. And of course there is no reason why each person cannot pray the rosary to oneself at any time not to disturb others. And as suggested the prayers on the leaflet may be said at anytime also.

Remember My child, I explained to you in the early days that it would not always be joyful and sweet sitting here, there would be dark days also but these days give Me much glory and help in the salvation of other souls. Have I not told you that this is your other calling? Relate all pain to My Thirst on the cross.

Thank you My little one for your obedience to My request, it was for your good and the faith of others will be strengthened through your obedience. Every little act of faith has repercussions elsewhere."

My Beloved, I cannot understand why You are so good to Me when I fail You so often?

28ᵗʰ September 1990
Before the Blessed Sacrament :
"My child, I am about to bring you into a time of great enlightenment. You must be very attentive to My calling, to come when I need you. It will mean many sacrifices. You will know that it is now time to live the life of a 'Carmel' in the world. You will suffer but I will be your strength. It will appear greater than it is to others. Remember at the intercession for the Falklands war, you will now be My intercessor for much greater and many souls. You will spend more time with Me but you must also make time for recreation, walking in the open to breathe in the air of My creation. Forget the past, live in the perfection of the present moment. I surround you with My little ones. Through your home many will find Me, follow Me, a great light will shine forth from this place of

worship. Last night was a sign of all that is about to happen. I showed and gave a sign to .... of a taste of the happenings before My Eucharistic Presence. This is only a beginning of the wonders when people begin to believe in the power of the Eucharistic Presence. My child, listen carefully, I will free you from the bonds that bind you. I want you free, free to carry out My plan for the days ahead. You will have much opposition, I will be your strength in times of temptation. The greater My work, the greater the opposition. Do not fear. As I have often said before, I never leave you, also My Mother. She has a special place also in your home."

29th September 1990 - Feast of the Archangels
Before the Blessed Sacrament :

"My child, I have been waiting for you to come. My child, I wait here everyday to meet Me in this room of prayer. We begin a new pattern this day. I will help you to be faithful to My call. Rejoice with the Archangels in My Presence."

'In the presence of the angels, come let us adore the Lord.'

16th October 1990
Before the Blessed Sacrament :

"My child, I did invite you here to write. Do not be afraid, it is an act of faith to write as I ask you in a strange place and before others. It is also an act of obedience and humility. My child be prepared now to answer this call at all times in many places. It is my desire My child that you give thanks for this place of Eucharistic worship in the centre of the city. I need many such places. I am never satisfied, the more I receive the greater My desire grows. This happens within the human soul also. As the spirit grows in Me, the more the spirit seeks and needs My Spirit.

My child, I give you an onerous task this day. I want you to follow through to have the Holy Sacrifice and celebration of the Mass said in this particular house. It will take much preparation in prayer and sacrifice to bring My healing and victory over evil.

My child, do not be afraid. I need your constant presence with Me before the Blessed Sacrament as far as it is humanly possible for you. I will supply and prepare the way. Be open to the urgings of the Spirit. He will lead you. Rest now in My Heart. Comfort Me for the many evils that are about that seek to destroy My little ones and bring discredit on their ways.

My Mother will protect you. Give her time this weekend, I will provide, do listen attentively to Me. Though evil forces are at work around you, I will protect you. Trust in Me, My little one."

29ᵗʰ November 1990
MARY :
"My child, I have much for you to write this day. Last night was a time of prayer and preparation. Now you are Our little messenger as you sit before the Exposed Presence of My Son. My child, do not worry, I never left you last night. Your pain brings much blessings on this day of prayer and adoration. Many are blessed and healed and how many of Our priests and religious find the strength and encouragement to continue their special calling through your faithfulness to this day each week. Never underestimate the power and love that emanate from this house of prayer.

Oh My child, My children, you do not have to come to My shrines when you can sit with Us before the Eucharistic Presence; and We must gather Our children before they can enter this form of prayer, but there are times when all are blessed by a change.

My child, I ask a special obedience from you to stay with My Son in the Eucharist. Not many are called to this ministry. It is a special calling My child. There is a great need for this form of prayer in these troubled times when men have war on their hearts as the only solution to peace. My child there are many evil forces at work. My child, My little one, you experience these yourself but I never leave you. I am with you at all times to give you the strength. Be alert, be aware and trusting always. My child, I do heed your prayers but trust Us. Your efforts are used for the salvation of many souls. Are you not aware of My need of you, reminding you, calling you to pray?"

4ᵗʰ December 1990
THE HEALING POWER OF THE EUCHARIST

"To receive My healing presence in The Eucharist one must also experience the pain of My Passion and Death. All are part of the Eucharistic Presence. Oh My child, I touched your heart this morning. Your heart will hence forth be more open to the sacredness of My Own. You will experience My pain, My thirst for souls. My child, My little one, I make you a victim for others. There are not very many who answer this call. It is a demanding call but, My beloved little one, have I ever failed you in your hour of need? Would you ask anything else of Me this day? Today is a milestone in our relationship. In all relationships one can pinpoint a time of change, a time of knowing, a time of deeper commitment.

My child, I arranged this week. I arranged this rest to spend more time with Me. My child, I call you to spend the next three days with Me. I ask you to sacrifice all or at least as much as possible for My sake. My Mother has great plans prepared. Ask the others to join you. Even though you seldom meet, T... . is the link. You are united in Spirit, you are united in calling, you are united in purpose. The prayers of others help also to bring My plan about in you and others. Nothing is insignificant to Me. I use all to My advantage when hearts are open. Although you may not be together on Saturday, you will be united in Spirit. Each will be a part of all - even to being a part of My plan for all My children scattered throughout the world. No one is an island to oneself. Goodness and love touch all as evil does also.

My child, I bring you now into a deeper awareness of the community of My Saints on earth - and also My Saints in Heaven. The Eucharist embraces all the temples of My indwelling Presence.

My child, prepare yourself. I will not ask more than you can cope with but, your writing now will take a different slant - the way of the Eucharist - the light of the Eucharist to share with others. I have been preparing you down the years. You are ready now to begin. With My grace I anointed you this day at the Eucharist for this work. I hide from you My child the depth behind My actions."

29th December 1990
MARY :
I will change the hearts of all who let Me
I will change the hearts of all who listen
I will change the hearts of all who seek to change
I will lead all to My Son.

For this I leave My heavenly abode
For this I suffer with My little ones
To bring to Him who suffered and died
That all might know His Love.

31st December 1990   -   After the Eucharist
Before The Blessed Sacrament :

Mary :

 "Yes My child, I need at least one member in every community to sit at the feet of My Son. How can a community operate without prayer. If lay people can spend time with My Son why cannot one person spend at least the same time with Me in monasteries and convents etc."

Jesus :

"My child, I need to be taken out of the tabernacles to reach the tabernacles in men's hearts. If enough people sat with Me, united their hearts to Mine, great changes would come about in their homes, their communities, their country and throughout the world.

My child, you read a little of the sin of mankind in the newspapers and on TV. That is only one area and the area that appeals to readers and viewers to sell, to make money. There is much evil under the surface. I am being pushed aside, blasphemed with no one to speak for Me. My child, sit at My feet this day. I will be your strength. Come back soon. I will be waiting for you this afternoon. Then later I will tell you My need of you tonight."

1ˢᵗ January 1991
Mary:

"My child, leave things as they are. I led you to say the words. My chosen ones will come around in time. In the meantime there will be opposition but there is always opposition to Our works.

I will bring you to this shrine soon My child and you will know that I came there and that I have made My abode in this place. My child, stay with My Son. Pray much during the coming two days of adoration in your house. They are very important days. They will have great repercussions for good in the world. My child, We will be in residence in The Eucharistic Presence. Many and myriad will be the blessings on all who visit your home. I am with you in

---

My child, I have a special plan prepared for your home on this day week, Holy Thursday night. Would you be open to a vigil My child? I will arrange it My child if you wish?"

Oh my Beloved, You know that I want to do all You ask of Me. If You can arrange it I will be happy to fulfil this need in You.

"Well child, seeing as you honour this day every week I will arrange it."

How come with all the church regulations.

"But child, I am above all regulations."

My Beloved, I thank You for all the people who come and find comfort and peace here on this day.

21st. March 1991

---

your pain. Offer all to My Son, for My Son, during these days of sufferings and trials. My child, say the first mystery to-night. I will help you to pray the fifteen decades each day. Do not fail Me My little one. I know, I see. I will tell you, explain My reason for asking you later. Thank you My little one. I understand your difficulties, your distractions. Your efforts comfort Me.

Your prayer time here is nearly ended. Turn to My Son who needs you My little one. I will teach you to respond to His Love, His infinite, constant and unconditional Love, to a Heart of Love. What more can I say to you My child."

15ᵗʰ January 1991
Before The Blessed Sacrament :

To-morrow morning at 5 a.m. our time - unless a miracle happens - the Americans will be free to press the button for war. My Beloved, You lift me above the dangers, the impending sufferings, the consequences that others suffer. My Beloved, I come as I am. I have nothing to offer You - no feelings but a lack of peace when I am reminded of my own weaknesses. My Beloved, You offer us as we are, You accept us as we are, with the little or much, to Your Father in Heaven. And as I sit at Your feet here in Your Presence You ask nothing else of me. Mary, embellish my littleness with Your love to make it into something to offer to the King of Kings in His hour of anguish and the pain and sufferings of all my brothers and sisters. I am numb to all the last minute efforts for peace as if it is not important. But, I do ask help for all whom I know that carry Your pain at this time. I ask for Your strength, Your light, Your perseverance that Your Holy will be done in them. Lord I am nothing in this situation, I carry nothing in this awful war situation. I do nothing but just by being here in Your Presence I believe I fulfil a need, I add some little comfort to You.

25ᵗʰ January 1991
Before The Blessed Sacrament :

My Beloved, my heart overflows with joy this day with the news that the 'prayer before The Blessed Sacrament' leaflets were saved in the fire. They have come to light now after three weeks (?) in a miraculous way. Lord, who says You are not Lord of everything that happens. Who can say that You are not in control of everything that happens. Lord, You want us to believe that You are Lord of every situation - all You ask is that we trust You.

My Beloved, You did direct me all along about this prayer that You spoke to my heart many years ago before The Blessed Sacrament. I pray now that when it comes to being circulated outside, it will bring many souls to sit with You before Your Eucharist Presence. Perhaps You will give me in time the words to write the story of this prayer from the beginning.

Thank You Jesus, I know that if this is Your desire. Your Will, will be done.

29ᵗʰ January 1991
<u>Before The Blessed Sacrament :</u>
My Beloved, My spirit is so restless I cannot pray nor be still. My mind keeps racing on instead of resting in Your Love, soaking up the Love You wish to share with me here and now, especially since I received You in the Eucharist. My Beloved, You are so good to me in my weakness and frailty - so I write now to express my grateful thanks from a loving heart for all Your loving kindness and goodness to me in the past days and now. You tell me to spend more time in prayer. If You want me to be still in Your Presence in the quietness of spirit You will have to gift me with this grace. Dearest One, I can only give You what I receive from You. Perhaps I am not making enough effort but I cannot concentrate like I used to so perhaps my present state of prayer is perfect in Your eyes; my intention You know, because I come to please You alone. Although I haven't been able to listen to You speak to my heart - perhaps later I will be able.

Mary, I am trying to pray the three rosaries each day as best I can as You asked me - help me.

30ᵗʰ January 1991:   "I will bring My justice to bear soon. I will administer My justice as I deem appropriate. I am in control, in the little things as well as the great. My child I have shown you an example of My power recently. Many will be touched through this prayer before The Blessed Sacrament, which was saved by Me in the recent fire. It will make many think, reflect and give thanks. You will begin soon to really see My power, My power in the Eucharist manifested throughout this land. My child, pray much during these two coming days. Oh the comfort We receive and the blessings are manifold.

My child, you cannot always be aware of My Presence. You are My little one, you freely give Me your home - your time - that is all I ask. Do not overwork your body. You are tired - do not worry about your prayer. You are present to Me, that is all I ask. Remember I have spoken much to you about My Presence. It all happens as I said in the prayer. You mustn't worry, you mustn't be over concerned. It is all My work. I will lead and guide you in the distribution of the leaflets. Be open, listen and be present to My Presence and you fulfil My need of you. Thank you for coming My child - bless you."

3ʳᵈ February 1991 - Marianella
Before the Blessed Sacrament :
Mary: "My child, My child, this is only the beginning of many disturbances. The reaction to the prayer has been phenomenal. The Spirit is working here very profoundly this weekend. The message is spreading, will spread to many places from this week-end alone.

My child, the evil one will try and disturb you, confuse you, destroy you. Turn to Me, My child. I will take you in My arms and place My Mantle around you.

My child, people are hungry, thirsting for any word, their hearts and souls have been emptied to receive every word of My Son. My child, peace will be restored to your heart. I will crush him. He cannot do any harm here in the Eucharistic Presence. He will try My child. All you have said and done this weekend has been guided by Me My child. Do not be afraid. Spend these precious moments preparing for the coming Eucharist."

4ᵗʰ February 1991
Before The Blessed Sacrament :

Mary, my Mother, after the past few days of soul searching I am only at the beginning of learning and realising all the healings that have yet to take place within me. Oh so much inner healing so much purification yet to come. Mary, it would be easy to allow despair to enter my spirit but that would be the greatest rebuff, hurt I could inflict on the Hearts of Jesus and You. Mary, You know that now I am at a very vulnerable stage in my spiritual growth. I could be as putty in the hands of the evil one without Your help and protection. Mary, as I prepare now for the coming Eucharist help me to retain the gift of peace and hope I have received. But open my heart to receive more love - to love like You, pure love that comes from an empty heart, made ready and cleansed by the living waters that flow through the Holy Spirit.

Mary, I know that I will never walk again to the altar of the Most High to receive the precious Presence of Your Son, body, blood, soul and divinity without You, without Your Presence enveloping me. And Jesus will expect it, now that He gives me to You and You to me in this intimate relationship to grow in fullness and depth day by day.

11ᵗʰ February 1991   -   Feast of Our Lady of Lourdes
Before the Blessed Sacrament :

Thank You dearest Mother, You always speak to my heart on Your feast days to help me take a step nearer Your Son. This morning at the Eucharist my heart was filled with the burden of all my weaknesses, it was as if I carried the burden, my share of original sin down all the generations. This was my cross and more acceptable and more fruitful than if I was completely unaware of this and aware only of my love, my eagerness to please Him. And I was reminded of the day long ago that I was brought through a similar experience to touch the pit of despair each time I thought of my sin against charity at a particular prayer meeting, simultaneously God kept pouring out His love and mercy upon me making me feel ever more despairing. I believe that this is to be my little offering now, my little cross at the elevation, to be in communion with Him through Mary at His moment of sacrificing

Himself in obedience to the Father.

Mary, I can only attempt to make this offering to fulfil His wishes if you are with me and I with you because I so easily forget and become distracted but I trust you will guide me in whatever way it pleases Him. Later I get a greater insight into praying the Magnificat in union with Mary specially after the Eucharist.

Later
Before The Blessed Sacrament:
"My child, I have to keep reminding you that you are always on Mount Tabor when you come into My Eucharistic Presence.

My child, My Presence is your food, your strength, your peace, your hope. Oh My child, I keep pouring out My graces and blessings on you. Give thanks My child. Here you find the consolation you need. I will give you the means of coming often again, so that you may be refreshed and restored to give, when others come to your home for consolation. This is truly a blessed place, blessed over the years by the prayers of all - priests and people. Here you will receive your guidelines on prayer again. Here your own peace will be restored to share with others. Bless you My little one for answering My call again."

21ˢᵗ February 1991   -   House
Before The Blessed Sacrament :
"My child, be tolerant, they have not yet reached your understanding of the Eucharistic Presence. I meet all where they are. I understand that you must keep order and you must be in control of each situation. I am with you to help you. They are so enthusiastic at times. They will learn from your example."

Oh Mary, I pray I didn't hurt you. That was the last thing I wanted to do. Forgive me for any offence given.

"My child, listen attentively this day. I have much on My Heart, much for you to write. I thank you My child, last night pleased My Heart. It was truly a call of prayer that gave Me much joy. I will answer the prayers of each one and fulfil your needs.

My child, I think you know already what I am going to say to you. All your needs will be fulfilled here in My Presence. Here I have called you. It will be easier on you also - the quietness suits you. I will tell you when to return. I have your programme already planned. You would not be able to go to all the places you are invited. I will tell you when and where to go to further My plan in your life. I know all that is best for you.

You are My own little child, whom I have called to be a messenger of My love and particularly My Love in the Blessed Sacrament. Here I can use you for My greater glory and your greater reward. Over the years have you not seen My words come to pass, My desires being fulfilled? Oh My child, the joy I receive as each tabernacle is opened to My people. How I can draw them deeper into My Eucharistic Heart as each one sits in My Presence - the comfort they bring to Me and I repay them a hundred fold. My child, this will be your future mission - to witness to My need, to witness to the power of My Eucharistic Presence. Others have other roles. Do not disappoint Me. This mission is very close to My Heart and will change the hearts of My people. My Mother gathers My people to lead all to My Eucharistic Presence. Man has created his own weapons of destruction. The Eucharist is My weapon to heal mankind, to gather My people together, to bring peace amongst all nations, to bring about My Kingdom on earth. My child, I hide from you all that happens here. You would not be able in mind nor body to continue My work, My calling. Believe, have faith. You touch the world, the ends of the earth. I am working in the Gulf. I have not forgotten My word to you. Trust Me child."

Before The Blessed Sacrament :
"I prefer silence My little one. It is not easy for some to remain silent and they make a great effort to spend the night with Me. Soon have another rosary. I will direct your writing later. We have much time together yet, the day is young.

This group has been very faithful. They have been used to sharing amongst themselves. Gradually I will bring them into the silence - to speak to their hearts.

It pleases My Heart to have so many here this night. See My child, there is a hunger and thirst in My people to respond to My need. If My priests would listen. My people are ready for Perpetual

Adoration and they have no place to go."

4ᵗʰ March 1991:   Dearest Mother, I believe that it is only through the darkness of faith that you can teach me true worship of the Eucharistic Presence, to worship the Father in Spirit and in truth. And the wind outside is indicative of the storm within the sanctuary of my own heart now, ever restless in seeking the Father who seeks me. This is the only way I know of adoring Him here this morning, yet somehow I can relate all to Him who carries the storms of restlessness in all who seek Him everywhere.

> WRITE MY CHILD, DELIVER THIS MESSAGE :
> I DO NOT CONDONE WHAT MY PEOPLE,
> THESE IN AUTHORITY ARE SAYING, ARE DOING,
> SOME EVEN IN MY NAME.
> I DO NOT PUT MY NAME TO SUCH REGULATIONS.

8ᵗʰ March 1991:   "There is much in this land, much happening in this land that is not to My liking. People in authority are condoning evil. It does not help the young people. Even if every other country flaunts My desires, it does not mean that this land should follow suit. The commandments are still My commandments, the laws have not changed. People try to camouflage My laws, the laws for good and evil.

I need people who will stand up and be counted, perhaps even ridiculed in both church and state to speak out and call a spade a spade. Who are you afraid of ?

The day of salvation is now, is at hand for many, souls are their calling, souls are My priority. Every age has its own difficulties, temptations but here My child before My Eucharistic Presence, I say to you, write My child, deliver this message : I do not condone what My people, these in authority are saying, are doing, some even in My Name. I do not put My Name to such regulations. Preach sin, preach about the evil that exists, the evil that is trying to take over My own dear little ones.

My child, much is at stake. These writings may be dismissed but I write them in My Blood, My own Blood poured out for all on the Cross."

9th March 1991 - Later
Before the Blessed Sacrament :
"My child, before this Novena ends you will know your future ministry, all will be made clear to you. Do not be afraid. I confirm every word spoken to your heart by My Mother this morning. We will be your strength, your inspiration, you will receive insights never dreamed of, or expected.. My child, I thank you for your faithfulness, your trust, you will be rewarded with greater gifts, the more gifts the more you will be tormented. But that is obvious My child, My little one. The evil one will always try to destroy Our instruments. I have told you previously that you will be used for My Church. Each one I call has a special niche, unique to each, one confirms the other. My little one stay close to Me in the Blessed Sacrament. Here is your protection. Here I speak to your heart.

21st March 1991: "My child, never under-estimate the importance of this day (Thursday). I do not want to overburden you. You must not feel that you neglect Me at times. I am a very gentle Master. I give the strength for all I ask of all My little ones. Then all the prayers of all My little ones are gathered together on this day, My Heart leaps with joy. I am comforted and consoled for the neglect and rejection of many.

My child, I have a special plan prepared for your home on this day week, Holy Thursday night. Would you be open to a vigil My child ? I will arrange it My child if you wish?"

Oh my Beloved, You know that I want to do all You ask of Me. If You can arrange it I will be happy to fulfil this need in You.

"Well child, seeing as you honour this day every week I will arrange it."

How come with all the church regulations.

"But child, I am above all regulations."

My Beloved, I thank You for all the people who come and find comfort and peace here on this day.

23ʳᵈ March 1991:   "My child, if My Eucharistic Presence is an embodiment of My whole life, body, blood, soul, divinity, it embodies My whole passion and suffering from the beginning. Why cannot I be exposed for adoration during all these times? It will encourage all My little ones to come closer to Me, to be closer to Me, to prepare for My resurrection and their own resurrection made possible for all through My sacrifice."

6ᵗʰ April 1991:   "My child, if you didn't accept that I was above all regulations you would not have received the special blessing at the Eucharist this evening. My child, thank you for coming, thank you for letting Me come to you in the Eucharist. Thank you for your response."

My Beloved, thank You for speaking to my heart. I am learning that the prayer before The Blessed Sacrament refers above all to the times when we receive You in the Eucharist.

Mary my Mother, help me to ponder the words spoken by Jesus to my heart in the Eucharist.
Mary, love and pain go together in all prayer of the heart.

Sr. Faustina, pray for us all this night in preparation for the feast of Divine Mercy tomorrow brought about through the word of Jesus in your writings.

13ᵗʰ April 1991:   "My child, I refrain from disclosing Myself in a deeper way to you here in My Eucharistic Presence, you are very precious to Me and I do not want to overburden you, your work is onerous enough, also your suffering. My child, be aware of My Presence always. Be aware of My Love. Be aware of My Mother protecting you, caring for you. Be aware of the evil influences trying to destroy you because of your calling and the work I have planned for you.

The Eucharistic Presence is your protection. You will always find consolation and peace here. I will remind you again.

The Eucharist embraces all the indwelling temples of My Presence. Everybody is called to be a temple of the Holy Spirit. Reading : 1 John 2. 27"

> As for you, the anointing that you have received from him remains in you, so that you do not need anyone to teach you. But his anointing teaches you about everything and is true and not false; just as it taught you, remain in him.

25ᵗʰ April 1991:

"You must believe in the power of prayer to receive the fullness of My graces and blessings. You live in the time of My Resurrection. I am Resurrected. I am as truly present here as I appeared to My apostles and disciples after the Resurrection. Healings and blessings are for all who come seeking My help and intercession. You do not have to go to healing services to receive My healing. Believe in the healing power of My Eucharist. Healings, healings of body, mind and spirit will come about depending on your faith. Nothing was happening to those whose faith was diminished. Now I ask you to believe in the power of My Presence and you will see and experience miracles in your daily lives and in the lives of others. People are hungering for a sign these days of My power in this broken and tormented world.

Here I come. Here I am, more powerful than when I moved about on earth after My Resurrection. Believe Me My dear children, you have been empowered with My Spirit to go forth in My Name to bring the power of My Eucharistic Presence to others."

7ᵗʰ May 1991 - Later
Before The Blessed Sacrament :
My Beloved, here I am. 'Speak Lord, Your servant is listening'.

"I remind you again My little one, be aware of My Presence, My Spirit but, be aware also of the evil spirits that try to destroy you - especially when you are praying against evil spirits and their plans to destroy the souls of My children."

8ᵗʰ May 1991
Before The Eucharist :

Mary my Mother, help me to offer my pain, related to His in the coming Eucharist for the person He places on my heart and the success of the discussions taking place presently for a political settlement in the North.

13th June 1991
<u>Before The Blessed Sacrament :</u>
My Beloved, it has suddenly come to me that all these years You have been teaching me 'to be we' and I do not remember to take this literally and precisely as You intended. Everything I do, think, say must always be with You. I cannot do anything without You, apart from You. You are one with me writing this letter to You. I know You are not with me when I do wrong or go away from Your plan but, because we are so united You will not allow me to separate from You for any length of time. I must learn to think always that because of Your indwelling presence I cannot be apart from You. Instead of always using I, thinking of myself alone, I must think, speak, act as We. I must move beyond the stage of relating every pain, suffering, joy, act to Yours, to seeing and expecting Us to be one in body, mind and spirit in all things, especially in prayer - praying to Our Father, praying with Our Mother through the Spirit of Love. My Beloved, I know You will not fail me in this great act of faith I dare ask of You. But, first I must really learn when We commune in the Eucharist, the daily Eucharist. If this does not happen, I mustn't have any awareness of the depth of gift of the Eucharist and because You are not lacking in giving, I must be lacking in receiving. This must be my first lesson in practising **'Learning to be We'**.

15th June 1991
<u>Before the Eucharist:</u>
My Beloved, here I am. Mary my Mother, help me to prepare for the coming of Your Son. Enclose me in Your Immaculate Heart in preparation.

"My child, I waited and waited last night. I ask much but do I not give a hundred fold in return. I do not ask you to neglect your family but, I need you more than your family. **I have given you a place of peace to answer My call at any time.** Of course I love to have you before My Eucharistic Presence but when this is not possible or feasible come inside to Me. My Presence has made this room holy down the years. It is truly a place of prayer and peace, whether you are aware or not. The more you sacrifice all other interests now the closer you come to My Heart. You need to keep close in prayer these times. There are many evil influences about trying to destroy all My little ones."

17ᵗʰ July 1991:   *Yesterday was the feast of Our Lady of Mt. Carmel. Words cannot express the thanks that is in my heart for the healing received yesterday, Mary, before The Eucharistic Presence. A great fear has been lifted from my heart.*

'Nobody who seeks Your intercession is left unaided.'

Mary, I continue to depend on You to receive the strength and guidance for this day.

Later :
My Beloved, may Your Love and the love of Your Holy Mother replace the void vacated by this deep fear in my heart this day.

19ᵗʰ July 1991   -   After The Eucharist
Before The Blessed Sacrament :
My Beloved, You never fail to bring comfort to my aching spirit at The Eucharist. Now I can relate my inner turmoil to those of Your chosen ones who are in crisis of vocation. My Beloved, not all are made aware of the relative cause and results of our sufferings. My Beloved, I know I should be rejoicing in my spirit for the burdens I carry without which, I couldn't serve and comfort You and fulfil Your need of Me.

"My child, My child, I will direct and lead you through the present crisis. Surrender all to Me. Do not be down-hearted. Be joyful in your calling. My beloved child, through your purification I will be free, because you will be free, to use you as I wish. I need your full and total surrender for the next stage of your work for Me. Your writings will change because of this freedom I bring you. Rest now with Me. Come with Me to drink at the fountain of all graces. Nothing can happen to you outside of My Will for you."

1ˢᵗ August 1991
Before The Blessed Sacrament :

My Beloved, I come to-day to drink at the well of living waters in Your Eucharistic Presence. You use the thirst in my body to remind me of the thirst in my soul and to relate this thirst to Your thirst for souls. My Beloved, I have been so blinded by my own sinfulness that I have neglected You - rejected You.

Here in Your Eucharistic Presence 'Teach me the power of Your Eucharistic Presence that I may know it, claim it, use it.'

Let me know in my heart by writing on my heart the reality of the prayer You gave me before the Eucharistic Presence on the eve of the First Friday many years ago now. How little my response to all the blessings You have bestowed on me down the years. Lord, do not look at my failings but, look to the response of all those who visit You here during these two days.

6ᵗʰ August 1991:

"Oh My child, you are truly on Mt. Tabor as you sit here with Me in My Eucharistic Presence. So few realise this My child. You cannot climb higher in this life. My child, the past while, you have been living in the Valley. Today I give you a taste again of the mountain top, but child, dear child, I prepare you for the days ahead. You must not be fearful. I have promised you, trust My Word, live My Word. T..... and yourself will complement one another on this journey through valleys and mountains, guided and led by My angels, My Holy Spirit and accompanied at all times by My Mother and I. Do not be fearful of the terrors of the nights, they will pass. My child, these are times of purification. These are times of preparation for the days ahead.

All My little ones suffer My sufferings one way or another. I share My sufferings with those I love, whom I have chosen for greater works. I give you souls. You have experienced a reflection of My thirst for souls."

2nd October 1991
Before The Eucharist :

"Rose, Rose, Rose, listen to Me My child. Confusion does not come from Me. Confusion is a ploy of the evil one.

Child of My Heart, there is nothing wrong in your mind. Your mind and heart is under the control of My Spirit. To-day is the feast of the Holy Angels. Today and everyday, your angel guardian, your guardian angels take care of you. Child, do not entertain thoughts that will disturb the mind. Rest in My peace - My Mother will teach you. She is your Mother and Queen of Peace. My child, you are being disturbed because of your work. You are My little instrument. You pray for My priests and religious. You suffer for My priests and religious. I will not let the evil around you take over your mind.

My child, how I suffered in My Mind. It was more painful, more disturbing than all the physical pain I suffered at the passion and at the crucifixion.

My child, I am in control. I take care of you. It is right that you take a rest from all mental exercises. Find Me in nature. Seek Me in My creation, My beautiful creation. Here you will find the healing you need. Yes child, go away. I have a beautiful and wonderful rest prepared for you. Do not be afraid nor fearful, nor feel guilty of neglecting Me. Remember prayer is as easy as breathing. I am everywhere. Child of My Heart, prepare now for the coming Eucharist. Here you will find comfort and strength for the day ahead. I will control every action of the day. Thank you child for your faithfulness."

8th October 1991
Before The Blessed Sacrament :

Mary, thank You for Your support and protection before the Eucharistic Presence of Your Son. Mary, we know that we can count on You this night. It is Your work, Your desire, we desire also. Protect us all, guide us all, use us all as Your little instruments. Open our hearts to the Holy Spirit. Bless all who come in answer to Your call.

Mary, won't You arrange the format. Oh Mary, keep us all united in love. Protect us from any agro.

Glencree
Before The Blessed Sacrament :
Mary :
"My child, My child, write:
My Son, My Son so defiled, so defamed, so disfigured for love of you. Oh My children, I bring you here to this holy place to-night to give praise and honour to My Son in the Eucharistic Presence.

My children I have been gathering you for some time now. Thank you Our dear children for answering My call.

This night I pour out My graces on each one. My dear children, My heart bleeds when I see My dearest Son rejected by so many.

My children, I call you to this holy place to give thanks, to make reparation for others.

My children, you have been faithful, very faithful over the past year. My Heart overflows with love for you all, the sacrifices you have made to answer My call. My child, I call you here this night. Remember in Lourdes I did not want you to look for Me at the grotto when My Son was exposed in The Blessed Sacrament in the church. I call you here to bring about Exposition of the Blessed Sacrament in this church. I have been preparing My people for this."

5ᵗʰ November 1991
Before the Blessed Sacrament :
My Beloved, today through the intervention of Your Holy Mother, You begin in our hearts a new phase in our realisation of the meaning of reconciliation. If this place is to become in time a place of healing and reconciliation for this land, much healing, inner healing within ourselves must take place first that we might be reconciled within ourselves to bring about reconciliation within our families, from which great healings will spread to others, to all who come truly seeking this same reconciliation. Reconciliation must begin at a very deep level within the spirit, at the root of our being to effect the same influence for good in others.

"Child, I begin here with you, the recent pain is a preparation for all I ask of the others. Child, child, it is truly painful but it is through your sufferings related to Mine I can bring about My plans, Our plans for this place, to make this ground, holy ground.

My Mother has already told you that We work through the efforts of man, We enlarge on the efforts of man. All the prayer of the past has helped, this was really the beginning of the great reconciliation now about to be brought to fruition.

My child, I do not ask the impossible, I am with you. I am your strength. I use your weaknesses. I use you because of your weakness. Your weaknesses are your strength. Yes, My child, the time has come to share the fruits with others. What I revealed to you in the early days of your writings is about to happen.

My child, the writing I refer to now, you have resurrected it because the time has come to bring this writing to the attention of My Shepherds. Child of My Heart, you cannot expect great things, monumental changes to happen except through suffering and times of temptation. The evil one will try and block this plan in every way he can.

My children, together through your united prayers and sufferings, I can bring about the great plan I have prepared, prepared to bring My fold, My different folds together into one."

TAKEN FROM 1979 WRITINGS

20th May 1979:   *Through the Pentecostals Lord You brought about this great Renewal or Charismatic Movement in Your churches. Through them and other Christian groups You brought back the power of the Word in the Bible. The Catholic Church You made the custodian of the Eucharistic Presence. You now ask them to share this Eucharist with all the other churches. You died for all Your people. You gave Your Body and Blood under the appearance of bread and wine for all Your people.*

21st May 1979:   *Our church says you must believe in the Eucharistic Presence. What is belief? Can any human being* *look into the heart of another and ask, do you believe? There are as many degrees of belief as there are people. I think that if one really believed in the Eucharistic Presence, we could not receive and live.*

Do you not think that Jesus knew when He instituted the Eucharist that there would be different interpretations amongst His people. Did this stop Him? No. He instituted it so that all people with all their interpretations and beliefs could receive it and in receiving would never die. Does it not follow that Cod, Who created us all like Himself, wanted us to receive His Son as One Body, not divided to give Him praise, honour, glory, worship and adoration. Lord, You want us all to press forward to attain to this unity in You. May the Holy Spirit touch the hearts of all people this Pentecost with a great sense and purpose of unity and together we will go forward to claim the victory of Christ before all the world over the darkness and evil that strive to keep us apart for its own end. Acts 10.

25th May 1979
My dear children :

"Do not be dismayed or hurt because of Me when I tell you to share the Eucharist. Did My Father not share Me to the extent of letting Me become man to die on the cross for the forgiveness of the sins of all men? If you had known and asked Him before My coming not to send Me as so many would not believe and reject Me, would He have changed His design? You do not and cannot comprehend My infinite love for mankind. My love is beyond all human understanding. You do not know the power of My love in the Eucharist. It satisfies Me that people come in love even without understanding and belief, My love is so great. Can you not understand, My dear ones, it is I you hurt more than yourselves. Do you not see that receiving in love brings belief. All things are possible, nothing is impossible with Me. If I could only make My people understand, so much goodwill could follow. Do help Me to bring all people together for My sake. I need you together, it is painful to have My Body broken."

23ʳᵈ November 1991: *Mary, today is Saturday, the day of the week dedicated to you. Give me a listening heart, a loving heart to prepare me for the coming of Jesus in the Holy Eucharist. Mary, I depend on you to welcome Him, to respond to His Love, to listen to Him and give praise and thanksgiving, for the perfection of His Love and Holy Will in all the circumstances of my life, that the graces of this Holy Sacrifice and celebration will touch the whole world. Oh if only we could empty ourselves of self how much we could share the Body of Your Son with the Body of Your Son.*

Oh Holy Spirit You see into the depths of my soul, make it possible for me to fulfil His need of me. I cannot really be Eucharist to others unless I am truly Eucharistic in the Eucharist.

"Oh My child, My child, listen to My Heart beat with yours in the Eucharist, converse with yours. Prepare now for this sublime union of Hearts and Spirits."

Later before the Blessed Sacrament :

"Yes, My child, as you look at the picture of the Eucharistic Miracle of Luciano, many of My priests need such a miracle nowadays to confirm in their hearts the True Presence in the Eucharist.

Child, pray much for My priests, suffer all for My priests, your night vigils are My design. They compensate, they bring comfort to My broken and bleeding Heart, for those who do not believe. Child, when they neglect their prayer, the evil one takes over. Oh My child, these are dangerous times but for the prayers and sufferings of My little ones, My Father couldn't restrain His anger.

Oh child intercede for My priests, My dearest of children. How I weep, and My Mother also, to see so many being sucked into confusion and disbelief in My Real Presence in the Eucharist. How can I ask them? How will they be open to My Word to share Me with others who often have more love in their hearts.

Oh My child, do not fear all I ask of you. My Mother, My angels protect you at all times. The other little worries you carry in your heart are of no consequence.

Oh My child, all I ask that you be open to My Spirit.

This meeting tonight (with V...) will confirm and bring you a step further into understanding My overall plan.

My child, I gather the pieces of the jig-saw. I am gathering you, you from different parts to come together in ways you do not comprehend. My child, keep your eyes on Me, keep your heart united to Mine. My Mother is your advocate now. How she cares for you! She sees all, knows My desires, your needs. Call on her. She waits. She waits."

28ᵗʰ November 1991: "Oh My Shepherds, listen to My little ones. Their hearts are open to Mine. I knock, they open up to My desires, My pleadings.

Oh My dear Shepherds, spend time before My Eucharistic Presence. Expose My Presence on the altars. I will enter your hearts, change your hearts to be Eucharistic Hearts to combat all the evil forces that seek to destroy you, take you from Me. You will then truly fill My sandals as you stand at My altars as you celebrate the Eucharist."

5ᵗʰ December 1991 - Later
Before The Blessed Sacrament :
My Beloved, I have found a new name for You - my Divine Repairer. Lord, where will You begin. I mustn't say this. You have been blessing me and healing me from the beginning. Before You created me You knew me and carved me on the palm of Your Hand. You knew all my faults and failings, besides the good and promising traits that I received from my parents and fore-parents, and all the outside influences and circumstances that have taken their toll over the years, some to build on what I had received, others to tear me down. Now dearest One, You are in the process of opening up all the wounds of the past, bringing all the memories out into the open to heal. It is very painful at times as You told me it would be, but with Your strength I am learning to cope a little because I know You are using all for Your greater glory. It is wonderful to know that You can use every emotion, good and bad, as we offer all to You. Oh Lord, how gentle You are with us, how mercifully You accept us because You can channel

all for good, because we know You love us and when we try to love You in return You can bring good out of everything.

My Beloved, there are many on my heart this night. First I must bring before You the priests I have heard of who do not believe in the real Presence. Lord I know that this is the greatest insult one of Your chosen ones can give You. Truly Lord, they are being led astray by the evil one.

Lord as we sit here in Your Eucharistic Presence this night we bring those priests who cause You so much pain and anguish. Lord, I give very little to comfort You. I spend much time away from You when I should be with You. Although I have very little feeling these times, I come in faith because I know this pleases You, comforts You a little for those who neglect You totally.

Oh my Beloved, I will try now with the help of Your Holy Mother to open my heart to Yours to rest in and with You.

12ᵗʰ December 1991

The Presence to embrace all Presence : The Blessed Sacrament

As I sit here in Your Presence Lord
Seeking searching the stillness
To allow Your Love take root
It evades me.

Oh the void that is within me
I must believe that love
Once desired and sought
Must respond.

I must believe that Your Presence
Suffices for all my poverty
Overcomes all the deficiencies
Of my immortal soul.

Oh Lord, Oh Lord,
There is nothing in the heart and mind of man
You cannot fulfil
In this Presence.
If in this Presence You are present
Both human and divine

Our poverty must become
Your resting place.

You are present everywhere I know
In creation, in man, in everything
Why then leave us this legacy
In death.

Why humble Yourself so
To become less than man
Inanimate, smaller than the palm
Of a new-born babe.

Lord, I am searching, searching
To find the answers
For those who say but don't believe
That the wafer and drop of wine contain all.

All that mortal man can surmise
All that mortal man can conjure in his mind
Faith alone is needed
To receive.

Faith of a mustard seed
Is all You ask of us,
Watering is Your domain
To move mountains.

If seed and growth are here present
Available to all who seek
Why search further
Than the mountain top?

Creation depicts Your majesty and power
People Your humanity
Eucharist Your passion and death
The pinnacle of Your humility.

God prepared the way from the beginning
When there was no beginning
That all paths would converge
To include all, at the mountain top.

11ᵗʰ January 1992 - Before The Eucharist
Before The Blessed Sacrament :

"Yes My child, you are beginning to understand why I call you here to spend time with Me. Before My Exposed Presence you fulfil My need of you, you fulfil My need for souls. Child, feelings do not matter, you know that now. Come child as you are in all your weaknesses and miseries. I will supply, embellish all into My divine virtues. I change you into an image of Myself. I give you My Divine Humanity. You become an intercessor for the world, the healing of the world especially My Church. By the Church I mean the institutional Church that is in great need of healing. Many forces gather to destroy this Church. Child, give Me yourself, surrender yourself to Me and I will astound you with My wisdom. You will not be believed because of your littleness but those I touch will know and not doubt. Child, I have shown you My Heart, through your own heart. I am within, abiding in you, changing your heart as you come to me daily in the Eucharist. Child you understand, do not doubt My power. So many of My very own do not understand. I will teach and touch many through these writings. Child, I will give you the strength

---

"When the Sacrament of Marriage becomes a stable institution, I will allow My priests - those who choose, to marry, not until then."
11th February 1992

"I fulfil your needs, not your wants."
29th. February 1992

---

and the courage to carry out My plan. Yes child, you will have Me more often in your home. Have I not made it possible for you.

How I love to gather you around My Heart in the Eucharist. Such a banquet we all enjoyed last night. Heaven and earth rejoiced together. Thank you each one of you. The one who was missing also rejoiced. You compliment one another. See the charges being brought about in each one.

Child, now that a great fear has been lifted from your heart you will be freer to hear and receive My word for others.

Prepare now My little one as I taught you many years ago. This prayer I spoke to your heart first for you, others will benefit also. Thank you.

I am here waiting, waiting also to give and receive to make all hearts one with Mine, to abide in each one to make Us all Trinity."

31ˢᵗ January 1992
Morning :
My Beloved, I know You want to speak to my heart. Should I get up and go to the church or do You want me to write now? Oh my Beloved, how indecisive I am. I never know what to do myself. I depend on You for everything. Do send me Your Holy Spirit. How I need Him.

"Child, child of My Heart, My Sacred Heart, I need you now. Listen My child, so few of My Elders, those in control listen to My Word. They are so engrossed in their own importance, their own knowledge, the extent of their own intellects; they close themselves off from Me and My Word.

Child, My Heart breaks to see My little ones neglected, lost, many going astray because of lack of leaders. Oh My dear children, My Church, those in control are in a time of great purification, also My people; my little ones especially. Do not worry, do not be afraid of all I ask of you. I will be your strength. Now you realise on your own you are nothing - nothingness - without Me. Without My Holy Spirit the evil one would take you over and lead you astray also, but dear child, I do not want you to be afraid of this mission I place on your little shoulders. Oh so little you are, a very small child to

Me - with Me. It is because of your littleness that I chose you. Others do not appreciate this, but I speak through My little ones, hence so few believe, because they do not understand My ways. Child, you see through My strength what you can accomplish. Little did you think when you woke up this morning that your mind would be so clear to write, but this is a little warning to remain quiet in Me. Child, I will direct you now not to become over enthusiastic, but I use this impulsiveness within you to reach those I send to you. I speak through you to touch their hearts, when their hearts are open to Mine. You have much ahead of you. Child, dear child, you now understand why I ask you to spend more and more time with Me, sitting at My feet before the Eucharistic Presence. Child, I hide from you all that is happening even in your own parish, city and country at this moment of time. Child, you will soon see the results of your many years of writing, many years of faithfulness - but remember dear child I graced you so with this grace. Your home is now a place of refuge for many. Oh dear child, your home will soon be an example for many. When others see, many people will be drawn, have been drawn over the years to a deep love of Eucharistic Adoration. Now child, I have a word of comfort for you. See the peace I placed in your heart yesterday while another mother would be devastated with anxiety and pain. You know My peace. Yes child, your daughter may have no fear. I use all these illnesses for My greater glory and her greater reward. Her willingness is come about through your faithfulness to My Eucharistic Presence. Child, assure her I take special care of her and all her care.

Ask her as a special request to please My Holy Mother to pray the rosary, the five decades, each night with the family, the way I taught you My little one. My dear Mother asks this of her especially. She will learn to know why, love it, as My Mother teaches you.

I bless you all now, all your family. I have all their deepest desires in hand, within My Heart. Child, arise now, come I wait for you, I long for your coming. Oh child, the pain until you come! Come, come."

Yes Beloved, I will go now. Thank You.

11th February 1992 - Feast of Our Lady of Lourdes
Before the Blessed Sacrament :
"Yes child, I do call you to write this day. I have much on My Heart. My Holy Mother is preparing you for My greatest and final work for you. Do not be afraid My dear child of what I ask of you in the coming days. Child, in the days past you touched on the area of these coming writings. Now I gather My little ones, chosen for this great plan I prepare to come to fruition. Believe Me dear child, you will have much opposition but do not doubt My power, My power over all evil, all evil spirits that will try and distort My plans. Get ready My child, prepare with much prayer. I gather others to support you in prayer also.

Child, your safeguard will be My Eucharistic Presence. You will become more and more aware of the power of My Eucharistic Presence in the days ahead.

Child, about the documentary you watched last night on the television, (*Priests of passion, Channel 4*); at the morning Eucharist I spoke to your heart again, My wishes, My desires for My priests. I do require celibacy in these present times. As I told you before that does not say the regulations may not be changed at a future time. But child, you are aware through My grace of the present state of the Marriage Sacrament in these times. All the forces of evil are bent on destroying this sacrament as unrealistic and of no consequence. They seek to destroy the idealism of My children everywhere. The whole media is responsible and used to destroy this beautiful and noble sacrament I gave to bring My Kingdom about in the hearts and minds of My dear children.

Why allow My priests to marry in such a temperature of evil, to double and treble sin in their lives? Child, My priests, My dear priests need so much prayer to counteract the temptations of this present modern age of lust and greed. Lust and greed are the two greatest evils that take My little ones. Beware all, all My children, priests, parents, children, married and unmarried of the temptations of this age. Prayer is the answer, prayer the only answer."

Later before the Blessed Sacrament :
"When the Sacrament of Marriage becomes a stable institution, I

will allow My priests - those who choose, to marry, not until then. Some may say that this would make it a stable institution through their example but this is not so, they too could be drawn into the mire of the present way of life.

See divorce, the repercussions in the countries where it is practised. We must think of the common good.

More preparation is needed for marriage and more counselling for those marriages that are shaky before they disintegrate. Provision is already made for special cases. This should be enough for the present time. This is all part of the process for unity. You will be a link in the chain of events I have planned."

16ᵗʰ February 1992
Before The Blessed Sacrament :

My Beloved, 'here I am, Your servant is listening.' Abba Father, in the name of Jesus, open my heart to the Holy Spirit.

Beloved, I am sad this day to see the Consolata Fathers leave Ireland, but I believe that in their place You send us these nuns 'Disciples of the Divine Master', to continue their work among us and to bring to fruition the seeds they have sown. I thank You for my link with them. I truly pray for each one of them. It is a great challenge, but Mary, Mother of Consolation, I know will truly guide and protect them in the days ahead. May the vision of Sister Mary Paula be fulfilled now to bring untold blessings on our city, country and the world. It is truly a mission for these troubled times. I already see the desires of Your Eucharistic Heart coming about in my own time.

Lord how wonderful You are, so faithful to Your promises. May we see the peace You promised for our own country come about in the days ahead, to make us again a land of saints and scholars, to emigrate missionaries to the other countries in the EEC and throughout the world.

MARY :   "Now child, I have a further writing for you. Listen carefully My little one.

Spread the writing of 11th February. This is an important

message. I will place on your heart the people to whom you will give it. Collect the other writings on unity also. They are very important for these times. **You are a link with the others who receive the same messages.** I bring you together."

"Do not worry and say 'I have no discernment'. I am guiding you; and My Holy Mother. We will not let the evil one misguide you about these important matters. He will try My dear child. He bothers you a lot lately but We are with you protecting you day and night. Do you not see dear child that he is trying to dishearten you, lead you into despair. Keep fighting, keep trying. I will relieve you in My time. I use your sufferings now. I need them. Oh how I need them. Child, do not let yourself be drawn into empty discussions. Your mind is a very delicate part of the body and must be treated gently and carefully. Do not try to solve the problems of others to the detriment of your own health. Be still, remain quiet in Me. I need you now more than ever. I need you to write and deliver My messages for the Church. **You will know hassle and persecution but remember dear child, that is part of the life of a prophet.** Your endurance and fortitude will serve you well.

Yes child, it is time to pray the Divine Mercy prayer. Child, order your ticket but I will tell you the times to attend. I do not want you to overstrain body and mind nor neglect your Eucharistic Adoration, although this is part, together with the Celebration of the Eucharist, the most important part of the Conference.

Bless you My child for coming. Remember the people I place in your heart. Come to Me later."

29ᵗʰ February 1992
After The Eucharist :
Jesus my Beloved, thank You. I know You will answer the needs of all Your little ones in Your time and in Your way.

All that was on my heart yesterday, You do not want me to carry on my own. Many others feel the same. How many parents are burdened so for their children?

"I will prepare the way for change. Yes My child, a change is coming. Many will not be prepared for this change. Many will

not welcome it, but My will, will be done. I am in control. I hold the hearts of all in My Heart, also My Mother. All My children are Hers also.

My own precious Mother has taken it upon Herself to prepare the way of the Spirit. Yes My child, before great happenings in the world, She comes to warn, to prepare, to intercede, to beg, to plead with all to listen, to hear, to see the signs, the forebodings before they happen and perhaps to stave off and maybe lessen and even prevent coming disasters in the world. Child, you have seen and heard in your own land, in the people, the anger, the resentments, the results of the degradation that has taken over. It is an insidious evil so subtle that people have allowed themselves to be duped - people in authority, in Church and State, even the parents, well meaning parents. I do not refer to those parents who are even a bad influence on their children but the good God-fearing family.

You have heard a few, only a few as yet of the youth I am preparing to change the climate of opinion, of morals, for justice to filter through. I have prepared men of principle. I have prepared men who will influence coming events.

Wherever My Eucharistic Presence is exposed, people through their prayer and commitment will see and know the plans I am preparing to bring about the change I envisage, I have planned.

My child, come back later. I will be waiting for you. Go in peace now My little one.

'I fulfil your needs not your wants'. You understand."

2ⁿᵈ March 1992
Before The Blessed Sacrament :
Abba, You have prepared a very busy itinerary for me this day. You will have to give me the strength to carry out Your will. I know You need me more than I need You. I must be a very heavy burden for You to carry. The turmoil seldom leaves me now. I wish I could willingly and lovingly give You all.

Oh if I could only understand in the minutest way how Your Son humbles Himself to give us Himself in the Eucharist.

I come each day to sit in the Presence, less and less I seem to appreciate and treasure this gift.

Mary, my Mother, help me to understand. Teach me to be humble of heart.

30ᵗʰ April 1992
Before The Blessed Sacrament :

Beloved, the worries of yesterday are solved by today. Oh when I read back my writings this strikes me. How futile and useless is worry and anxiety and yet because we are human we cannot help ourselves. Every Thursday I become more and more aware of this truth as I hear the pain that others carry in their hearts. And how can our pain be compared to the pain You carry in Your heart for all Your children everywhere; and we come to unburden our pain unto You.

Beloved, we want to share in Your pain, to lessen the load You carry, to help, comfort and console You in Yours, or perhaps now that we are in the time of Resurrection in the Liturgy of the Church You would rather we praise You in Your new found glory, midst all the evil and confusion in the world around us. We must look to Your victory instead.

Later:

"Yes child, tonight is very precious and dear to My Heart. Look at My Heart. I am here open to all in the Monstrance, in the Host therein.

Child, look deeply, see the scars, the wounds, so deep, so hurting. Man rejects My Love.

Child of My Heart, recall now the writings of this night over the years. All happens, all is happening."

Beloved, do You want me to do the vigil to-night?

"No child, go to bed as usual. Unite in spirit with the others. I need you tomorrow to pray, to write. I have much on My Heart. My Heart cannot contain the love, the graces I have prepared for all.

So few come to receive. Thank you My little one for giving Us your home. See child, they answer My call. Truly I will bless all and all they carry in their hearts."

19ᵗʰ May 1992
<u>Before The Blessed Sacrament :</u>

Yes Beloved, more and more I realise that in fulfilling this desire of Your Heart, that in opening the tabernacle doors, we will find the peace and strength we need in this time of purification for the world. Look at any country in the world, with no exception, turmoil, unrest, crime, sins of all dimensions exist. To bring about a change all the pillars of society that man has built must be destroyed before You can build a society, a welcoming society for Your second coming. Lord, You Promised us a time of peace where Christian values would be the norm. Who could possibly say, we are ready in such state to receive You. Truly Lord we live now in a time of great mercy. We live as You told Sr. Faustina and many others but we must not let this time of mercy pass without answering Your call, Your invitation to all mankind to repent.

Lord, the people of this land are in a quandary about this **Maastricht Treaty**. *The politicians tell us to vote yes, but many others who speak in Your name say no.*

We are a country of very high unemployment. Unemployment very often leads to crime etc., and we are promised that united to Europe we will have better prospects in the area of unemployment etc.

Lord, You know the answers to all our problems. Lord, You have the answers to all our problems. Lord, we have many young people seeking work, leaving school with no prospects. What should we do? Help us, we seek to be guided by You, to do Your Holy Will.

"Child, child, am I not confirming for you everyday all I have been teaching you over the years about The Eucharist. Are you not surprised to see the very words I gave you to write now appear in a recent book?

Child, there is a mountain of wisdom and knowledge in the writings over the years. They need to be edited and compiled in book form now. I will send you someone now to help you. **I want these writings to be made public, the time has come**. I will take care of the others. You mustn't take on the worries of others. It is a time of great healing for all. Child, I need you free now to complete My work. I gave you a special calling that I want fulfilled now in these times. Child, believe that you will receive and have My strength in the daily Eucharist. I will recall to your mind all I have taught you in the past. The darkness will pass now and you will receive a clarity of mind through My Spirit for this work to be completed in the near future.

Child, children, you are both in this together. You have both been so faithful, so faithful. We make allowances for your weakness.

My Mother and I appreciate the efforts, the sacrifices you have both made for Us. See, you will see Our light directing you both now and always."

Later:
Here I am Lord, to make myself present to Your Presence. Mind to mind, heart to heart, spirit to spirit, to fulfil Your need of me.

22ⁿᵈ April 1992:   *Thank You Mary, thank You for directing me just now to make that phone call.*

Oh Mary, You never fail me. I wish I was more trusting. I know all will be well, because You are guiding all concerned. Mary, thank Jesus Your Son. He did answer my prayer for another before the Eucharist last night.

I am so scattered these times, so confused and indifferent and yet He never changes. He seems to do more for me when I neglect Him. Oh Mary, do help us to give Him joy and glory to-night when we come before the Eucharistic Presence. We hope to join with all Your little ones who pray before the Blessed Sacrament especially these days in preparation for the march next Sunday. May our 4O hours Adoration beginning on Sunday 24th in the parish be well attended to bring and receive all the special graces and blessings You have prepared for us and all we carry in our hearts.

26th April 1992
Before The Blessed Sacrament :
'Here I am Lord, Your servant is listening'.

"Yes child, I have been waiting for you, always waiting. Thank you My little one.

There is much on My Heart, there is much confusion in yours. It is the state of the Church in your land, not only in your land but throughout the world. The time of purification is upon all My people. The evil one is truly making a great, great attempt to destroy all. My Heart bleeds to see so many come under his influence. So child, children, all My children everywhere need to pray, pray more, pray constantly to destroy the evil influences in your midst.

> *"...but the rosary must be recited as She intended, slowly, gently, prayerfully from the heart."*

My Mother gathers the people of this land under the banner of the Rosary, also under other titles but, as the rosary saved this land in the past it will protect it again. Through the Rosary, She is sharing Me with you all, drawing you ever closer into a more intimate relationship with Me, but the rosary must be recited as She intended, slowly, gently, prayerfully from the heart.

When you learn to know Me you will seek Me. Where? In the Eucharist. Here I give Myself in all My fullness in unlimited love to all. And Eucharistic Adoration will spread throughout the land.

Already dear children Eucharistic Adoration is taking place in many parishes, so evil forces are in battle now. Wherever they see defeat looming they increase their efforts to destroy.

Children, yours is a very special calling, never forget this. You compliment one another in your calling. Rose, as you are the elder partner, you remain and spend more time before My Eucharist Presence, to cover and protect Teresa as I send her out into the world."

'Victorious Queen of the Universe, show us Your power'.

27th May 1992   -   Teresa
Before The Blessed Sacrament :

"I am the Victorious Queen of the Universe. I am your Queen. I am your Mother. Thank you, My Son's faithful friends and My own dear children for your faithfulness. You are both the joy and consolation of the two Hearts of Love. I envelop you both in My Mantle of Light. I ask you both to pray the Rosary this morning in the way I have taught you. I need your prayers My dear children. If only We had more like you and Our other faithful little ones, all wars would end, would stop instantly. All the works of the evil one would be blown away as a puff of smoke in the power of a people united in prayer. Continue to pray dear children. Be vigilant. Your enemy prowls around you like a roaring lion. You have nothing to fear. He cannot harm those who are covered with the shield of prayer and dwell in the powerful light of the Eucharist. I have much to say, but right now I ask you to pray. I will speak to you both again. Peace Our dear precious children. Peace always."

8th June 1992:   "We do understand you are a people good at heart but can be easily led astray as affluence comes and greed takes over and much is lost. Family life is changed, not always bad but the spiritual is neglected. My Mother comes again to bring the Rosary back into the homes of Her children. How true, the family who prays together, stays together. My Mother's Heart breaks to see so many marriages break up, unhappy, only held together with a string. Peoples hearts must change. We have Our faithful little ones. Thank you Our dear little ones for the comfort and consolation We receive from you all. We know it is not easy. Because of original sin it would not (be easy) but the reward is great, very great for all who try. Many carry heavy crosses for Our sake. Do We not know and see their struggle. Some are chosen for special work in the vineyard, sometimes amongst the laity to prepare the way for the shepherds. Shepherds sometimes fail to see the heart, My Heart in the law. Laws were never meant to be rigid, but to be interpreted with the heart. Never white and black, black and white. There is a seed for good, a seed for bad in each one. The seeds for bad came from original sin and through the generations one or other may have been developed more for better or worse. So dear children, no one is immune from the

forces of evil within oneself and outside of oneself. Child, I have much for you to write but I will spread it out - not all at one session. I want you to pray much. Sit with Me. Be aware of My need of you. Open your heart to Mine and I will take away all confusion to clear the mind for further writings.

Yes My child, My Mother invites you to G..... to-night. She has a special blessing for each of the 'five'. Pray much for one another. You are under attack."

2ⁿᵈ July 1992
Before the Eucharist :
" Child, you live in a time of great turmoil, of much sin and division. The forces of evil are at work in all areas. The work of the evil one can better be redressed through Eucharistic Adoration. There too I ask My shepherds to respond to the call I have placed in the hearts of My little ones, to spend time before My Eucharistic Presence in adoration. Here the forces of evil can be dispersed, put to flight. They seek above all to bring division and confusion into the Church, and no longer is the institution of marriage a stable commitment - hence family life is being disintegrated. Children suffer the consequences. They lack the security of Christian upbringing and are open to all the snares of evil that come their way as they reach adolescence and adult-hood. Child, children, pray much. Be an example to others. My Mother comes amongst My people to speak to My people, to call for a crusade of prayer for families, to bring stability and Christian values back into the homes of My little children to face all the perils they will encounter in their daily lives.

The Rosary is a preparation for Eucharistic Adoration later, and Eucharistic Adoration brings about a change of heart in all who practice this devotion. A change of heart amongst My people can bring about the peace I promised for all nations."

Before The Blessed Sacrament (House) :
Dearest Mother Mary, give me the words to write to Jesus to thank Him for the wonderful gift of healing He brought about here this afternoon before The Blessed Sacrament.

Mary, we knew You were leading us in the Rosary. It was prayed just as You asked, gently, slowly and in unison and from the heart - a fitting preparation of what was about to happen. We know dearest Mother that R….. is a very special and precious child of You Both. The healing of her cancer was a most wonderful honour and experience to happen here in our midst.

Truly He has shown us the power of the Eucharist, and He did promise that soon we would see it .

29ᵗʰ July 1992
Before The Blessed Sacrament :
Beloved, thank You for the insight received at the Eucharist this morning, letting me see the wisdom of Your ways.

I ask and ask to be healed of a certain weakness and now You tell me that without it my soul would have been impoverished. It must be like the thorn in his side that St. Paul speaks about in his writings. Beloved, help me surrender all to You. You ask and ask and I always hold back my will, except when You give me the grace to respond. So really without Your grace I can do nothing and I am reminded for the umpteenth time, I have nothing to offer You but the burden of my weaknesses. So here I am, just as I am to give You all my weaknesses and miseries to change into Divine virtues. This You promised You could do here in The Eucharistic Presence. I believe dearest One in the power of The Eucharistic Presence. I believe that You will not and cannot fail me because You are always faithful to Your promises. So whatever that is in me that You do not like You are capable of changing. So now my burden becomes Yours and my struggle must end in the victory of the Cross. It is all so simple when You explain and write these mysteries in our hearts. Thank You, thank You Jesus my teacher, my healer.

13ᵗʰ August 1992
MARY :
"Yes child, there is an attack on all My little ones, especially those I choose to lead and guide others and work for Me in the world. All need much prayer. Child, your calling is to sit here in Our

Presence. Child, My Son asks very little, just your presence. Your example will inspire others to do likewise and will also speak to the hearts of priests and religious to realise that this is their prime and foremost calling - the celebration of the Eucharist and prayer before the Exposed Presence. So few are aware of the power of prayer, their presence before the Eucharist. Child, no matter what others say or think, this exercise cannot be diminished in any way. We know others have other work. There must be Marthas as well as Marys in the world, but when a man or woman is called to the priesthood and religious life, the Eucharist is the centre, the first and foremost obligation of the day and prayer before The Eucharist.

Child, do not think that your prayer is wasted here, even when you are confused and the mind is in turmoil. Nothing is wasted. Was not My Son in confusion and turmoil all during His passion? Child, the torture of His mind was the most painful of all His sufferings. Child, as We have already spoken to your heart, the Church and World are in turmoil because of the evil influences of the present time. Does not the media, especially the visual media, mostly reflect and purpose to highlight the evil in your midst? Compare this with Our little ones who sit before the Eucharistic Presence. Oh how the evil ones shudder, curse, cringe, to see the power that emanates to counteract their influences. Child, the thought that came to you the other day concerning the power-house was only just a little inkling of the reality. Child, We keep you in the dark to write, prepare you for the coming rosary.. Priests and religious are so in need of your prayers in the present climate of evil and temptation surrounding them. We call them out of the world, but they are still of the world.

Little one, do not be anxious about the writings. All has been arranged. Have I not sent you someone now. Child, the name you have received has been chosen by Us. She will be a great help and inspiration to you also. Oh child, dear child, you will now begin to see the fruits of the past years."

Oh Mary, I feel so far away from You and You are so close to me, so protective, so loving, so wonderful to me. Oh Mary please help me to become just a little like You. Last night I was in the company of those who do great work for You out of the love they carry in their hearts. How come that at times You give me a word for these people. Oh Mary, I feel so inadequate, so unworthy of Your love and care. Oh Mary, You know Your Son's need of me. I disappoint Him so often. How I must cause Him pain when I reject Him, slight Him, especially after the Eucharist. Oh Mary, help me, change me to become the child He created me to be. Mary, I know You are as truly present to us here this day as Your Son because wherever He is You are.

Mary, how can we help to speed up peace in Bosnia? Oh Mary the evil one has taken control of men's hearts. Mary, You have the victory over all evil. Help them, also the people in Somalia who are dying from hunger because of the war and drought there. Oh Mary we are all so in need of Your help. Help us.

"Thank you dear child. Please stay. Oh how We need you this day. I have much to speak to your heart. Oh dearest child, if you only knew how much I love you, all My children. How I grieve for all who do not answer Our call. Souls are so dear to Our Hearts. Oh My pain to know the pain of My Son. Child, I cannot express in words, I cannot let your heart see the wounds of sin in the world, but believe Us dear child, that sitting here in the Eucharistic Presence, We receive the ultimate in comfort and consolation in Our sufferings and you help other souls to see the pain and sufferings they inflict on Us. We touch their hearts to repent. We touch the hearts of those you carry in your heart and the hearts of all those who have asked your prayers. Child, do not these few words help to answer some of the questions you carry in your heart; and have you not perceived the peace and healings that others receive when they visit your home, especially on this day each week. Remember child, the priests who are on retreat these days, that their hearts might be touched and changed to meet the very many difficulties and temptations they encounter daily in their ministry."

15ᵗʰ August 1992   -   Early morning
Feast of The Assumption of Mary :
To be Eucharistic one must become as vulnerable and naked as He, who became all things to all men by giving Himself to us in The Eucharist, the culmination of all He became on the cross of

Calvary. In the Eucharist He makes Himself the littlest of all mankind in the morsel of bread and the sip of wine, all word, all flesh, nothing - nothingness in the eyes of the beholder, ... nothingness in the mind of the beholder.

"How can My people become Eucharistic people unless I am allowed to become Eucharistic first? I will make My people Eucharistic when I am exposed in My Eucharistic Presence for everyone to partake, to behold; when My people will be changed through a change of heart. Hearts of stone will become hearts of flesh.

My Mother through Her Assumption on this feast of Her Assumption will further My plans, but hearts must first be reconciled to one another, to allow My peace fill their hearts when My little ones sit with Me, allow Me gaze on them, to gaze on Me. All can begin and the slow gentle process will take place."

17ᵗʰ August 1992 - After The Eucharist
Before The Blessed Sacrament :

Yes God is alive
God is living
In the living Eucharist.
He reminds me as I gaze on Him
That He is alive in me.

Pain and suffering mingle together
With Love.
Love is fullness, love is emptiness,
We cannot have one without
The other.
Thus we experience the
Contradictions of life
Inherent in our humanness.

Thirst begins in emptiness ,
Emptiness in our togetherness,
Spirit yearning for spirit
To respond.
Will the torment ever end?
Not until the beginning of eternity.

18ᵗʰ August 1992 - After The Eucharist
Before The Blessed Sacrament :

'Holy Spirit, I believe that with God, all things are possible.
Change my heart so that God alone is my true treasure.'
(Today's gospel reading - Matt. 19: 23-30)

Beloved, I await Your healing touch, but first let me gaze on the Face that gazes on me.

Beloved, how often have You to remind me of the healing power in The Eucharist. The irregularity in my heart beat has now settled and I wasn't going to come. Truly You could say to me 'Oh one of little faith' but You do not, we say it to ourselves.

21ˢᵗ September 1992
Later before The Blessed Sacrament :
Beloved, it is difficult to learn and accept that when we pray for the conversion of another, we must expect that we may be asked to become a victim for that person and the person themselves must suffer also.

We forget the cost of our own salvation.

Before The Eucharist :

I come to give You all
My nothingness
What have I got that I
Haven't received from You?

You say You have a need of us
Almighty One
Why stoop so low to beg,
To wait, to implore.

It is as if You're not complete
Your void is ours
Alone to fill.

It is the vacuum that
Draws us together
To be fulfilled.

You offer us communion
Of hearts and minds and spirits
To make us One.

One in one another
To complete the union
In The Eucharist.

Being kept alive by You
Breath of life
Nourished by Your Body and Blood
Then being allowed decay.

It is never ending
Because it has no beginning.
We dangle in space
'Till eternity.

24th September 1992 - (House)
Before The Blessed Sacrament :

Oh Jesus, the pain of wanting, of desiring to love You more and not being able. The pain of wanting to pray well and not to be able. But perhaps Beloved, that is the way You need me now, accepting with grace my inadequacies, my poverty. At least dearest One I can unite with others in their prayer this day to channel my distractions and lack of attention by accepting myself as I am now and seeing the times when I could spend time with You when my heart and mind were centred on You as times of special grace.

Beloved, may I see in my present state the perfection of Your love and holy will and if my praying is entirely due to my own neglect and failure to respond, please forgive me and heal me of my miseries.

"Child, there are many ways of loving, not always apparent to the human heart. Child, the intention, the desire is all I ask. Obedience is most important. The failures and miseries of My little ones attract Me to hold all closer to My Heart.

Oh child, I have allowed you to experience a very little glimpse of My Mercy. Oh child, **teach** My Mercy, **witness** to My Mercy. So many souls hold back, are fearful because they do not know My Mercy. You are now in the age of My great Mercy. Oh child, offer all for souls, especially the souls most in need of My Mercy. Child, look deep into My Heart. You will see, you will know. Pray, pray, child of My Heart. Child, a great new mission opens up to you. You will help and counsel My priests, those I send to you. Do not be surprised. You have opened your home on this day each week for all to pray for My priests, My ministers, My religious. I reward a hundred fold, do I not? and so much more than you could ever comprehend."

13ᵗʰ October 1992
Before The Blessed Sacrament :
'Speak Lord Your servant is listening.'

"Thank you child, thank you children. How I long for this hour to give Myself to you both. Yes children, a time of change is here. Yes children, I am preparing you both for great work in My Kingdom, in My vineyard. So much is at stake. The world is in great turmoil because My Church is in great turmoil. Child, children, when I call you to prayer, Eucharistic prayer, you bring My Church in your hearts. Yes children, make these next few days, days of prayer, days of unity with My Heart. I prepare you for the feast of St. Margaret Mary, whom I used to bring about devotion to My Sacred Heart. She brought about the devotion of the nine First Fridays. Now children, I ask that My Eucharistic Heart be made known throughout the world. Eucharistic prayer will defeat the wiles of the evil ones. When My Eucharistic Presence is adored and worshipped throughout this land, much light, much hope will fill the hearts of My people. A time of change is about to happen in this land. Life and living will not be as comfortable and easy as before, but My people will grow through all that is about to happen. Sufferings bring about change. Sufferings related to Me and Mine, bring about great rewards. My people will find the peace they seek. People will find a purpose in life. Children will benefit. The next generation need this change if they are to survive the evil influences of these times.

Children, I bring you here to pray for your country, so in need now. Child, children, do not worry about your families. I take care of all. All will be well I promise you, but remember My ways are not always yours, but you will see in time that My ways are best. Children, I will direct you about Friday. I have a plan for My five little hearts. Oh children, your unity and love gives Us much pleasure. Oh to welcome five such united hearts - you cannot comprehend."

22ⁿᵈ October 1992
Before The Blessed Sacrament :
"Thank you child, thank you children for your generous hearts. You welcome Me again on Fridays. Your hearts are open to My touch, My grace, the grace of My Eucharistic Heart.

Child, you read about the cross of Dozule - I assure you My little one, My glorious cross is here, here in My Eucharistic Presence. All the promises I made to M... I make here. Child it is not possible for the human mind to understand all that is contained in the mystery of the Eucharistic Presence. Little by little I will reveal to you, through aspects and insights, for My people. Child remain little and you will not be burdened by the knowledge I impart to you. You will continue to wonder and be amazed but dear child, it is because of your poverty I tell you the secrets I withhold from the learned. Do not worry about your weaknesses, they help you to remain humble in My eyes and in the eyes of others. Yes child it was My Spirit speaking through you this morning. Surely I will heal her of her fear through your intercession.

> "Child, when you read about the Second Coming and all the messages about all that will happen in the days ahead, remember dear child that I never left My people. My Presence is always with My people. Are you not in My Eucharistic Presence? Do not seek Me elsewhere."

Remind her again of My Holy Mother's request. Child, the insight I give you is a special gift for your faithfulness.

Child, when you read about the second coming and all the messages about all that will happen in the days ahead, remember dear child that I never left My people. My Presence is always with My people. Are you not in My Eucharistic Presence? Do not seek

Me elsewhere. Oh child, dear child, give yourself to Me here, always here. Child, I have been preparing you for many years, taking My time, gently leading you to where you are this day. Child, I have much more for you to write. It is through these writings I will touch the hearts of My shepherds to fulfil My need, to destroy evil, to be the victor, to have the victory - when My Eucharistic Presence will be exposed everywhere to be adored and glorified by all My people."

30ᵗʰ October 1992   -   (House)
Before The Blessed Sacrament :
"Child, child, child, you will be busy this day. Listen to My Voice speak to your heart. Much of what you have read recently is all happening here in My Presence. Child, here is the glorious Cross. I invite everyone to drink at the well of My Eucharistic Presence, always full, always available, always satisfying and fulfilling the needs of mankind. I fulfil every need, every void in the heart of man. My Eucharistic Heart cries out again and again: 'Come to Me all who are weary and burdened ...'. Your home will confirm these words, this invitation I issue to all My children. Everywhere My Eucharistic Presence is exposed and worshipped is a place of healing for body, mind and spirit.

Oh children of My Eucharistic Heart, do come to satisfy this need within Me to give, give, give of My fullness to each and everyone who answers My call.

Oh child, children of My Eucharistic Heart come, spend some time in My Presence, satisfy this need, this thirst I carry within Me always and forever.

Children, you are truly blessed. Children of this parish, you are truly blessed to have this home in your midst that has opened it's door to My Eucharistic Adoration. You now have Me two days a week. I have made it secure, blessed from intruders that you may worship and adore Me in safety. Do come dear children, do not reject this opportunity. Come to Me with all your burdens. Give them to Me to carry. I will lift you above the pain, the pain of life, of living in these troubled times. I do not say that I will take away all your burdens, your crosses, but I will carry you to carry them.

My Mother waits now to pray this rosary with you. She carries you all in Her Immaculate Heart, loves you all beyond your comprehension."

16th November 1992: "Child, little one, do not overtire the body to safeguard the mind. Indeed My little messenger, to write much in the days ahead I have prepared you My little one, and here in the Eucharistic Presence the evil one may try to destroy you but he cannot succeed. Here you are safeguarded against all his attempts to twist the writings for his own advantage. Pray this Mass for your country, so in need of repentance, reparation and conversion.

Many of those with power have turned their backs on Me. They seek to destroy My little ones, to allow the evil that has entered their own hearts destroy others. Thank you My little one. Come back to Me now with all your heart."

25th November 1992
Before The Blessed Sacrament :
"Thank you My little one and all My little ones for your response. Great credit is due to the organisers of this 72 hour vigil. Your prayers of intercession rise like incense before the Throne of your God.

Your prayers will bear fruit in a way you least expect. You may think the evil one has succeeded in his endeavours to take My unborn from Me, but children I will have the victory over all evil.

Child, I speak to you, I will speak of My plans later. Do not let the evil one take over. He tries to take away your peace. He tries this on all My little ones who seek to be My disciples, all who seek to do My Holy Will. Your pain, your efforts are your sacrifices, your love in action. Do I not lift you above all your family worries and anxieties to carry Mine. Child, relate all to Me - your pain to Mine, your sufferings to Mine - especially during the night time. The human body and mind is then at its lowest resistance to the evil one. I may ask you for a vigil soon My little one. I will tell you and give you the strength to answer this call.

The burden of the debt will ease with the coming of Perpetual

Adoration. I am ready, waiting for a response, a stepping out in faith. Open the doors, I will supply."

Beloved, help us to fulfil Your need of us during the next two days of prayer at my home.

28ᵗʰ November 1992:   "Child, all My plans will unfold during the day. Do not be anxious. Thank you little one for your promptness in delivering My messages. Thank you My little one, I use your impulsiveness for My greater glory. The words I place in your mouth come from Me. Do not worry, did I not say so My little one?

Many need you child this day, but you must take care of yourself also. You do not have to answer all calls. I want you free and at peace to answer Mine.

Yes child all will be made clear. Come back later My little one. I will be waiting, always waiting and longing for a visit to My Eucharistic Presence, child of My Eucharistic Presence. Thank you My little one for your faithfulness. Bear with Me the little cross. Relate to Me, it is Mine."

<u>Later before The Blessed Sacrament :</u>
Oh Abba, how restless I get at times and I run away, but I try to come back when You call me.

"Yes My child, I called you and you listened. Oh child, how many of My own do not listen to My call so I tell My secrets to My little ones and I give instructions for My shepherds."

Oh Abba, there are times when it is so easy to stay with You. I wouldn't be able to listen without You. Every good I do comes from You. Other times I fail You and You always bring me back.

"Yes child, I do need you to come to the Mass later tonight. I will arrange the transport. All will be well. You will stay as long as it will be My pleasure to have you, then you will return home. Tonight is the night for the vigil I mentioned some days ago. Do not worry little one. You will offer the night for the community, they have a big debt, a big problem but am I not the provider for all I ask."

4th December 1992 - 1st. Friday
Before The Blessed Sacrament :
Speak Lord , Your servant is listening :

"Child, child, listen carefully, I speak to your heart.

Child, the night of the eve of the First Friday is very precious to Me. Child have no worries about this night in your home. Surely I will supply. All I ask is your trust, your openness. No matter where else opens it's doors - each place has a place in My Heart. Remember from here many doors have opened to My need. Child I prepared you for many years to fulfil this need in My Heart. Child it is more important than ever to open your doors on this night. I issue the invitations - always there will be people to answer My call. Do not fear. Oh the comfort and solace I receive on this night. Child, little one, if I need you, I will speak to your heart. Remain always open My precious little one.

My child, I have truly entered your heart. I am changing your heart, your attitudes, your ways, in a way you cannot comprehend yet. I am pleased My little one with your efforts. The evil one will try and discourage you. Encourage others in the way I encourage you. Do you not realise the hope people receive in this home of prayer. Do you not see the peace I pour into the hearts of all who come seeking Me, answering My call. No one leaves empty-hearted. Do I not give them the strength to carry their burdens?

See the way S. and E. return and return as I predicted. Child, great healings are taking place. They receive here the strength and grace to live day by day and all are blessed and touched by their coming. They will draw others to My Presence also. Child, My graces extend and pour forth from this house of prayer and faithfulness. Child, be at peace, I am your Prince-of-Peace, always was, always will be. Christmas will confirm it My little one.

Every prayer from the heart pierces My Heart with love, touches My Heart. Oh child, I have truly blessed you from the beginning. Continue to give praise and thanks. All will be well in your family. Do I not always fulfil your deepest desires. I will fulfil theirs when they know and realise them in their own hearts."

Beloved, I do not have the words to express my thanks, my love.

"Speak with your heart My little one, that is all I seek. My Love is restricted also. My Heart is deeply hurt and wounded by those who do not believe and accept My Love.

My Eucharistic Heart gazes upon you all from My Throne. Who sees, who knows, who realises - it is not possible for the human heart to comprehend this mystery, clothed by the veil of mystery in mystery. Do not worry My little one. Remain little. I understand, accept you as you are. You do not doubt My words, the words I ask you to write."

15th December 1992
Before The Blessed Sacrament :
Beloved, thank You for the insight and the grace I have just received here in Your Presence. Oh the importance of offering one's life - past, present and future - as a life offering - even if it be just one moment of grace only, it is forever Yours. It also gives meaning to the following words: **Today will be the happiest day of my life when I see the perfection of Your Love and Holy Will in all the circumstances of my life**. *Thank You Beloved. You are always waiting, longing to shower us with Your graces but we are not always ready to receive. Beloved, give me the stillness, the peace to listen, to hear You calling, longing for a response to Your ever thirsting Heart. Your ever loving Heart is ever laden with gifts to distribute to all and we fail to respond.*

Beloved, You keep reminding me to sit in Your Eucharistic Presence. Oh how I fail You - day after day and You wait and wait.

This was a moment of light in the darkness.

24ᵗʰ December 1992
MARY :   "Child, child, I have been waiting for the moment to speak to your heart to speak to his. He is truly My son, My messenger. He now will cover many of the ways of St. Paul. I have already lead him along many paths including the way of St. James.

Child, I confirm for you the thoughts that came during the Mass. You will cover him on his journeys. You will be part of his work. You will be a co-worker on his journey in prayer. Offer all. Remember him especially in the daily rosary.

My Son speaks to your heart also this day. Child, you now experience a taste of His thirst on the cross. Do not be afraid, We are with you at all times to comfort and console you. Do not worry about temptation, I am here with you always to protect you against all evil. Child, I will help you abandon all to Me, to offer all to My Son for souls. Yes child you are beginning to accept your mission. We will deepen your understanding, help you, help you. Yes child there will be times of suffering intermingled with times of great joy. You will never be asked to suffer beyond the strength you will receive.

Child We thank you for your sacrifices. We thank you for your home. We thank you for your heart, now lived, contained, one with Ours, the Eucharistic Heart of My Son and My Immaculate Heart."

Mary, my Queen and Mother, You bestow on me a great honour. Mary, You know my weaknesses, my miseries and yet You choose one like me and in the words of another I pray -

'O the wonderment of Your
   Calling O Blessed Mother
Heavenly mission that
   Transcends all human understanding
Only You Mary know the ultimate
   Fulfilment.'

Oh Mary, I offer myself in prayer to You before the Eucharistic Presence that Your plans will be fully accomplished as You desire.

'Lord pour out over the whole world this Christmas, the treasures of Your infinite mercy.'

29ᵗʰ December 1992:

"Oh My child, do not fret nor be anxious. I call you to a special mission during the coming year. Child, it will be a time of purification. Relate all to the purification of the Church. The

Church is My people, My little ones.

Child, take the words I gave you through another to rest more in My Heart. Spend more time before My Eucharistic Presence. Here you will be an intercessor for all, especially My priests, My religious and every day will then be as every Thursday. I ask this of you My child. I will make it easy for you to fulfil My need of you, My desire for you. It will come about in an unexpected way. I will prepare the heart of another to allow it happen.

Child, do I not direct you day by day, moment by moment. Do not dwell on the confusion, distractions. Give all to Me, I mean all. I have already entered your heart. I will bring about the changes I desire. Do not struggle. Leave all to Me. I speak to you in the little booklet you refer to often. In the same way these writings will speak to others.

Do not worry about the family, All will be well I assure you My little one. Help when you can and where you can. Your example will be the most powerful way possible."

EXTRACTS FROM WRITINGS
1993

1ˢᵗ January 1993: "Continue My dear children, continue to bring Us comfort by spending time with Us, specially before the Eucharistic Presence. So many in these days do not comprehend the need, the necessity for such prayer. Even as I said before, if you do not understand - I ask, I beg that this special exercise of love come about in every parish, area, diocese of this land to counteract the evil forces that seek to draw all My little ones away from Me.

And as I have given you previously, these two days are very special. I come bowed down with graces and blessings to bestow on all and so few come to receive."

12ᵗʰ January 1993

Oh wounded and tormented Heart,
Before Thee I come
To ease the burden of unrequited love.

Oh bleeding Heart, crushed by the sins of men
Of warring hearts,
Before Thee I come.

Oh turbulent Heart, before Thee I come,
The elements outside are turbulent too
In sympathy.

Oh Eucharistic Heart, before Thee I come,
To sit and gaze, to receive and give
In waiting.

Come Holy Spirit. Come.
Enkindle a fire with Your kiss of love
To inflame a heart now dead and empty,
To come to life before the end.

12ᵗʰ February 1993
Mary :
"Oh child of My Immaculate Heart, I will not allow you be led astray. Child, the priests you mention need much prayer. You will carry them in your heart during the coming days. They will be healed through your intercession. T... and yourself will pray and remember them together. The other problem is a more complicated matter. Good and evil operate together at times.

There is no need for priests here to be running to such places to find My Son and I. Their prayer life should be centred on the Eucharist and Eucharistic prayer. Child, here they will find the truth, Us. Child, encourage such priests through the writings. These writings will help them to live their vocations, strengthen them in their vocations.

I gather all, shepherds and sheep to bring to My Son. Child, as I told you it is not necessary to seek out My shrines. The greatest of all shrines and places of prayer are before the exposed living Presence of My Son in The Eucharist.

Child, they are in crisis. Here My Son will speak to their hearts, direct and guide them in the path He has prepared for each one."

1ˢᵗ March 1993:   "Yes child, that is what I ask, that is what I desire. Child, did I not die for all, consecrate the Host to be exposed for all. Child, the more I am exposed, the more people will be drawn to come into My Presence. They (priests) are over protective. I know the evil that is about. Am I not aware of the

"Child, dear little one, I am preparing a way for you, a door will open for you that My priests may listen and take heed of this burning desire within Me to be present, in the living Presence of The Eucharist to My people."   26ᵗʰ September 1993

109

dangers, but child, I have My army of Angels to protect Me wherever I am. When I am desecrated, it is not because of lack of protection but the evil that has entered into men's hearts. That is a ploy of the evil one to block My priests from exposing Me. Does it not happen that people are more ready to visit Me when and where I can be seen. Oh child, you will be rejected because of this, you will be persecuted because of this. Child write, spread this word My Eucharistic Presence will dispel the evil in your midst."

24ᵗʰ March 1993
Before The Blessed Sacrament :
"Oh child, now that I have you here to Myself, please child listen to the words I am about to speak to your heart. Child, I keep you in the dark concerning the power of My Eucharistic Presence. Otherwise I could not use you. Child you must be free to write, free to absorb all I speak to your heart, as free as a little child listening to a parable that he or she does not understand. Your faithfulness is all I ask now My little one, your faithfulness and fidelity. Oh child, I love for Us both. My Heart, My Eucharistic Heart covers and encloses the universe. Oh child, men of great intellects cannot see, cannot hear - they must have a reason. Divine wisdom is above and beyond all human reasoning. Oh child, as you read in the gospels, if man had only the faith of a mustard seed, he could say to the mountain move and it would move. Oh dear child, instinctively you believe. You do not reason, hence I use you to write concerning the needs of My Eucharistic Heart.

As I have said down the years and I repeat again, when My Eucharistic Presence is exposed throughout this land you will have peace and not before.

Child, there are wars brewing everywhere throughout the world. Men would destroy themselves were it not for the faithfulness of My little ones. Child, prepare for tomorrow's feast, truly an important day, a day to pray, a day for praise and thanksgiving, a day to give glory to My Holy Mother.

Child, give Me this day. Come back again. The sun is shining outside but I will shine the sunshine of My love within you to grace you and bless you abundantly. Yes child, visit the sick, to please

Me.''

8th April 1993   -   Holy Thursday
Before The Blessed Sacrament :

Beloved, help me to see the institution of the Eucharist at the last supper in the present 'now'. May it fulfil Our need of one another. You know the emptiness of my heart but You remind me that You have enough love for Us both and to embrace the whole human race and beyond.

Today was betrayal, is betrayal, yet You manifest the ultimate of Your Love for mankind in giving us the Holy Eucharist. Purify our hearts in our betrayal, strengthen us in our poor efforts to respond. We are family with Your apostles. May all priests share their love on this night, to receive hope for these times.

11th April 1993:   *Your church is being purified and sanctified. Oh Lord, we are responsible, we do not pray enough, we do not give our priests the support they need. I see now why You ask all the faithful to give each Thursday, to offer prayer on this day, if possible before the Blessed Sacrament for strength for all priests to be faithful to their sublime calling.*

15th May 1993
Cian's First Holy Communion :

Cian, you are a little man of few words.
Few know your thoughts
And you think a lot.

I am The Silence.
I am in that Silence
Waiting, longing for your response.

Some day you will pierce the Silence
I will no longer be that Silence,
Our Hearts will be one.

Today is a beginning,
The beginning of a great journey

Into the silence of union.

It seems a lonely way
But you are never alone.
Alone accompanies you always.

20ᵗʰ June 1993: "Child, child, thank you for being open to the change of plan. Here is where I needed you this day before The Eucharistic Presence. Child, this is your calling, this is the sacrifice I ask. Child, you no longer live alone, I live in you. You are now under the control of the Holy Spirit. He leads and guides you to where I need you. The torment relate to Mine in these troubled times, to the suffering and pain I carry in My Heart - oh child so wounded, so tormented by mankind.

Yes child, you have now received an awareness, the significance of the 8th day of the month. More about this later. It is still mystery but all will be revealed in time.

My Holy Mother has a plan, the steps to be revealed one by one to Her little ones. She is gathering the little ones throughout the world - preparing them - inviting all into My living Presence.

Child, I thank you for Thursday night. You were aware of My need and fulfilled it. Simple but oh so profound."

22ⁿᵈ June 1993
Before The Blessed Sacrament :
Oh Mary, behold Your Son. He needs You so. You suffer in one another the pangs and pains of all mankind. We join the crowd. We are one of those who need You too. We need Your protection and perseverance to survive the onslaughts of the princes of evil who seek to destroy our hope and trust in Your victory over all evil.

Today and everyday we come to find the strength and courage to continue the search to climb the ladder that leads to Him who died for all. Before He died He gave us You to be our Mother, to suffer with us the pangs and pains of our daily struggle for conversion and salvation. Mary Immaculate, join our hearts with His, who became man to suffer, die and rise again, that He might live with

112

mankind in The Eucharist.

Beloved, oh Beloved, I come to comfort You. You are lonely, oh so lonely in Your emptiness. So many reject and neglect You. They do not understand Your need of each one. When I think of the pain of Your thirst, my mind cannot comprehend. You are so gentle, so tender. You do not want to burden me with Your sufferings. I am only a little child to You, so fragile, so weak and yet You give me the words to write of Your need for each one. Seldom now do You allow me experience Your emotions and even if You do not, I remember at times when You did. And now that I find it very difficult to be still in Your Presence and keep my mind at rest, I can write my thoughts to You because I know You rest within me. But how I wish I could be more aware of the privilege of being present to Your Presence - that You are truly God and Man in the Eucharistic Presence, and I take it all for granted because You have made Yourself so available to me each day, and You come to my home two days a week, and I can even receive You in the Eucharist every day.

Beloved, do we allow ourselves to become so familiar that we offend You. And yet You tell me that You want all tabernacles opened to combat the evil forces that are everywhere now and also that it is in sitting here with You I fulfil Your need of me.

I know I must never question nor doubt Your love - always giving and seeking less and less for Yourself. So little comforts and consoles You. It is as if You want to show us all that Your Love has no bounds - limitless - beyond our comprehension. You employ every ploy that man can comprehend to reach us now. Is it Lord the urgency of these times? Is it Lord an explosion of Love, Your Love to warn mankind, to draw us back before it is too late. You speak of a time of judgement. Is this to be a last chance to count on Your mercy? Beloved, we come in all our miseries now, with all our miseries seeking Your forbearance, seeking Your mercy. Mary, Mother of Mercy, here we know we are safe, in this place, in this Presence that gives life and hope to all mankind. Now You come and are present above and beyond when You came at the Incarnation, You the risen merciful and glorious One, to heal our miseries, to burn away all the impurities within our souls through the burning rays of Your love in the solid reality and yet mystery of Your Eucharistic Presence.

1ˢᵗ July 1993   -   Feast of St. Oliver
Before The Blessed Sacrament :

"Yes child, I share My secrets with the humble and humbled. Thank you child for the sacrifices you make each week to allow Me come to your home. Oh the comfort and solace I receive here in your midst from all My faithful little ones. Here I do not fail them. I give the strength and hope to meet all trials. Here they will find My comfort and solace in their hour of need. Yes child, there is much violence in your land in these troubled times. The evil one has entered all spheres of life, of living. He is trying to seduce all My people, My little ones and above all the youth. Child, prayer alone will bring about a change in your land and as I have said time and time again, wherever and whenever My Eucharistic Presence is exposed and adored the evil forces will be overcome. It takes time but their time is limited and you will see My victory over all yet My child.

These writings are not for yourself alone - they will speak to the hearts of many.

Yes child, today is the feast of one of your martyrs, St. Oliver. Pray to him, ask his intercession for your country, for peace and reconciliation within the church, government and families. Child, remember the special causes I place on your heart. Keep in mind all whom I ask for your intercession. This is important. You do not realise the power of intercession. Follow the urgings of the Spirit, the call to pray. I do not wish you to be or feel overburdened, but to be always aware of My need of you. We wrote about this some years ago. Refresh your mind, it is a word for each day, everyday. You will know where to find it My child - on the completion of the categorising of your writings into years. I will direct you in the next step. These writings are not for yourself alone - they will speak to the hearts of many. I will help and give you the strength to carry out My desires in respect to these writings."

1ˢᵗ August 1993:   "Happy birthday dear child. Give Me all your worries, your anxieties. Am I not here to comfort and console and take upon Myself the burdens of all My children.

I have Myself already arranged all for the anniversary. Remember men propose but I have the last word. My ways are not always the ways of mankind. I am always a gentle and loving God, but so many oh so many do not believe in My Love, the perfection of My Love for one and all. Man brings about so much suffering, unnecessary suffering on himself at times, when My plans are of the utmost simplicity.

Child, I will write of My plans later. Give Me your whole attention now. I wait for your love, your comfort also. Pray for others, those in most need of prayer at the present time, to fulfil My need of you.

Yes child, about another matter. You see how important not to place one's relationship with Me on rules and regulations. The time is not far off when I will change, make the changes I deem necessary in My Church. I seek to change the heart of My Church into a Eucharistic Heart, into it's full meaning and potential. It is better to allow the heart rule the mind than the mind rule the heart, in the end.

Of course we must have regulations in all spheres in Church and State, since I gave Moses the Tablets. Over the centuries I have been changing the hearts of mankind to become the heart of My Son. The sins of mankind and the wiles of the evil one seek to  destroy all My plans. Look around at the state of the world. Hatred gives way to warfare, but I have My army of peacemakers everywhere, hidden, unnoticed, unrecognised, unheralded, working unobtrusively to bring My peace to others. Time will bear this out. My little ones suffer but remember suffering is never wasted. When related to Mine and willingly accepted, all becomes redemptive to further My plan for My people. Yes child, give Me all your miseries. You may go now. I go with you and remember the word I gave you in the writings of an other."

3ʳᵈ August 1993
Later at home :
Beloved, there is a restlessness within me I do not understand. Are You calling me back to Your Eucharistic Presence. You know why I stay here presently, but I will do whatever You ask of me.

"Thank you My precious little one. I am here with you. You are in My Heart as I am in yours. You comfort Me here and now, as you are, the way you are."

25ᵗʰ August 1993: *Oh Beloved, turn my thoughts and prayers to suffering humanity, the starving in Mostar, all peoples suffering the effects of wars throughout the world. And as I sit here in Your Eucharistic Presence Beloved, hear the cries of Your little ones everywhere, all hearts suffering with You and for You. May the evil in our midst be put to flight. Oh Beloved, I pray and hope that Your priests will listen to Your cries, Your need, Your deepest desire for these times, terrible times, to open the doors of the tabernacles everywhere that Your Presence in the Eucharist exposed in all It's nakedness and vulnerability, the pinnacle of Your humility, will be allowed to draw Your people back to You when we come face to face with You in Your living Presence, where soul meets with the Divine to become divine. And even though my spirit appears to be numb to all, I believe. I believe I am in the Presence of the Risen, Resurrected Christ, Father, Son and Spirit, the Alpha and Omega.*

Truly Lord, I miss Your vibrant Presence as I sit now before the Tabernacle. I know You are hidden away behind locked doors. It is not the same to me now, since You called me to pray before Your exposed Presence. I am aware of Your pain. The church is empty but for myself. I may ask why is it empty? People who seek You now seem to look for You where You are exposed to the human eye, which reflects the attraction of the soul to look on The Beloved. When we become aware of Your need, we cannot rest until this need within You is fulfilled. Beloved, there is a great drive now in Your people in this land to seek to have You exposed on our altars. I know the priests encounter many difficulties, many reasons for not complying with this desire of Your Heart. There is the danger of vandalism and desecration in many to deter them and others who do not see the need, and then there is always the temptation to fail in our faithfulness to keep You company when we make promises, and yet Beloved, You override all the objections, all the regulations as You did the other night. How many will agree? How many will be afraid? How many will condemn, and yet Beloved, I feel You ask me to walk on the waters of faith now and write whatever You speak to my soul, be it ever so unworthy, ignorant, weak and miserable.

Beloved, You led me here this afternoon to show me the difference, but many will not believe what I write. Many will condemn, but I pray only to do Your Holy Will.

Mary, my Holy Mother, teach me wisdom, teach me love, and since You are taking care of me I mustn't be afraid. And You remind me now of the vast difference between the churches that contain Your Eucharistic Presence in the Tabernacle, and the churches that do not contain the Eucharistic Presence. We understand that there are varied definitions of presence, in the person, in the word, where people gather in prayer, but as You explained to me in earlier writings, The Eucharist embodies all states of presence. Here is contained the living Presence of the resurrected Christ, body, soul, spirit, in the pinnacle of His humility. Here all evil forces are put to flight. Here is the victory over all evil.

Lord, increase our faith in the power of the Eucharist to change us, to change all peoples, to change the climate of our land and all nations.

21ˢᵗ September 1993
Before The Blessed Sacrament :
"All I ask My dear precious child, is that you be present to My Presence. Schools of prayer are not for you now. I lead and guide you Myself. Others will come later to be guided in prayer through these writings. Does this not answer the thoughts in your mind this morning child."

Later at Willow
Before The Blessed Sacrament :
Beloved, I cannot wait to write of Your feelings as I witness the priest take You out of the Tabernacle and expose You in The

Blessed Sacrament .

"Oh child dear child, so few realise and specially My own, the joy in My Heart as the Tabernacle door is unlocked and I am released. No prisoner on earth experiences such joy. But how difficult to explain to My priests, the pain I experience to be locked away behind locked doors.

Can they not realise the pain they cause Me? Oh My dear priests, do step out on the waters. You must trust Me to take care of Myself. I have My army of angels around Me now, all rejoicing with Me - and Heaven and earth are one. I am here visible, available in the most vibrant Presence possible to My people.

Come, come, My dear people. Here you will learn My Heart's desire. Here I will open this Heart to love, to embrace all, to give all, to fulfil all the needs of mankind.

Why listen to the prompts of the evil one who seeks to, at all costs, place so many fears in your hearts. It is a ploy to dissuade you, to block adoration of My Eucharistic Presence because in the end here and through My Eucharistic Presence, all evil, all forces of evil will be dispelled through the power of My Eucharistic Presence, that embodies all Presence."

My Beloved, it is easy for me to write Your needs because I am not involved, nor is it my responsibility.

"Oh child, cannot you see, understand that because of this I use you to write My desires, My needs for My Church for these troubled and turbulent times. Evil forces have taken over in many areas. They are intent on taking this land from Me also, in their subtle ways. My Mother takes great care, has great regard for the peoples who have remained faithful down the years. She will not allow Your country sink to the degradations of other lands. But, people must be made aware of the dangers that seek to engulf all, but, because of the faithfulness of My little ones here, We will not allow the evil forces that seek to destroy, take over. But, all must be vigilant. Continue to pray and make sacrifices and as the exercise of Eucharistic Adoration spreads throughout the country, peace will be seen to touch the hearts of the men of violence. Child, I will let you know later My desires for these writings."

26ᵗʰ September 1993 - (Willow)

Before The Blessed Sacrament :

"Thank you child for answering My call. I know it was a sacrifice, thank you. I call so many and so few answer. Oh child, you know a little reflection of My pain now. You realise that I am the most unhappy suffering prisoner on earth.

Oh child, you realise how little it takes on the part of one of My own to release Me, to unlock the chains that bind Me, that make Me a prisoner day after day, night after night. I do not dare child to touch you with the thirst that overwhelms Me, with the love that consumes Me and yet to whom shall I go, to whom will I share My grief, My pain, when I only seek to open My Heart, My Eucharistic Heart to all My people, My little ones everywhere. Many are not aware of the cause of their emptiness, their aloneness, their unhappiness. They search and search and do not know where to find that which the soul seeks and doesn't know where to find, what alone will satisfy the hunger within them. You remember the joy I shared with you on My release. Share with My priests. It would soften their hearts if they knew how easy to fulfil My need for one and all. It is a time of great confusion, a ploy of the evil one to take away the peace I came and come to share with all.

Child, if they really believed, if they really listened, they would come to realise the desire of My Heart, My Eucharistic Heart for these times. In this church the Holy Sacrifice and celebration of The Eucharist will follow the Adoration, to lessen the pain of being locked away again. Child, dear little one, I am preparing a way for you, a door will open for you that My priests may listen and take heed of this burning desire within Me to be present, in the living Presence of The Eucharist to My people."

29ᵗʰ September 1993:   *Beloved, in all the recent writings You say You want all the Tabernacle doors opened to allow You be exposed to Your people.*

Beloved, please help those priests who listen and know Your wishes, but are not allowed to carry them out by their superiors. I also ask Your help in the particular case that has been brought to my notice for prayer. In a particular town where there is no Exposition of the Blessed Sacrament, the curate has a prayer meeting in the local convent and is not allowed to expose the Blessed Sacrament during the meeting. The nun in charge believes it would be irreverent to Your Eucharistic Presence.

"Child, My child, pray. Pray much during the coming days. Offer your wakefulness at night for this particular situation. It is the desire of My Eucharistic Heart to be exposed to My people. Many are blinded and deaf to My appeals. Oh My dear child, they do not understand. When will they understand? Oh child, the evil one uses every ploy as you know to block Eucharistic Adoration everywhere he can, whenever he can get a footing.

Child, do I ask much of you when I come to your home? Have I ever asked more than to sit in My Presence. When I need you to write I need your attention. When people gather to give Me worship - listen to My word, pray and share together - would I not wish to be exposed in My Eucharistic Presence, specially when they cannot find Eucharistic Adoration in the church. Oh child pray, through the prayers of the people

"Please, please I ask to be released from prison."

who answer My call here in your home, I will touch the hearts of My priests and religious to answer My call, My invitation. Oh dear child, what pain I suffer, what thirst I suffer. Very few realise that I am a prisoner in the Tabernacle. It will, take much prayer and suffering to touch the hearts of those closed to My desires. Oh how they already pain My already pained, suffering Heart.

If My Holy Mother and Holy St Joseph had kept Me to themselves while I was on earth, how would My people have come to know Me, how could I have touched the hearts of so many. Oh child, pray for all who are not listening, do not want to listen.

Please, please I ask to be released from prison. Child, it is so important for these times, these terrible times."

1st October 1993 - First Friday
Feast of St. Teresa, the Little Flower
Before The Blessed Sacrament :
"Child, the inner picture of the rain like monsoon pouring down is a

reflection of My graces pouring down on the world this day. Yes child, I have so, so much to give and so few come to receive. Yes child, the roses gave a special significance today for the feast of the Little Flower.

Remember an early writing - the three buds - husband/wife and Me. Also the three stages along the path of holiness.

Yes dear child, We have come a long way together, a long way. Child, you are now to enter the final stage. Remember - full blossom. All is as it was, is, will be, is present to Me here before you. I take up residence here, so homely, so peaceful. Do not worry about little things, little disturbances. I will teach you how to deal with all that I do not like.

You are My instrument. You I have chosen to have My Eucharistic Presence perpetually exposed in The Blessed Sacrament throughout this land. You will have much opposition and persecution before all the Tabernacle doors are opened to release Me from bondage. Child, do not be afraid of what I ask. Remember I will carry you, to carry the burden of new pastures. Time will prove these writings to be Mine.

It is significant that the three buds will come into full blossom in My Eucharistic Presence.

> 'Oh Most Holy Trinity, I adore Thee.
> My God, my God, I love Thee
> in The Most Blessed Sacrament.'   (Fatima)

12ᵗʰ October 1993
Before The Blessed Sacrament :
Romans 1. 16-25.

"Yes child, I write the readings of the day on your heart. I read your thoughts and I remind you, one day is as a thousand years to Me. Have no regrets. The daily readings of the Mass now will leave an indelible mark on you to increase your faith as you sit here in My Eucharistic Presence, to see with your soul the power of, the Eucharist and sitting in My Eucharistic Presence. These writings will become meditations for My priests to grow in faith, to help them to answer My call to sit with Me, to be an example to My flock, to share with them and not deprive them of My

Eucharistic Presence. Yes child, the Eucharist is the word become flesh. Here I am the word. Here I am flesh and blood. Here I am the Resurrected Christ. Here I am more present to My people than when I lived on earth. Here I am fully human and fully divine. Believe Me child. Child, My people look forward to My second coming - wondering, hoping, trembling maybe, but I am here, I have come and I do not want to be imprisoned. I come to be with My people. Oh child, do I ask much, demand much of you? Child, look at Me with the eyes of your soul. Gaze upon Me. Come in your weakness. Come with your weaknesses. Share with Me your miseries. Give Me yourself as you are. I wait, I long, My Heart, My Eucharistic Heart waits, longs to receive all, the whole person to make you whole and holy. Oh My dear children of light, share My light with others, with everybody. You were not given this light to hide away, to keep to yourselves. Oh children of light, share this light, spread this light to shine in the darkness of an unbelieving, wicked world that seeks to live in the darkness, rather than accept My living Presence all around them."

16ᵗʰ October 1993   -   Feast of St. Margaret Mary
Before The Tabernacle :
St. Margaret Mary, again like St. Teresa I forget You except on Your feast-day. I have so much to thank you for, the wonderful days of prayer and peace I spent at your shrine at Paray-Le-Monial over the years. I felt so close to Jesus who spoke to my heart. Today I am more undecided than ever. I am that much older and I find it very difficult to concentrate on prayer and at prayer, and yet The Good Lord accepts me as I am. I pray now for guidance for this night. I do not feel fit enough for the vigil to-night for priests, and they need all our prayers in these times of division and confusion within the church. And yet they are wonderful times also. The Holy Spirit works in extraordinary ways amongst His people to have the victory over the evil spirits who try to destroy His church, His people - in times of great extremes of affluence and poverty, joy and suffering, indifference and great piety.

After The Eucharist
"All is well, all will be well. Child, thank you for answering My call. Be assured dear precious child that all that is happening is part of My plan for this day. I will see that I

come to your home this night. It is My desire that you pray together here in My Presence. What more fitting place for you and for Me on this feast-day of St. Margaret Mary, who was My instrument for spreading devotion to My Sacred Heart throughout the world. Now child, as I spoke to you on this day a year ago, I wish the devotion to The Eucharistic Heart to spread throughout your land, to spread to all lands. Collect Me now. Release Me from prison."

Oh Beloved, I bring before You specially this day, those in authority in the church who are not open to Your needs, to the hunger of those priests and people who have been touched with Your hunger for Eucharistic Adoration.

Beloved, are You not the God of the impossible, Spirit of the humanly impossible. Your bishops and priests are afraid that You will be desecrated and insulted through lack of reverence and love. They do not understand Your need.

Beloved, You continue to favour me with Your Eucharistic Presence in my home. Do I treat You with the love and reverence You deserve? Allowing that no human being can do this, but many make great efforts to do so and You ask so little of me because I have so little to give and often nothing at all. See how if they opened the Tabernacle doors and released You from Your prison, how much more love and respect You would receive. So many would run to answer Your call to fulfil Your need for these terrible times. Beloved, how can we reach those in authority in church and land to listen to Your appeal? Oh Beloved, You did promise years ago that we would have peace in our land and not before Your Eucharistic Presence would be exposed throughout the land .

"Child prayer, Eucharistic prayer is your calling. Your home is a place of prayer. Others are called in other ways. I will speak to My shepherds now :

I call on My Shepherds to have a day of prayer before The Blessed Sacrament. I ask that all tabernacle doors be opened for a day, to allow My people come in Adoration, to make reparation for the sins of the past and the present in this land, that My people may be released from the terrible fear and slaughter of life itself in the North. Without prayer and fasting the trouble will worsen."

11ᵗʰ November 1993: *I believe now dearly Beloved, that all the prayers, Eucharistic prayer of 6th November throughout the land are now bearing fruit. It was truly a preparation for the prayer of Adoration called for on the Feast of Christ the King.*

How wonderful Your ways. The response of Your priests and people have touched Your Heart. You give us another chance on the Feast of Christ the King to call us to Eucharistic Adoration, to make reparation for the sins of the past and the present in this land.

Before The Blessed Sacrament :
"Yes child, I will confirm for you both (P. and yourself) My plans for the coming Feast of 21ˢᵗ November.

Truly child, all will come about as I have planned for this nation and it's people.

Many left this land in pain and suffering, with heavy hearts, some steeped in great hatred, who still carry this hatred in their hearts. They left because they believed that their country had failed them. Now I give them through My messengers an opportunity to pray, to ask pardon, to make reparation, to join with the living and the dead of this land.

I call together all My children. I have no divisions in My Heart. Everyone I create is My child. There will be no divisions in Heaven. All will be one. Did I not pray this prayer to My Father.

(John 17).
The Prayer of Jesus
When Jesus had said this, He raised His Eyes to heaven and said, "Father, the hour has come. Give glory to Your Son, so that Your Son may glorify You, just as You gave Him authority over all people, so that He may give eternal life to all You gave Him. Now this is eternal life, that they should know You, the only true God, and the One whom You sent, Jesus Christ. I glorified You on earth by accomplishing the work that You gave me to do. Now glorify Me, Father, with You, with the glory that I had with You before the world began.

I revealed Your Name to those whom You gave Me out of the world. They belonged to You, and You gave them to Me, and they have kept Your Word. Now they know that everything You gave Me is from You, because the words You

124

gave to Me I have given to them, and they accepted them and truly understood that I came from You, and they have believed that You sent Me. I pray for them. I do not pray for the world but for the ones You have given Me, because they are Yours, and everything of Mine is Yours and everything of Yours is Mine, and I have been glorified in them. And now I will no longer be in the world, but they are in the world, while I am coming to You. Holy Father, keep them in Your Name that You have given Me, so that they may be one just as We are. When I was with them I protected them in Your Name that You gave Me, and I guarded them, and none of them was lost except the son of destruction, in order that the scripture might be fulfilled. But now I am coming to You. I speak this in the world so that they may share My joy completely. I gave them Your Word, and the world hated them, because they do not belong to the world any more than I belong to the world. I do not ask that You take them out of the world but that you keep them from the evil one. They do not belong to the world any more than I belong to the world. Consecrate them in the truth. Your word is truth. As You sent Me into the world, so I sent them into the world. And I consecrate Myself for them, so that they also may be consecrated in truth.

I pray not only for them, but also for those who will believe in Me through their word, so that they may all be one, as you, Father, are in Me and I in You, that they also may be in Us, that the world may believe that You sent Me. And I have given them the glory you gave Me, so that they may be one, as We are One, I in them and You in Me, that they may be brought to perfection as one, that the world may know that You sent Me, and that You loved them even as You loved Me. Father, they are Your gift to Me. I wish that where I am they also may be with Me, that they may see My glory that You gave Me, because You loved Me before the foundation of the world. Righteous Father, the world also does not know You, but I know You, and they know that You sent Me. I made known to them Your Name and I will make it known, that the Love with which you loved Me may be in them and I in them."

Child, remind My people that no one owns the ground they walk upon. Their divisions are grounded in history. History is past. All must look to the future. The bloodshed must stop. People of prayer, you have the power. You can and will destroy all the evil forces who seek to destroy My people. Yes child, I will touch the hearts of My Shepherds to listen.

Invite all peace loving people to pray with you. I invite all peace loving people into My Presence, My Eucharistic Presence. Did I not die for all? Did I not create the Eucharistic Presence for all? Remember the writing concerning the Eucharist, sharing the Eucharist with all who come in love. How many of your own come in love? I see into the hearts of all. Remember the word child. It is for now. The time is ripe.

I invite all to pray together, to come together."

After The Eucharist
Before The Blessed Sacrament :
  Mary said yes to the angel
  Mary received the Spirit
  Mary said yes to the Spirit
  Mary received the Son ......

May our hearts be open this day to receive the united Hearts of Jesus and Mary by saying yes to our angels, to say yes to the Spirit. And here in The Eucharistic Presence I join with all the angels and saints (in Heaven) in giving praise to Your glory.

19ᵗʰ December 1993
<u>Before The Blessed Sacrament:</u>
Mary, thank You again for protecting me as You did now, entering the church for Adoration and also on Thursday night last as I carried the Eucharist, when I fell and broke my glasses and the broken glass didn't enter my eye.

Beloved, heal Willie of his bad cold that I will be able to spend more time with You before the Blessed Sacrament in preparation for Christmas as You asked of me. If I cannot visit You, will You come to visit me? I want to fulfil Your need of me each day now. Bless and comfort those You place on my heart. Thank You Jesus and Mary and specially I ask that the politicians will respond to Your word and the men of violence will be touched to answer the call to respond to Your pleas for peace. Let the healing begin in me and through me, Beloved. I become disheartened when I see in others the virtues I haven't got. But then I remember to thank You for the burden of my weaknesses and that pleases You. How wonderful to know that when I write to You, You receive it before I write. Thank You for giving me the words and for the millions and millions of gifts received down the years. I wish I answered every call to come and sit with You. Give me a listening heart, to be still in Your Eucharistic Presence. Soon You will be all around me and I will not have far to go to find You, as many churches are now beginning to expose Your Presence as You requested down the years and not be kept a prisoner in tabernacles. You will always then have someone to comfort and console You. Thank You for the health to be able to visit You on the days You do not come to my home. Perhaps soon You will come to stay. I am reminded of Your promise !

20ᵗʰ December 1993
Before The Blessed Sacrament:
You did come to my home unexpectedly this morning.

Thank You. Now I come to You. Oh Beloved, You teach me the different meanings of flesh in my writings. The heart of flesh against a heart of stone and Your Presence in the world against human nature as a consequence of original sin.

Abba Father, I must soon leave. Oh the emptiness that is within me. You leave me with a heart of stone. I cannot give what I do not receive to give. Oh Abba, Your little one hungers for the love to give, to share. You are Trinity. We are Trinity. Oh the abyss that separates us. Is this the precipice that we must meet before unity?

Oh how I long for The Eucharist but when You come, I have nothing to give in response. I am one with the lost souls You place on our hearts.

My Beloved, heal me of all judgement and criticism of others in my heart.

31ˢᵗ December 1993
Early morning.
" Child, yes child, I call you to write even in sickness. My Heart is sick also.

Men of violence I call you to lay down your arms. Nothing will be achieved by you continuing your acts of violence. You terrify My people. You try to achieve your aims through violence. There will not be another time. The more you insist on your rights, the more you will lose. This is the last warning I give you. I am in control. You are all My children. I love you. I seek your souls. Turn back before it is too late. Think of My humiliation. I

did no wrong. I have implanted a desire for peace in the hearts of all. Listen before it is too late. This is My last word on this last day of 1993."

Morning: *Oh Beloved, thank You for coming to me in The Eucharist and being present in the Blessed Sacrament in my home. I was so reluctant to answer Your call last night to write. Your pain must have been unbearable - Your thirst for souls. I have been no comfort to You in the past days, only that You had already warned me of this particular stage of my spiritual growth, I would have believed that I had turned my back on You altogether, to become the worst of sinners, but it was nothing to the darkness You suffered for us in Gethsemane. But all Your faithful friends did not fail You. You have truly blessed our home with Your Presence and all who come to pray.*

Beloved, You will tell me what I should do about this morning's writing. One, perhaps two people come to my mind particularly.

4ᵗʰ January 1994
In bed :

Beloved, thank You for coming to me in The Eucharist this day and You had a special surprise and gift for me also. In my present state, I cannot see the wonder of Your ways, but that does not mean they are not happening all the time. I seem to have lost the joy and wonderment I used to have when I would recognise Your blessings in hidden ways, and yet You do not fail to continue to treat me as before.

6ᵗʰ January 1994   -   In bed
Blessed Sacrament in the house :

Beloved, I know You are present in the Eucharist during these two days and nights. I unite with all who come to visit You. I accept my emptiness because I know You accept me as I am.

Beloved, I did not take the care I should have in my ignorance since I got sick, but You protected me as You promised.

Bless all Your faithful little ones.

22ⁿᵈ January 1994
In bed :

"Yes child, I hide Myself that you might search for Me again. Child I never left you. Search for Me, I abide in you - abide in Me. Child you will see that I am faithful to My promises. When you cannot come to Me, I will come to you in the Eucharistic Presence.

You have been faithful over the years. Now you know the emptiness that many of My priests carry in their hearts. Day after day they must live on faith, and in dark faith teach My people My need, My greatest need for These Times - Eucharistic prayer and Adoration. But I remind you little child, do I not ask very little, just your presence. To sit with Me comforts Me for the rejection of many. Child, rest with Me. It will be a while yet before you will be able to return to your daily chores. Spend the time with Me in intercessory prayer for your country. You are a land of many blessings. Do I not protect you from the extremes of other lands. You will learn much from your own writings. You may not feel the same emotions now, but all are part of your growth in the spiritual journey of the soul."

29th January 1994 - In bed
After The Eucharist :

Beloved, I am only beginning to realise Your goodness to me, Your faithfulness to Your word, the privilege of coming to me in the Eucharist during my illness, and today You sent me a priest to receive the sacraments of penance and of the sick.

How blessed I am. How unworthy of Your goodness and loving kindness. Help me Lord to begin again. Thank You for Your peace and may Your peace bring about the fulfilment of Your need of me. Prayers without heart are only empty words. Help me to respond to Your request to 'abide in You', to be aware of Your Presence within me, to quell the restlessness of my spirit and racing thoughts. If these are all You need, may I accept with loving acceptance my present state without question. Praise and

"The Eucharist is sharing, is thanksgiving, the Eucharist is for one and all. Until the regulations allow the sharing of the Eucharist for all as I intended, I ask My little ones at the Eucharist, at this Eucharist, at every Eucharist, to include all mankind, all My children, to satisfy My thirst for all, each and everyone I create and created. You limit My power, specially in the Eucharist. THE PEOPLE WHO STAND ON MY WORD UNITE AND BECOME ONE WITH MY FLESH. YOU ARE ALL PART OF MY BODY, MY CHURCH." 14th February 1994 *thank You for the perfection of Your Love and Holy Will in all the circumstances of my life this day and everyday.*

I believe dearly Beloved that the healing of my body, mind and spirit will take place through the Holy Eucharist.

In Sickness
Beloved, Beloved,
The day is long in bed
Yet not long enough
To satisfy Your need.

I come and go because my sickness
Does not confine me
The pain in body is very light indeed
Minimal.

But Lord the pain of purification
Smarts at times
When You allow me see
The darkness of my soul
Darkened by cancer.

And yet You say :
'My light shines within you'
How can this be :
When light is brighter than the darkness.

Oh Lord, oh Lord, You bless me. I fail You.
You show me mercy
How can I be reconciled
When I have mercy not on others.

And yet of myself I am nothing, nobody,
Less than dust.
I depend on You to give, to receive,
To give to others all You ask.

Living is a paradox
Our struggle is Your struggle within us.
We all become one struggle,
One hope along life's journey.

You carry us,
We carry one another.
We may not be aware
Because life is mystery.

You're a mystery Lord,
Unsolvable, unattainable
In our humanness
In this life.

3ʳᵈ February 1994   -   (House)
Before The Blessed Sacrament :

Beloved, to-day is the first time since Christmas that I felt able to spend some time in Your Presence. Beloved, forgive me for neglecting You for so long. I could have made the effort, more of an effort, because I believe that here in Your Eucharist Presence my healing of body, mind and spirit will take place. You did tell me that You would take away all desire for You, that I would experience the dark faith that some of Your priests experience. Now I realise the difficulties and emptiness of this state. Truly Beloved, everything, every good thought, word and deed comes from Your Holy Spirit. It takes us so long to learn, that of ourselves we are nothing. We think we are growing closer to You yet look down, judge and criticise the actions of others. Oh Beloved, how patient and tolerant You are of us all.

Beloved, I ask for the strength to be able to sit with You again. I know now the emptiness of not being able to sit with You in the Eucharistic Presence. May my desire grow, to be an incentive, a deep longing to renew my relationship with You, to deepen my relationship, to answer Your call to be present to Your Presence in the Blessed Sacrament.

4ᵗʰ February 1994   -   First Friday
Before The Blessed Sacrament :

I see in others the rewards of thanksgiving
When praise is ever on their lips
Give me Lord the grace to see
To know Your needs.

A change of heart I need
To fulfil Your need of me
Oh Lord, oh Lord
The burden of my weaknesses bear heavily upon me

The struggle, oh the struggle
Truly it is a moment to moment existence
The soul must suffer
To overcome the world.

Oh Lord, oh Lord
It is not easy to follow Your commands
Our efforts are of no avail
Unless ordained and sustained by You.

Oh Lord a change of heart I seek
To ease the torment of my mind
To allow love, Your love
To command, to control.

Or is the answer in my sickness
When our resistance is attuned
to our bodily weakness
Evil takes over.

Lord You say, Your power is manifested in weakness
Shine Your light upon me,
Dispel the darkness
Here in Your Eucharistic Presence.

4ᵗʰ February 1994   -   First Friday
Before The Blessed Sacrament :

"Yes child, I must remind you again and again, no evil spirit can overtake you, overcome you here in My Presence. Now My little one as you come back, seek My Eucharistic Presence again he will increase his attacks. Child, place your trust in Me. The words of the poem you have just written are My words. Child do not be fearful. All is well. Your health will be restored soon. I need you My little one, to sit with Me again. The loss of the past weeks have pained Me more than you. My light within you never went out. Child, the darkness is another stage as I explained to you, in your journey, in our journey together. We have much more, My Mother and I, to have you write. Child, you will be busy again, busier than before because We have much to teach others through you. We are gathering all Our little ones. We are gathering all Our victim souls. Remember We are your strength, your hope in these difficult times. We are showing Our people that We control the elements, nature. People have forgotten that there is a God, the Creator, their Creator and Creator of the world. I seek the souls of My children, all My children. Many will not listen to the bearers of the Good News. They must be brought to their knees, dispossessed of all possessions. Even the good suffer for the sake of others. Remember My child, to-day is special. It pleases Me now that many churches expose My Eucharistic Presence on this day. Remember the promise for this land. The time is not far off when the men of violence will be brought to their knees. They continue not to listen and distort My plans. Pray child, pray children for a change of heart. Goodness will overcome the wickedness in your land. I come with My victory."

'Your word is a lamp for my steps Lord.'

5ᵗʰ February 1994
First Saturday :
Beloved, thank You for yesterday's word which prepared me for the result of the recent X-ray. You are giving me more time to spend with You, to rest with You.

Mary, today is the first Saturday. Teach me to spend this day in unity with You in loving Your Son.

6ᵗʰ February 1994
After the Eucharist :
"There are so many evil forces trying to destroy My people every-where, that My Presence in the Eucharist will help to destroy all in their efforts to destroy My people. Yes child, My children, I do ask all to sit with Me, to give Me time, and unless My priests will comply with My desires, My needs, My people cannot.

Yes My dear, dear priests, it is My greatest desire that I be taken out of the Tabernacles and exposed on the Altars of the church or some place within the confines of the church to allow My people come in worship and adore Me. I gave Myself, did I not, at the Last Supper? I know the Holy Sacrifice of the Mass comes first, but here in My Eucharistic Presence I will change the hearts of My people, strengthen them against the wiles and subtleties of the evil one to combat all the evil in your midst. Yes child, I will give you writings to pass on to My priests. Child, I have much to say, to speak to your heart. I give you these days to spend with Me, to waste time with Me, to give Me the time that I may speak to your heart. I take all the distractions of home chores and outside commitments to spend this time with Me.

Yes child, I wait and wait. Wait on Me My little one and I will fill your heart with My love, My need."

8th February 1994 - At Mass
After The Eucharist :
"Yes My child, I specially ask you to have My Eucharistic Presence collected and brought to your home. I desire My little one that you spend this day in My Presence, for the sake of My Mother also, to pray for those who visit Glencree to-night. I know you cannot be present yourself, but here in My Presence you will be in communion with the others and in intercession for the group.

Yes child, you now understand that because of your lack of concentration, through no fault of your own, I come to you in the tears. My tears denote My Presence. Child, I cannot be more explicit now. Child, you know when they are My joy, My pain. At times I am sharing My joy with you, other times you are partaking in My pain. Yes child, a new path, a renewed path is opening up, a new walk with Me.

Child, be ever attentive to My call, My needs. It will mean many sacrifices to deny the flesh, to answer My call. Child, to write on My Eucharistic Presence, you must spend much time with Me. Sometimes you will be aware of My Presence, My Consolation, but mostly it will be in dark faith I ask you to come.

Thank you My little one. Now I ask that you come to daily Mass. Here your healing will be completed. We take care of you. Trust Us, We are always with you, within you, in communion, in oneness in one another. Now go My little one. I thank you. Our blessings go with you."

Before the Blessed Sacrament in the house :
Thank You Jesus and Mary for blessing me so this night.

9th February 1994 - At Mass
After The Eucharist :
"Thank you My little one for coming. A further healing will take place at each Eucharist as I promised you. Child, relate the attacks of the evil one to Mine in the desert and at Gethsemane. They will increase, be not afraid. I will heal the rift in the five group. It is the work of the evil one to divide. Take action. Nip everything in the bud. I have given T... this gift of discernment specially. She **will** use this gift, she **will** need this gift more and more in the days ahead. Child, do I not treat you very gently. I fit each one for the burden they carry, never beyond the strength that goes with it.

Child, take rest until you get the all clear from the X-ray. I use the medical team in My work of healing also. Child, give Me time to speak to your heart. Soon you will be able to visit Me in The Blessed Sacrament again daily. I wait for you, I long for you."

10th February 1994 - House
Before The Blessed Sacrament :
"Yes child, come to Mass this afternoon. I will confirm 'word' for you. I will give further instructions to clear matters. I use you My little one in this situation, to restore peace in the group. Truly this little hamlet, chosen by My Mother, will become a place for peace and reconciliation. Your prayers, your example, your sufferings will bring all this about. You will see the results in the days ahead."

11th February 1994 - Feast of Our Lady of Lourdes
Before The Blessed Sacrament :
Mary, I ask a special request of You this morning. Truly I have seen this prayer answered in an extraordinary way. On all Your feast-days You truly receive a special blessing for me. Oh thank You dearest Mother and how I neglect You. Mary, I know You will direct us about to-night and as a true loving Mother, You will bring

about peace and reconciliation amongst us.

Beloved, to-day's gospel (Mark 7. 31-37) speaks to my heart in a special way. Truly I am often deaf to Your word. To-day You also said to me 'Be opened'. **My ears were opened and the ligament of my tongue was loosed (further) and I was able to speak more clearly.** *Beloved, more and more You teach me the significance of the word that becomes flesh at the Eucharist. Beloved, teach me from the beginning, the length and breath, height and depth of the Eucharist. Now that I am able to attend Mass again, help me to make my daily Mass the centre, beginning and end of my daily prayer through my encounter with Your living Presence.*

With a singing heart to-day I pray the Act of Consecration to the Sacred Heart of Jesus and the Immaculate Heart of Mary and like the man in the gospel may my 'admiration be unbounded' for my new found freedom. And may this new freedom that I have received be used for the greater glory and praise of the Most Holy Trinity in my daily life. Beloved, You never fail to answer our prayers, but in Your perfect time be it long or short.

12ᵗʰ February 1994
Before The Blessed Sacrament :
Beloved, it is good to be here, to be able to visit You again.

"Yes child, I was waiting for you, preparing a great welcome. See child, you have another place to visit now. Have I not opened up many places to expose My Eucharistic Presence in the past years? Yes child, and I will keep all the promises I made to you in your writings. Oh My child, the joy of being taken out of the Tabernacle, to no longer be held prisoner - to gather My little ones to My Eucharistic Heart where I can bring comfort and solace in all their cares and trials of these times. Dear little ones, you will see more and more Tabernacles opening up. Keep praying and the desires of your heart and Mine will be fulfilled.

Yes child, I spoke to your heart this morning at the Eucharist. Your thoughts were My thoughts. Unite now with the others at today's conference on Divine Mercy. I know you would have wished to be there. You will receive the same blessings and more here because you are not yet fit. Here I can speak, do speak. Remember it was this church many years ago I gave you the prayer to be said before the Blessed Sacrament. This prayer has travelled far and wide and the blessings received through this prayer are manifold, unknown to man. Child, there is much on your heart that you would like to write, but you must take it easy. The body and mind is not recovered fully yet to take such writings. Later child I will explain and answer the desires of others. Now child, rest in My Heart. Abandon yourself to Me. Let Me minister to your needs and the needs of those you carry in your heart. Thank you child for coming."

14ᵗʰ February 1994
Before The Blessed Sacrament :
"Yes My child, I read again the doubts you prayed about. I will take care of all. There is no need for worry nor anxiety. Yes child, leave everything to Me, in My care. I have a plan for Glencree. Now is a time of preparation. Pray much. We will direct each one called and concerned. As you can see and know, the evil one tries to distort Our plans.

Remember children, We are in control, but one step at a time. To execute Our plans We ask much prayer and sacrifice from Our little ones. First Our little ones must strive specially for peace and reconciliation within and between one another before Our plan can be born. During these days of preparation, many hearts are being touched, hurts healed, divisions mended and unity in families and homes.

In the days ahead these reconciliations will be broadened far and wide and have repercussions throughout the land North and South, to bring peoples of different cultures and above all, Christians of different denominations, to pray together and work together. But firstly, hearts must be changed in individuals, in families, in communities and within each Church and denomination. Only then will My Spirit be free to unite, to bring all together.

Child, children, as you come to daily Mass, here bring all these intentions of Ours for this holy place in your hearts. Share your

Eucharist with everyone. Multiply as I multiplied in the gospel. The Eucharist is sharing, is thanksgiving, the Eucharist is for one and all. Until the regulations allow the sharing of the Eucharist for all as I intended, I ask My little ones at the Eucharist, at this Eucharist, at every Eucharist, to include all mankind, all My children, to satisfy My thirst for all, each and everyone I create and created. You limit My power, specially in the Eucharist. The people who stand on My word UNITE and BECOME ONE with My Flesh. You are all part of My Body, My Church.

My Mother, your Mother, is equally Mother of all I create. She must not be excluded. What human mother does not seek and desire each of her children to be united in love. How much more Her spiritual children. No one is excluded. She received and accepted one and all at the foot of the Cross. Is it not the desire of Her Heart also to gather all Her children into one fold.

My Mother, your Mother, is equally Mother of all I create. She must not be excluded.

Man created the divisions. It is the desire of Her Heart to make, to complete the circle of love to exclude no one.

Children, look to My Mother. Pray to My Mother to heal the divisions in the Church. Each Church represents the people of that Church. When Christians unite, your example will draw others into one Fold, under the one Shepherd."

17th February 1994 - House
Before The Blessed Sacrament :

Beloved, give me the words to write for others the beautiful insight at the Mass this night. Oh my Beloved, truly our bodies can only take so much. The parable of the loaves and fishes takes on a further meaning for me now and adds to the above writing. At the Eucharist You allow us share in the miracle of the multiplication of the loaves and fishes, You allow us share with others the multiplication of Your Body and Blood in the same way when You worked the miracles of the loaves and fishes. You power is unlimited. We limit You but You allow us share in this power also at the Mass. Beloved, it is mystery beyond the comprehension of the human mind but You allow us at times to receive a glimpse of this. Oh Beloved, as You told me once early on in my writings that even if You gave me an insight into the Eucharist at every Eucharist I received during my life, I would only be at the beginning of learning to understand.

19ᵗʰ February 1994   -   After the Eucharist
Before the Blessed Sacrament :
It is good to be here Beloved again, to be able to come to this place as I have come down the years.

Beloved, thank You. Truly You have kept Your promise. If only I could in some little way keep my Lenten resolutions. I always fail, but I will try with Your help to fulfil Your need of me - one day at a time. Beloved, if I could only retain in my heart all You have spoken to my heart in the past weeks. You carried my burden. You didn't allow the cross to touch me. Oh Beloved, I pray for a change of heart. Oh Mary, my Holy Mother, thank You for last night. May we the five, be united in Your care. May we support one another at all times.

21ˢᵗ February 1994
Before The Blessed Sacrament :
Mary, Mary, I thank You for the wonderful surprise this morning. Lead and guide me in Your wisdom, to choose the writings to send.

I thank You for making it possible to visit Your Son here again this morning. May our morning prayer continue as before my illness. Oh it is so good to be in the Eucharistic Presence of Your Son. He missed me I believe but I wasn't aware of my loss in my own darkness. Oh I believe, I believe in the absence of any response on my part, yet I know my soul is one with His in the depths of my being.

24ᵗʰ February 1994   -   House
Before The Blessed Sacrament :
"Child, please carry out the doctors order for My sake. All is well

140

but you will know why later.

Thank you My little one, others need you. See all that sought your help this day. I gave you the words of wisdom for all, but now child I give you the words to write. Surely the church, My church is in great disarray. Priests and people are confused. This is because of the evil in the world. Yes child, they do not spend time with Me, listen to My need of each one. Priests are bogged down by regulations. Those who step beyond the regulations are reprimanded and lose heart. Child, as I told you before, I wish to put a heart into My Church. I come, I came to change the hearts of all, but over the years regulations were added to regulations, and now the Church is bowed down by these regulations. Child, as I have spoken to you, as I speak to all My priests, the Mass is the centre of the Catholic faith. Unless the Mass is at the centre and the most important prayer of the day for any priest, he is not obedient to My calling. All others can supply every other need for My people. Child, I have begun to teach you, to give you an insight into the Eucharist. Truly child your body is not made for such knowledge and insight but I will sustain you. I drain you My little one but you are all Mine now. Remember and believe, you will then learn to accept all the happenings of each day and live one day at a time.

Yes child, if My priests only listened, they would comprehend the power of the Mass and as I said before, every need for man is contained therein, but other matters, other exercises block out the importance and power of the Mass.

Oh child, the more I teach you, the more insights I reveal to you of the Mass will cause you more pain, but I will be your strength from day to day. Therein you will receive the strength for the body to receive and write all I reveal to you.

Yes child, you are right. You need to say this Novena from the heart to join with the Immaculate Heart of My Holy Mother for these writings that you are about to receive. The past years were all a preparation for now.

My child, you have been faithful from a very young age and I reward you now and choose you for this onerous task I give to you, but My Mother and I will carry you through the dangers, the persecutions, the trials ahead, but remember child, always I am your Abba Father. I will never fail you. I will never leave you prey to the attacks of evil and evil men.

The writings now will embrace all I have taught you from the beginning. They will be simple, clear and yet profound, readable by all, for all but particularly My priests.

This task child will call for changes. I will lead and guide you, one day at a time, to sit at My Feet, to sit before My Eucharistic Presence It will not be all joy and ecstasy, but My shield of peace will surround your soul at all times."

1ˢᵗ March 1994
Before The Blessed Sacrament :
"Oh child of My Heart, My Eucharistic Heart, do I not show you, overwhelm you with My Love, My gifts? Have I not chosen you above many, many others to this special calling to write on the Holy Sacrament of the Eucharist? Do I not share all My innermost secrets with you? Do I not answer all your needs, your requests?

Child, oh child, truly I need you above all others for this task. Truly I seek you above all others.

Child, oh child, truly I need you above all others for this task. Truly I seek you above all others. Have no regrets of the past. I was there, was I not, leading and guiding you every moment of everyday. All fail, all have regrets, but must I not teach you, help you to accept, show you a little of My pain to draw you to Myself. Only through suffering, My suffering in you can I lead, direct you, guide you along the path of holiness and truth. Child, I am preparing you for your greatest work. Child, listen, take heed, when your body has recovered I will be able, free to start the most important writings. All that went before was only a preparation of all that is to come. Child rest now. Rest in My Heart, My Eucharistic Heart. My Holy Mother will take care of you, lead and guide you through Her Immaculate Heart to that state of soul that will free you to enter into the last phase of these writings for My Church, your Church, during this troubled and turbulent time of change and challenge."

4th March 1994 - After The Eucharist
Before The Blessed Sacrament :

The pain of longing
The pain of desire
No words to express
The emotions within.

You give, we take
Nothing to give in return
Words, thoughts, confused
Into nothingness.

The heart cannot lie
We're as transparent as glass
You see what we hide from ourselves
And from others.

You ask for an open heart
But You hold the key
That we are helpless to turn
In ourselves.

We wait, we wait
Perhaps to-day, perhaps to-morrow
How long must we wait
For the knowing?

The knowing we know
Believing in faith
The end is the beginning
Of enlightenment.

What does it matter
What lies in between
You use our struggle
To bring us perfection.

Silently You sit on Your Throne
Lovingly, smiling with tenderness
Gazing, longing beyond our longing
For that day.

Your waiting is more painful
Than our darkest hour
To bring to fruition
Our hearts desires.

18ᵗʰ March 1994   -   After the Eucharist
(House) - Before the Blessed Sacrament :

"Make Me a living Presence, give Me a living Presence. I seek to live amongst My people, to be seen by My people, be One with My people. Here in the Eucharist I am that living Presence, the Presence that embodies all Presence.

My Church, My priests, listen to My word. Listen to Me. Do not close your ears, your hearts to My pleas. You are living in a time of great need, great change. We are in battle. My Eucharistic Presence will have the victory. Make available My Eucharistic Presence to My people. Do not make excuses. Excuses are the ploy of the evil one. My Eucharistic Presence will destroy his power over My little ones. My children, My own, I knock at the doors of your hearts. Listen, take heed before it is too late. Here I will change the hearts of all, all My people.

I plead with you My ministers, My shepherds. Do not deprive My people of My Body, My Blood. I am the food and drink for their souls. The Eucharist will bring about the unity I seek in My Church. You will see, you will see.

Child, let Me use you. I take care of you, do I not? Others mean well. Listen to Me. No one else can fulfil this need, My need of you. Yours is a special calling. Give thanks. I bless you. I have prepared you. Do not seek emotions. I give you the faith. I know you do not doubt My Love. This is most important.

My Mother is preparing you. She speaks to your heart in this novena. Continue My little one."

24ᵗʰ March 1994   -   House
Before The Blessed Sacrament :
Beloved, today being the fifth week of lent, the last Thursday before Holy Thursday, we pray as You asked us for a fresh outpouring of the Holy Spirit on the Church.

Beloved, we pray specially for Your priests for an ever deeper realisation of the Eucharist. Imprint on their hearts that only in allowing the Eucharist to be the centre, be all and end all of their priestly vocation, can they answer Your call, their special call that makes them different from all others. They alone have the power to change bread and wine into Your Body and Blood.

Oh Beloved, if only we had a little understanding of this great mystery and miracle that takes place at every hour every place throughout the world, would they, would we, realise the cost to the Father, the Son, the Spirit, of our redemption. Beloved, write this love on our hearts, infuse this love in our hearts, that we might be instrumental in bringing about a change, a healing in the Church in these times of great confusion. Mary of the Immaculate Heart, Mother of the Church, may this novena dedicated to the Triumph of Your Immaculate Heart, help us to help as You ask of us. May our prayers, through our prayers united with Your Immaculate Heart bring about His Kingdom on earth as it is in heaven, for these times.

Mary, I cannot carry out, do on my own all You ask, but with You all things are possible. I place my trust in You. As Jesus told me on an occasion **'I want you to go back to My Mother now. She can do for you all I can do, give you all I can give you.'**

Mary, I believe the time is now. Open my heart to Your Immaculate Heart to-morrow, the feast of the Annunciation, that His Will and Your will, will be done in me. Amen.

Beloved, thank You for making the Mass the most important part of the day for me.

"Oh child, dear little child, would that it be so for all My priests. Oh child, pray, pray, pray for My priests. They are being attacked by Satan on all sides. Child, children, they need the prayers of all My little ones in these turbulent times, to ward off the attacks, the temptations. Oh My Church that I founded on Peter, the Rock. It will never be rocked but the evil one will try. It will appear that he has succeeded but remember, I promised My Church I would always be with it. I will have the victory over all evil. You will see child, you will see."

25ᵗʰ March 1994:   "Child, do not worry about Holy Thursday arrangements. Your arrangements are Mine. This is My desire that I come to your home and be exposed there for the day. I will give you confirmation through another. All will be well."

26ᵗʰ March 1994
Before The Blessed Sacrament :
Mary :

"My beloved precious child, do not tax your mind. I take care of all. I will answer all your questions, all your requests in time. A little at a time child, a little for My little child. You are to Me as the little baby who is being baptised to-morrow. How I care and love My little, little ones.

I hold you all close to and in My Immaculate Heart. Oh child, the joy of yesterday (day of Consecration). There was rejoicing in Heaven. Do not be afraid of the evil in the world. I have My army of handmaids to counteract all evil. You are all so precious to Me. Child, leave your family to Me. I will answer all your prayers. I bring you to sit at the feet of My Son. He has much work for you in the days ahead. Turn to Me in your needs. I am always with you. Call on Me. I like to hear your call. I like to know you trust. I like you to know I keep My promises.

May the blessings of My Son be upon you. You give Him great joy every time you visit Him in the Blessed Sacrament. Come often, come often. He needs you. Your letters give Me great, great joy."

31ˢᵗ March 1994   -   Holy Thursday
Before The Blessed Sacrament :

Beloved, You asked me to bring You here today though this is not according to the liturgy of the day.

Beloved, thank You for the confirmation. You surely have a sense of humour. You are the God of surprises. What is past You make present. Did You not give us the Eucharist to be Your living Presence in the world. Should we not give thanks by worshipping Your Presence instead of dwelling on the darkness of these days. You came to bring light into the world and You do continually say in the writings that You want to be released from Your prison (the tabernacle) and be present to Your people. Perhaps this is one of the regulations of the church You want changed? Perhaps this is a time You ask us to drink the new wine. Surely we cannot offend You by sitting in Your Eucharistic Presence this day. Oh Jesus tell Your priests, they are confused, so confused because at heart they just want to please You.

"Thank you My little one for inviting Me to your home this day, on this very special day. It is truly the feast of the Eucharist. Surely I want to be present to My people, truly present, visible and viable. Oh child, so many regulations that they confuse My people. One by one they will be taken away, to make room for My Heart, My Eucharistic Heart. My Mother knows My need. She will bring My need about. Through My Mother now I bless all mothers, specially those in pain for their children. My Mother takes care of one and all. Trust Her, trust Her. She holds one and all close to and within Her Immaculate Heart, specially when mothers hearts are one with Hers. All will be well. Trust in prayer. Praying is loving and loving is trusting.

Oh child, so many regulations that they confuse My people. One by one they will be taken away, to make room for My Heart, My Eucharistic Heart.

I ask My priests to move with the times, but I understand that it takes time to study and mull over so many regulations, now all part of canon law down the ages."

9ᵗʰ April 1994
Morning :
Mary, You show me how vulnerable I am. Help me to see others and accept others as You do me. It is now brightening, the rain is lessening. Mary, I would love to go to Mass at 1 p.m. Would it be possible. I know obedience is foremost. Tell me Mary and I will do whatever You say.

Mary, could I have Jesus here in the house when I cannot visit Him in the Blessed Sacrament? Oh Mary, I have been so lukewarm of late. Open my heart, change my heart. Enclose me in Your Immaculate Heart to please Him, to fulfil His need of me. Please Mary.

MARY :
"Stay child, it is a greater sacrifice to stay at home. Offer to Me the disappointment, the loss. Your longing for My Son in The Eucharist will increase. When the pain of longing grows, increases

to the extent to fulfil the need of My Son, then He will come to stay. Yes child, you have received great blessings. You have a special grace that you can collect the Blessed Sacrament. This you can do when the longing is great. Do this for today and tomorrow, the feast of the Divine Mercy. See what tomorrow brings."

10ᵗʰ April 1994 - Feast of Divine Mercy
(House) - Before the Blessed Sacrament :
Beloved One, to-day You sit on Your Throne, King of Mercy. Oh to see You as the Father of all fathers, to know You as Father of all fathers. We believe what we cannot comprehend.

You know all those I carry in my heart this day and specially the people in Bosnia where fighting has broken out again and many are being killed.

King of Mercy, have mercy on us all for the sake of His sorrowful passion.

Thank You Most Holy Trinity for this day, this moment of peace and happiness - happy family. Truly this is the answer to perfect living, living in the Resurrection, living in You. Is this the answer? Is this the solution to our present needs? Is this the fulfilment of Your need of us? You give us our freedom, now do You ask us to give You Your freedom, to release You from behind bars, from imprisonment in the Tabernacle?

"After the Resurrection I could go where I willed, be seen by whom I willed. I visited those who carried Me in the Tabernacles of their hearts. After Pentecost, the Holy Spirit descended upon all He enlightened with the truth."

13ᵗʰ April 1994
Before The Blessed Sacrament :
'The word was made flesh and dwelled amongst us.'

In today's reading (Acts 5. 17-26) 'an angel of God opened the prison doors and brought them out.' (the Apostles)

Immaculate Heart of Mary, Spouse of the Holy Spirit, open my heart to my Spouse also, that my thoughts are His.

15ᵗʰ April 1994 - House
Before The Blessed Sacrament :
My Beloved, You come again. Oh how I take You for granted. Beloved, change my heart of stone into a heart of flesh, but now I am reminded that when You were on earth You visited those who needed You most. Thank You Beloved for the peace and solace You give to so many others when You come.

Beloved, I do not have to tell You all the requests I carry in my heart. Instead I should be thinking of Your need of me.

Now I come through the Immaculate Heart of Your Holy Mother to fulfil Your need of me this day.

20ᵗʰ March 1994
Before The Blessed Sacrament :
Thank You again and again. Through another's suffering I see the perfection of Your Love and Holy Will in the present circumstances. Oh Beloved, if only I could know this lesson and practice it in my daily living how peaceful my life and the lives of others would be. Beloved, we continue to intercede for Bosnia and South Africa and our own country. All are Yours. All You control. May Your Holy Will be done over all the earth as it is in heaven. Amen.

As I sit here in Your Eucharistic Presence I am reminded that 'all is well', 'all will be well'.

May I abide in You as You abide in me and may the rays emanating from Your Eucharistic Presence, heal the cancerous areas of my soul to make it more like You each day, as my concentration diminishes.

24th March 1994
Vocation Sunday:
O Immaculate Heart of Mary, gather us into Your mantle of protection, Your maternal embrace - into the refuge of Your Immaculate Heart. Help me to know my place in God's Divine Plan.

After the Eucharist:

"I am the Shepherd of the shepherdless. Remember this always no matter what others think or say. Surrender yourself to me - body, mind and spirit. All are Mine. You are nothing without Me. Turn to me before you make any decision, for any decision. I chose you for a special mission, did I not?

Rest in Me now - all is well. Give me your nights specially. I use all My little one, My precious one. Come back later, I need you."

Later
Before the Blessed Sacrament:
Here I am Beloved, to fulfil Your need of me.

"Yes child I called you to minister to you. I am your healer. You do not seek others as others do. I am your all as I often tell you. I speak to your heart, I give you the gift of tears for inner healing. Your soul is Mine to care for, to protect. Child, I have been moulding you down the years, from the beginning. You were free to respond or not. You have been faithful. Now you will see the fruits unfold in the writings. **Hither fore I was teaching you to teach others, now the writings will speak to My shepherds, My pastors for the years ahead.** Do not be anxious about what I ask of you, ask you to write. My Spirit will lead and guide you, My Mother has a special care of you. You will grow closer to her as you pray to Her each day. Depend on Her. Call on Her."

Come Holy Spirit. 'Sanctify all that I think, say and do that all will be for the glory of God. Amen.'

1ˢᵗ May 1994
Before The Blessed Sacrament :
Beloved, I believe that You have all the answers to all our needs, the needs of the whole world. Today we celebrate the feast of St. Joseph the worker. Most celebrate because it is a bank holiday weekend. It is good for the worker to have an extra day of rest, but how few of us use it to find our rest in You. You seek that all may find some form of happiness, healthy, holy happiness. Many give over their days of rest to help others, share with others. This gives You happiness and pleases You.

Mary, our Queen and Mother, the month of May was always dedicated to You. May processions were always held in the past to honour You, to give glory to Your Son. May these devotions be renewed as they were in the past, or perhaps exchanged for a greater need by opening the tabernacle doors to expose the Eucharistic Presence of Jesus, as He continually asks of His priests now for these times. If the priest would respond to this special desire of Your Heart, they would find that the people would respond, because You have already planted the seed for Eucharistic Adoration in their hearts.

I know dearest One that it is difficult to respond when one has been conditioned to guard and protect You at their peril in case You are humiliated, vandalised in any way.

They think they are doing the right thing by You and You on the other hand say that they make You and keep You a prisoner in the tabernacle when You want to be with Your people, present to Your people at all times.

Beloved, I do not doubt what You give me to write. I must believe, even though I come to You mostly in dark faith myself. I understand the difficulties imbedded in priests through their training and formation in the seminaries and specially in these present times of widespread vandalism and crime, when respect for God and man is being diminished by the day, or it would appear to be. Beloved, You are the omnipotent God, nothing is impossible to You. Since You came to visit my home over 10 years ago now, many churches, oratories and places of Eucharistic prayer have started throughout the land. You can touch the hearts of all to seek and bring about the deepest desires of Your Heart for these times. There are many willing souls eager to help. Give them a lead, speak to their hearts.

Beloved, it would appear that peace in the North is being pushed further and further into the background by the men of violence. Perhaps more days of prayer and fasting would help to turn the tide of events.

Beloved, through the Immaculate Heart of Your Holy Mother, speak to our country, speak to the Church leaders and political leaders for a way forward. We do need the Holy Spirit. Perhaps we should all be doing something special in every parish in preparation for Pentecost. We await Your instructions. This is my prayer of intercession for the country on this day. I unite now with The Two Hearts of Jesus and Mary and all Your little ones that peace will prevail in our land.

"Let peace begin with me."

5ᵗʰ May 1994   -   House
Before The Blessed Sacrament :

Oh my Beloved, I wasted so much time this day that I could have been present to Your Presence, when Your need is so great. If others had this same privilege how faithful they would be. What a truly merciful God You are, to one so miserable and weak and so easily distracted. My Beloved, I know that these two days are very precious to You and specially the night vigil. Beloved, bless all who come to spend this night with You. I wish I had the health and strength to spend these precious hours with You, and yet if I were faithful during the day that is all You ask.

"My child, listen, take heed of what I speak to your heart. Child, be attentive until this writing is finished. Nothing else matters now. What you are about to write is very important. Now child I ask you to wait up this night until I tell you to go to your bed. Remember these are the three days of prayer I spoke about last week. Child, I do not rebuke you for today. You mustn't feel that you must remain in My Presence all day. That would be impossible My little one. You please Me as you are. It is a big commitment to open your home two days every week and have a night vigil on the eve of every First Friday. That is all I ask for the present. Child, I ask you to pray this night specially for My priests and bishops, in this land. Child, I do not ask much. I do not overburden them with many requests but I do ask them to spend more time, make more time for Eucharistic Adoration. They should be an example to My people, give leadership to My people. More than ever priests need personal prayer. They have the Eucharist at their disposal at all times. How many give Me the hour each day? Nowadays and in the present climate in this land, that is a minimum. Above all else I ask of them to give Me at least one hour, invite their flock to spend this hour with them. It will take much Eucharistic Prayer to bring about a change in your country to counteract the evil forces that seek to destroy the land that once I could call My own. I do not say that I haven't an army of little ones to carry out My wishes, but the majority live as if I didn't exist. Where does all the violence originate? Why does all this violence erupt in your midst? Parents where are your children? Do you know how they spend their time, where they are at all times? Parents are you at home, available for your children? Society is deteriorating. Why? Because of lack of leadership and parental control. Parents you have a grave responsibility. Every parent is responsible for the upbringing of their children. Example speaks louder than words. Parents, you cannot hope to fulfil your duty without prayer in your lives, in your homes. Never before has the adage 'Families that pray together, stay together' been more applicable. Oh My dear children, I plead with you, I beg you to take heed. Many suffer for My sake. Every suffering related to Mine I use.

Oh children, every little effort will be rewarded. Nothing will be wasted. My Holy Mother speaks to you also. She knows My suffering, She sees My pain, but also She is aware of the joy and comfort I receive in your home during these days of adoration and in all places of Eucharistic Adoration throughout this land.

My child, you will see in your lifetime that as this Eucharistic prayer is extended, the graces and blessings will multiply and peace will be restored.

People and even My priests have not yet realised the power of this prayer, why I beg them to open the Tabernacle doors, release Me from My prison to be amongst My people. How often My little one have I asked you to write on this. Many do not believe, do not want to listen, see it as a waste of time.

Child, every excuse as I have said before is a ploy of the evil one to block it. He knows the power of such prayer. It is in his interest to apply every excuse to block My requests to release Me. My child, I repeat again, no prisoner on earth can experience the joy I receive each time I am released. Oh the joy they give Me is beyond all human comprehension.

Oh to sit on My Throne, to be amongst friends, even to be alone is preferable than to be locked away, such is My desire to be with My people.

The priests do not have to worry. I will draw My people, I will place the desire in their hearts to answer My call, to be with Me. I will be waiting to unburden them of their burdens, share in their suffering, take upon Myself their pain. No more will they have to draw on the comforts of the flesh, of the world, to ease their pain. No more My child, no more.

My child, I died for all. I created the Eucharist for all. Here in My living Presence in the Eucharist I wait for all. I want to be free to go where I will, to whom I will. Oh My dear, dear priests, free Me. I long for the day I will be free. After the Resurrection I was free to go as I chose, to whom I chose. Why not now? Did I not send My Spirit to lead and guide you to fulfil all My needs."

18ᵗʰ May 1994
Before The Blessed Sacrament :
"Now child that we are alone, I wish to speak to your heart. You mustn't let the emotions that rise up within you at times, disturb you.

There will always be occasions when different emotions will erupt within you. This is part of the process of inner healing. Others may go to counsellors who help in the healing, but your healings come through your faithfulness to Eucharistic prayer. This is in My plan for you. Each day I take you a step further in the Eucharist. Child, you cannot realise the power of the Eucharist, daily Eucharist, but as you have been faithful all down the years, all your needs will be fulfilled therein. Child, many of My priests do not know nor experience the insights I give to you. You are easy to teach in your simplicity, but remember dear child, that the evil one will try to destroy in every way possible your faith with doubts, now child, as I bring you into deeper insights in the days ahead, for My priests.

Child, come when I call you. All I ask is that you sit with Me. Open your heart to Mine, I will do the rest."

21ˢᵗ May 1994   -   Eve of Pentecost
Before The Blessed Sacrament :
Mary, my Immaculate Mother, why must Your statues weep? Why do You have to humiliate Yourself so, for many to ridicule and

154

blaspheme You? Oh Mary, we weep to see You weep, but more so to see You humiliated and ridiculed.

MARY :
"My child, My little one, how much more My Son is rejected, ridiculed and blasphemed in the world to-day and by so many in your own land. Child, I come, I use every possible way to draw My children back to repentance and conversion. Child, I come throughout the world to every country, to some souls to plead, to remind My children that the wrath of God is not far off. Oh child, would that My people would repent. I remind you of Nineveh in the old testament. All down the ages I come, I come. So few take heed of My warnings. Oh dear, dear children, listen before it is too late. Pray child, pray children. I know that many listen but more do not. I thank you child for visiting My Son in the Blessed Sacrament. Here child He calls you. Here I need you also. Here child, you will receive all the healings you need for soul and body. Child, live your consecration now. I am your Immaculate Mother. I never leave you. Call on Me in all your needs. I know all. I come when you call and even when you do not. We are present to you always. Live in this Presence. It protects you from all the wiles of the evil one, day and night. Child, I direct all My children into the Eucharistic Presence of My Son. Would that all priests listen to Our need for these times.

My Son cannot give more than His Eucharistic Presence. It is the ultimate in sacrifice and love. Thank you child, My own precious child for answering Our call this night."

26ᵗʰ May 1994   -   House
Before The Blessed Sacrament :
"My child, My little one, now you see why We use certain phenomenon to draw Our people back to repentance and conversion. People can be very fickle at times and are drawn only by the unexplained phenomena My church was empty. Why? Oh My dear child, I repeat again and again, when My Eucharistic Presence will be exposed throughout this land, My people will return to a life of prayer again. I will be better able to touch My people when I make Myself present to the human eye, human heart. It is a greater sacrifice for Me, a greater humiliation. Do My

people not realise this? Oh My children come."

Oh Beloved, through the Immaculate Heart of Your Holy Mother, renew my zeal, my desire for Your Eucharistic Presence. How I wish I could be more reverent and grateful for the honours You bestow upon me. I unite with each one who comes in response to Your call. I thank You for the love and unity that unites us all in Your Eucharistic Presence. Oh the wonder of Your ways continue to amaze me. I cannot thank You enough.

30th May 1994
<u>After the Eucharist :</u>

Oh the pain of emptiness
No heart to respond
No heart to embrace
The gift of the Eucharist.

How long must we wait
How long will it last
All giving, all taking.
Will it be always like this.

The abyss is too deep.
An insight to encourage us.
It leaves us thirsting.
A reflection of Yours.

The journey is long
As long as life.
Preparing, being purified
As we struggle along.

But the ending is only the beginning
Of a life beyond our grasp,
Beyond all knowledge
'Till the last breath is taken.

Then the veil will be lifted
The reason He hides
Keep hidden from mankind
His secret.

1st July 1994:   "Yes child, you sought Me for a long time before I revealed Myself to you. So must it be with the others, but through your prayers of intercession I will draw all to Me. You mustn't worry nor be anxious but trust Me. Do I not listen, answer every prayer? Child you see at the Eucharist this morning - I welcome you, I invite you no matter what the emotions. You sought Me in your heart, you trusted Me. Oh the pleasure I receive in solving the little problems of My little ones, but so few give them to Me.

My child, the new catechism may not be to the liking of all, but I say be patient. All I ask is that people do their best to keep to the present regulations. **Women particularly are disappointed. I specially ask them to be patient.** I am moulding them, preparing them not to take over the role of men, but to compliment men in the running of church affairs. As the saying goes, Rome was not built in a day. As I said before, I mustn't be rushed into making quick decisions but the time will come - Yes child the time will come when women will be ready to take their place with men at the altar of sacrifice.

> "Yes child the time will come when women will be ready to take their place with men at the altar of sacrifice."

Much has to happen before this can come about. As I said before much healings have to take place in the attitudes of both sexes. They must be patient with one another, tolerant of one another. Remember it takes time for attitudes of long standing to change. All must come into the light to be healed, and circumstances will hasten this happening.

Oh My child, My dear child, I will prepare you for further writings relating to the Church. Be faithful to Eucharistic prayer. Be attentive to the urgings of the Spirit. See child My Mother is using you also to write for Her. Remain small and simple. Yes see Us in all the little happenings that take place in your daily lives. Be aware of Our Presence. So few know Our present day needs. Do not worry about your weaknesses. Remember to praise and thank Me always for the burden of these. My strength is manifested in weakness."

9ᵗʰ June 1994   -   House
<u>Before The Blessed Sacrament :</u>
Thank You Jesus, thank You Mary for yesterday and specially for last night. I feel I write Your words and others give them heart and bring them to life. I met one such priest last night.

Truth is the image of God.

<u>Later :</u>
Beloved, tomorrow is a great feast-day in the Church's liturgy. May we give praise, honour and glory to You for all the graces and blessings You have bestowed on our country down all the years. There was a time when every home carried a picture of Your Sacred Heart - were it so again. Hasten this day when every home will be a little Nazareth. Oh Lord, how we have neglected and rejected You of recent years, yet You seek to give Yourself to us, to humble Yourself more and more each day for us, to be present to us in the Eucharist.

Beloved, I haven't the words to write how I feel because I have no feelings and You make Yourself available to me whenever I seek You, here in my home, in the convent and in the churches. Because You are so infinitely generous with Your Presence, we, at least I, lack appreciation of this momentous gift of Yourself. You have never asked another human being to humiliate oneself as You do in the Eucharist. How difficult we find it to accept the least humiliation from others and we fail to see the greatest of all Yours at every Eucharist, and in every Eucharistic Host that embodies a living Eucharistic and Sacred Heart.

Immaculate Heart of Mary, touch our hearts to prepare our hearts to receive with open hearts His tomorrow.

12ᵗʰ July 1994
<u>MARY :</u>
"Yes child, your country is in great need of prayer at this present time. So much violence. They do not believe that life is very sacred. God alone gives and takes away. Child, children, pray constantly for your land. Offer all for those who do not know, do not listen, those who reject My Son, blaspheme and scoff Him. Oh

children, My Son suffers much to see this land follow the example of other lands. The prayers and faithfulness of His little ones have preserved this land in the past. I come to warn My children. So many do not believe. Oh children I plead with you to listen to the pleas of My Son. Shepherds of the Church take heed. Prayer, much prayer is needed. Pray in the churches with the people. **Expose the Eucharistic Presence of My Son as He desires this prayer above all other now**. The Eucharistic Presence will dispel the evil forces bent on destroying Our children, specially those chosen to lead and direct. Oh shepherds take heed. There are many oasis of prayer in this land. These holy places, these holy people help to stave off the punishment that surely fits the evil in your midst. Children, children, pray. We have blessed this home. We have blessed all who come to pray. We bless all you carry in your hearts. Yes children, We carry your burdens. You will find peace, Our peace in the Eucharistic Presence. Would that all shepherds would heed the cries of Our Hearts. We come in person. Do they not believe in the power of Our Presence. Oh children, pray that the shepherds will listen, will heed this request that comes from two broken, suffering Hearts, united in love."

12ᵗʰ July 1994
Before The Blessed Sacrament :
"Yes child, I see all, I know all. Nothing is impossible to Me. Remember this always. I choose, I mould, in My own way. Remember the leaking watering can? - a reflection of the soul. All things come together in time.

Now child, pray the prayer of repentance for your land, so necessary during these days of tension, specially to-day. I take care of those you carry in your heart. Think of the dangers of these days in your country. Men's hearts are still full of hatred and retaliation, but I also know of the prayers for peace and reconciliation taking place. The evil one is bent on dividing My peoples in all areas - in the church, politics and economics, but particularly amongst My own chosen and faithful little ones. Be careful dear, dear children not to allow him take control. Pray together, pray for one another. How many call on Me to settle their disputes, their problems. I wait, always waiting to take all burdens, to carry all burdens, to solve the needs of My people but above all to give peace of mind and soul. Distribute the prayer I gave you on 26th June for 2nd July. It is a prayer specially for the healing of your land through the healing of individual hearts. Since you are My child of the Eucharist I give you, I place upon you the burden of teaching and sharing with others the power of the Eucharist and Eucharistic Adoration. Remember always dear precious child that feelings do not matter. Faith I ask, faith I need, and openness always to the urgings of the Spirit. Thank you My little one for your faithfulness. As far as possible keep to this routine here (*convent*) until I tell you otherwise."

22nd July 1994: "My child, My little child, My Heart is heavy today - so much unnecessary suffering in the world. My little ones suffer the consequences of sin in their midst. So it has been down the ages. It is My little ones who suffer. Cannot My people see the power of the evil one at work in their midst, in your land. When I am exposed in the Eucharist in all churches more hearts will be changed, because My Eucharistic Presence acts like a magnet to draw people into prayer, Eucharistic prayer, prayer that heals. You can never envisage the power of My Eucharistic Presence in your home - the effects on those who visit Me, on your parish and in the country. You are My army scattered throughout the land. All sections come together, all have a part to play in My overall plan."

May Your plan for Glencree be furthered each week when we meet in Your Eucharistic Presence to pray together for this specific purpose, and when You unfold for us Your needs, but more often You tell us of the joy we give the United Hearts and fill us with Your Love and blessings.

27th July 1994: *Oh Beloved, why do we delay. Beloved, we pray, we offer ourselves this day in our miseries that more hearts, more priests and bishops will be open to the desire of Your Eucharistic Heart for these times. Our own needs we realise through Your grace are of little importance to Your greater need, but we also know that in desiring Your need to be fulfilled, You will fulfil the deepest desires of our hearts. You are ever ready to go before us, to show us the way, lead us along the right path and all* *those we carry in our hearts.*

23ʳᵈ August 1994 - After The Eucharist
Before The Blessed Sacrament :
Beloved, thank You for the privilege of being able to take You out of the Tabernacle, Your prison. And as You are present to me as I am present to You, we can communicate more deeply, more intimately, specially after the Eucharist. When will I ever begin to realise after all You have taught me that You have come to me in the most intimate and ultimate of all Presence and relationships. You give me the words to express the desire of Your Heart for these times. We lament the past. We think of them as the good times when there was peace in our land. We could walk our streets and live in safety, relative safety. Drugs had not been a problem. Organised crime, greed had not entered the hearts of our people to the extent that materialism and secularisation have brought into our society. We cannot take the evil of unemployment. But You come, You offer Yourself. You ask to be present, to be seen to be present to Your people, to lift their burdens, to take upon Yourself our burdens, our pain, our sorrow, our sufferings, to give us new life, a new way of life before we destroy ourselves or allow evil spirits to control us, rather than Your Holy Spirit.

Beloved, are You asking that all the laws that have grown up and been enacted over the years to keep You locked away from Your people, be changed to allow You be present to all? It would appear that more people answer Your call to visit You in the churches that expose Your Presence. Is this not a sign of the need You have placed in our hearts and that is being ignored perhaps through over-caution or deaf ears? Beloved, I write these words - I pray that I write under the guidance of Your Spirit. Beloved, I pray for the coming conference on the 'Two Hearts' next month, that hearts will be open to Your need, Your desire, Your holy will for these special days. We long that this conference will change our hearts, will change the hearts of the peoples of this land. Next week we have our three days of prayer, Eucharistic Adoration, vigil and Mass of the Generations. May these days be a special preparation for the success of the coming conference, that the Two United Hearts will unite the hearts of the people of this land as never before. Beloved, give me the grace to respond to the Two Hearts of love by being faithful to my calling, to begin to fulfil Your need of me each day, beginning today.

28ᵗʰ August 1994
Before The Blessed Sacrament :
Beloved Jesus and my Immaculate Mother, thank You both for inviting me into Your living Presence in the Eucharistic Host. Because You have made Yourselves available to me daily I cannot appreciate nor give You the worship and honour that is Your due. My senses are numbed, not like others who have a great sense of Your majesty in this great sacrament of love.

Beloved, how come You use me to tell others, to speak to others of the desires of Your Eucharistic Heart. Beloved, somehow I cannot forget the words You gave me about the coming Congress in September on the Two Hearts. You told me that when I delivered the first message my work was finished, but I cannot rest until I am made aware that Your need will be fulfilled. More and more I feel that evil forces are at work creating division amongst the organisers to block Your intentions. It is just a reflection of the present attacks and division in Your Church to discredit the Pope and his teachings. I believe dear Lord that all and everyone who is trying to be Your disciple is suffering the same division within oneself. We must never forget that Your strength is manifested in our weakness. "Create in me a clean heart O God" since I deserve nothing, I can therefore hope for all things from God's great kindness.

30ᵗʰ August 1994
Before The Blessed Sacrament :
Oh Beloved, what a privilege that You allow me roll back the stone and take You out of Your tomb.

Beloved, You show me that You are the essence, the ultimate in love and humility. How lower can You make Yourself become for our sakes. We search for You in books in lectures, in seminars, in conferences, in discussions. We search for You everywhere. Here and now You allow Yourself to be all things to all mankind. The Presence to embody all, the human, the divine, the Three Persons of the Trinity. How we doubt Your sincerity, Your word, Your invitation to be amongst Your people. You do not ask anyone to take responsibility for You. All You ask of Your priests is to listen, to be doers of Your present need for these times.

"Priests and people you sit on a time bomb. I alone can dismantle this bomb. I invite you all into My Presence. My Eucharistic Presence is for all My people. There I will speak to all hearts, challenge all hearts, change all hearts, heal all hearts. Child, children, the Masses of the Generations will help, will bring about peace in your land when hearts are healed."

4ᵗʰ September 1994: *Beloved, do try to instil in us the power of prayer, the power of the Eucharist, so few now have this gift to pass on to us. Beloved, we pray for this gift specially for our shepherds, the gifts of faith, hope and love in the Eucharistic Presence, to pass on to us to give renewed life, peace and joy into our hearts, to prepare us to face the difficulties of present day living, to change attitudes, to see the emptiness of our secular and materialistic society.*

Please Jesus, may the coming Congress on the United Hearts be first of all a Eucharistic Congress, the unity of the Two Hearts in the Eucharist. If we are to believe that Mary is Co-Redemptor of the world with Her Son, we must believe that She is also present to us in the Eucharist. It is now over 62 years since we had a Eucharistic Congress in our country. Lord, You were then carried through the streets of our city, and the Eucharist celebrated in open places. Now we are given an opportunity to glorify You again in the Eucharistic Presence at this coming congress. May all hearts be open to the urging of the Holy Spirit to allow this congress to take place in a Eucharistic setting - we pray, we pray.

Later : Before The Blessed Sacrament :

"What you seek now My child is for later (*stillness at prayer*). Time is urgent now. I need you to write, to be My messenger for these times. I must repeat My desires again and again. My messages are never new, always a repeat of My needs. You see the same, I repeat the same down the centuries. My child, My very own must never forget why I called them into the religious life. I call all to fulfil a need within Me. This is their prime calling. So many forget as they become engrossed in the day to day chores that make up their communities - overall administration etc. All will follow fully from hearts of prayer. My priests also must let go. Let the laity take over all that is not essential to their calling. How I wait for all to spend time with Me in My Eucharistic Presence. This Presence, My living Presence is always available to them. Oh child, it pains My Heart when they neglect Me, leave Me alone, lock Me away from My people, many who seek to be present to Me. Child, do not be fearful of becoming over familiar. I understand. Did I not tell you on that special occasion that I wanted to be treated as one of the family, instead of being institutionalised in the Tabernacle. These are dangerous times. These are times of change. Oh child, in your lifetime you will see many changes. It is only through great changes that My plans can be fulfilled."

> "... I wanted to be treated as one of the family, instead of being institutionalised in the Tabernacle."

13ᵗʰ September 1994
Before The Blessed Sacrament :

Who cannot but believe in the power of prayer. Beloved, nothing is impossible to You.

'Mary, Queen and Mother, we call on You
Listen to the cries of our hearts
For peace to prevail in our land
And throughout the world.'

Beloved, You alone as You said, can dismantle the time bomb. If only we would answer Your call to pray Eucharistic prayer in Your living Presence. Cannot they see why You ask for the coming congress, that Your Presence be exposed at each session. We need Your protection. Tallaght shopping centre is not an unlikely target for the men of violence.

We pray that hearts will be open to listen for Your needs. Lord, You have promised peace when Your Eucharistic Presence is exposed throughout the land. You ask so little for so much. Let us listen to the cries of Your Heart and the Immaculate Heart of Your Mother.

We pray for a fresh outpouring of the Holy Spirit on the Church, our divided Church, the governments, all in authority, on us all. We all are in need of Your Spirit for guidance, for wisdom in the present situation. Truly we sit on a time bomb and we know You alone can dismantle it.

18ᵗʰ September 1994
Before The Blessed Sacrament :

Do you believe in My Presence?
Do you believe that I am here
In My humanity and My divinity?

When will My priests listen to the cries of My Heart?
Crying, crying in My aloneness in My prison,
My priests, you hold the key to My freedom.

All I ask, to be made present to My people
That all might come and gaze upon the Face
That keeps searching for you all.

People came from far and wide in days long past;
Wherever I went the little ones followed Me
To look upon My Face and listen to My voice
And in their eagerness I could touch their hearts.

'Tis the same Presence and more
As you sit with Me.
I am the Resurrected Christ
That smiles upon you all.

The smile of happiness

That comes from a heart
Rejected and neglected by mankind.
Oh the comfort that I draw from you all.

Listen, My faithful little ones,
As I speak to one and all.
Oh the joy I have prepared I cannot share with you.
But the day will come when Face to face
You'll know it all.

2ⁿᵈ October 1994
Before The Blessed Sacrament :
"Child, dear child, who can teach as I do? Child, you do not understand yet the length, the breath, the depth of My Love here in the Eucharistic Presence. Child, I have chosen you specially to be an example for others, specially My own chosen ones, that here in My Eucharistic Presence, the teachings and healings that take place are above and beyond all that you can learn from human knowledge. Child, you have no need to go to the lectures that you seek. Here I will teach you all. All I ask is that you be present to My Presence. Oh child, I ask that you go only where I send you."

3ʳᵈ October 1994
Before The Blessed Sacrament:
Everyday is so different. Our needs and Your need of us change from day to day. The troubles of yesterday are no longer the troubles of today. But Your Love, Your strength never changes. Oh to see the perfection of Your Love and Holy Will in all the circumstances of our lives in the present moment, is Your gift for peace to be found most often here in Your Eucharistic Presence. Truly here is where You seek us to spend time with You, to give to us all the world cannot give. And yet Beloved, how often I seek to find You elsewhere and You keep reminding me and call me back. Oh Beloved, the burden of my weaknesses bear heavily upon me these days.

Later
Before The Blessed Sacrament:
"My child, listen to the cries of My Heart. My priests do not listen.

They are listening instead to rules and regulations that are out of date." (Gal. 2.)

The meeting at Jerusalem

It was not till fourteen years had passed that I went up to Jerusalem again. I went with Barnabas and took Titus with me. I went there as the result of a revelation, and privately I laid before the leading men the Good News as I proclaim it among the pagans; I did so for fear the course I was adopting or had already adopted would not be allowed. And what happened? Even though Titus who had come with me is a Greek, he was not obliged to be circumcised. The question came up only because some who do not really belong to the brotherhood have furtively crept in to spy on the liberty we enjoy in Christ Jesus, and want to reduce us all to slavery. I was so determined to safeguard for you the true meaning of the Good News, that I refused even out of deference to yield to such people for one moment. As a result, these people who are acknowledged leaders—not that their importance matters to me, since God has no favourites— these leaders, as I say, had nothing to add to the Good News as I preach it. On the contrary, they recognised that I had been commissioned to preach the Good News to the uncircumcised just as Peter had been commissioned to preach it to the circumcised. 'The same person whose action had made Peter the apostle of the circumcised had given me a similar mission to the pagans. 'So, James, Cephas and John, these leaders, these pillars, shook hands with Barnabas and me as a sign of partnership: we were to go to the pagans and they to the circumcised. 'The only thing they insisted on was that we should remember to help the poor, as indeed I was anxious to do.

Peter and Paul at Antioch

When Cephas came to Antioch, however, I opposed him to his face, since he was manifestly in the wrong. His custom had been to eat with the pagans, but after certain friends of James arrived he stopped doing this and kept away from them altogether for fear of the group that insisted on circumcision. The other Jews joined him in this pretence, and even Barnabas felt himself obliged to copy their behaviour.

When I saw they were not respecting the true meaning of the Good News, I said to Cephas in front of everyone, 'In spite of being a Jew, you live like the pagans and not like the Jews, so you have no right to make the pagans copy Jewish ways'.

The Good News as proclaimed by Paul

'Though we were born Jews and not pagan sinners, we acknowledge that what makes a man righteous is not obedience to the Law, but faith in Jesus Christ. We had to become believers in Christ Jesus no less than you had, and now we hold that faith in Christ rather than fidelity to the Law is what justifies us, and that *no one can be justified* by keeping the Law. 'Now if we were to admit that the result of looking to Christ to justify us is to make us sinners like the rest, it would follow that Christ had induced us to sin, which would be absurd. I were to return to a position I had already abandoned, I should be admitting I had done something wrong. 'In other words, through the Law I am dead to the Law, so that now I can live for God. I have been crucified with Christ, and I live now not with my own life but with the life of Christ who lives in me. The life I now live in this body I live in faith: faith in the Son of God who loved me and who sacrificed himself for my sake. I cannot bring myself to give up God's gift: if the Law can justify us, there is no point in the death of Christ.' [The Jerusalem Bible]

"Child, dear child, I cry, I continue to cry tears of pain, of neglect and rejection. They do not listen. Open the doors of the

Tabernacles. Release Me from prison. I ask again and again for My release. Child, spread My word. Begin again to send out these messages to My priests. I will touch their hearts to respond. Child, I know it is happening in your land but My need is urgent for your sake. My Mother is sharing Her tears also. She knobs My sufferings. Some suffer My sufferings for the sake of others. Visit Me later My child. Short visits will not tire you. I will be your strength.

Return to W... He needs you now."

4ᵗʰ October 1994   -   Feast of St. Francis of Assisi
Before The Blessed Sacrament:
"Child, do I not call you again and again and My priests do not hear My call. They are too busy with works that can be left aside to answer My call. Dear, dear child, I place a heavy load on your shoulders now. Be prepared to gather these writings on Eucharistic Adoration. I will send you someone to help you.

Child, I repeat again, these writings are for today, these days. Pray, pray, pray for priests to answer My call, My need to be with My people, present to them in My Living Presence in the Eucharist, to combat the evil forces that seek to destroy and take from Me My very own. What about My sheep?"

5ᵗʰ October 1994
Before The Blessed Sacrament:
Beloved, You truly bless us both. You give to each of us confirmation for the other through Gal. 2. - to-day's reading. Beloved, we truly need Your Spirit to write in truth. Preserve us from all evil. We trust in You, our Wonder-Counsellor.

6ᵗʰ October 1994
Before The Blessed Sacrament:
Yes Lord, are seeing a broken church. Your brokenness is being spread far and wide through the media. Beloved, how You must suffer. Yet we believe in Your Promise. You will never leave her, and we must never despair, but hope and trust in the mercy and goodness of God, always ready to forgive repentant souls. Let us

pray specially and offer this Thursday for those priests most in need this day. May we help to refill with wine the Chalice of Strength for their sake. Amen.

16th October 1994
<u>Before The Eucharist :</u>

Beloved, I bring all my miseries and gifts received, to the altar of all graces now, knowing that Your need of me is much, much greater than my need of You. I come only with the burden of my weaknesses to offer You but in faith. Thank You for all the graces about to be given to all who come and all we carry in our hearts. Oh what a truly bountiful God You are. Your Love has no bounds nor limits. May our communion in Communion bring us a step nearer to You in our struggle along the path to holiness.

21st October 1994:   "Oh My dear little child, My Heart is joyful to read your words of appreciation and love. Truly child, children, We look forward to this night of love also. Oh the comfort and solace We receive in your company. Yes child, your prayer together bears much fruit, oh so much fruit. Now you will see much happening in the days ahead. People will flock to this place chosen by Us to be a haven of peace and reconciliation, so needed, so necessary in the present climate of your land. Physical violence may have ceased but the inner emotions of all need so much healing. You will see and experience the fruits of the Masses of the Generations in the months ahead. Yes children, it will open up many areas, areas that need healings in the hearts of all, hearts that come seeking help and healing. Hearts will be touched beyond the expectations, but at a cost. You know child, you realise children that purification is the fruit of prayer and suffering for yourselves and others. Yes children, you are victims of Our love, Our Two Hearts of Love. Remember always We are with you to strengthen and sustain you. The battle is ferocious at the moment. You know it, you feel it, but, We are your hope. We give you hope to share with others. You are Our messengers of hope for your land in the days ahead."

25th October 1994:   "Child, child, I use you as you are. I use your impulsiveness. Were it not so I would change you. I use others as they are. No two are alike. Oh the uniqueness of each person I create. Each has a special part to play in My plan for all. Child, do not worry about your health just now. I am taking care of you. I will advise you when you need medical help. I ask that you rest more in Me. I need you. I need all but so few listen, respond to My need. All that you have written over the years, you will live and pray now.

Remember specially your preparation for the Eucharist. This child is the most important exercise of the day. I give all, I expect your all. Oh child, have I not always touched you, specially at the Mass, spoken to your heart. Here all the writings are born to bear fruit. Here you will help all whom I send you. Here I will bless all you carry in your heart. Do not forget to pray specially for the Celebrant. One can never see nor judge the state of his mind and spirit as he ascends the altar. You cannot comprehend My little one the omnipresence of this moment for him, for you, for others, for the world. Now child, give Me your heart, your attention. Comfort and console Me. I am so in need of love. You cannot understand this My child, I will teach you. Ask My Mother to help you respond to My need of you. She has special care for you now. Did you not consecrate yourself to Her Immaculate Heart?"

8ᵗʰ November 1994
Before The Blessed Sacrament :
"Rose My child be prepared to write much this day. I call the others to Glencree but you will pray at home before the Eucharistic Presence. Be in unity with the others. These are special days. My Holy Mother prepares My little ones for the days ahead. Prayer as I said before will bring peace to your hearts, retain peace while the world may be in turmoil. Already you see disturbances in the elements - the beginnings of great changes, consequent often on man's greed that disturbs. I do not disturb. Many prophecies have been written about the present generation, many of which will come to pass because man does not heed the warnings. On the other hand, the prayers, fervent prayers of My little ones, My faithful little ones will help to prevent disasters that would by nature follow the disturbances. I do not desire to frighten

My little ones. All I require to live in peace and hope, not to be anxious about the morrow."

16th November 1994
<u>Before The Blessed Sacrament :</u>

Beloved, now I understand the meaning that prayer, Eucharistic prayer as we sit here in Your living Presence, we can be one with our government and politicians as they decide the future of our country. We bring Your Presence into this situation. It is also a confirmation for me for T…'s vision the other night about Glencree. Tomorrow night as they hold their meeting, controversial as it may be, that as I pray before the Eucharistic Presence I can be present with You to bring Your light into the situation. It confirms for me when You tell me that prayer, specially Eucharistic prayer, is beyond all time and space. We may not be visibly present to others, but You can bring us as it were into these situations and places to influence those concerned through the power of the Eucharistic Presence. Oh Beloved, truly this is the power of intercessory prayer in all it's fullness, if only we could surrender and abandon ourselves to You.

17th November 1994
<u>Before The Blessed Sacrament :</u>
'A pure heart create in me O God.'

O God, help us all in this land of ours during these days of great confusion and division. Church and state appear in great disarray and yet we can see Your print, Your hand of victory in all that is happening. You truly can bring good out of evil.

Our Lord, we trust in You, our faith is in You, our hope is in You. You are truly a God of infinite love and mercy and hold us all in the palm of Your hand. May the Spirit of truth and holiness invade all our hearts - who can throw the first stone? Prayer is a bridge, Eucharistic prayer is our thanksgiving and hope for the future of Church and State. (Government resigns)

22nd November 1994: *Our Lady, You have given us Glencree. It* *is for everyone in need of peace and reconciliation. Who is not in such need?*

I would have loved to have been with the others on Sunday but I knew I was where I was called. Thank You Mary for Your loving guidance. You direct me to where My Beloved calls. Prepare me for the Eucharist, the centre of my day where I receive the strength and hope to live out my mission. Wrap Your mantle of love around us all and specially over our land, oh Queen of Ireland.

22ⁿᵈ December 1994: "Yes child of My Heart, I have much for you to write this day. Truly child, My Heart bleeds for My people on this day - for all who reject My Love, doubt My Love. Child, it is difficult for the human mind to grasp My Love. I do not expect you, but I do ask all that know Me to try, and I will teach each one to learn to know My Love - but hearts must be open to receive. Child, I continually knock but few hear because they do not spend time with Me. And to know Me is to know My Mother also - and likewise, to know My Mother is to know Me. (knowing is loving) We are the Two Hearts of Love, united in Love, bound by Love.

Child, children, in this land so privileged so blessed in the past - you spread Our love throughout the world - now We desire that the time will come again to bring Our Love, the Love of the Eucharistic Presence throughout the world. We seek to prepare you. Already My Presence is exposed in many parishes - some still hold back but through the prayers of My faithful adorers all will answer Our call. Yes child, yes children, in preparation you are being purified. All that was hidden must be uncovered and brought into the light to be healed, to be forgiven. All will be affected by the revelations taking place in your land presently, but there was no other way My dear little ones that the light would shine again. Repentance brings purification and purification brings resurrection. And the healing Masses of the Generations help to open the graves of the past to My mercy, My Love, My forgiveness to all souls, living and dead, bound by sin.

Now child, pray the prayer of Divine Mercy for all souls (3 o'clock). Now child, the tears you shed are My tears, My tears of healing for this land. Remember child, each day is a new beginning, a growth along the path of perfection. It is a daily struggle My little one."

172

EXTRACTS FROM WRITINGS 1995

1ˢᵗ January 1995:   *Beloved, You heard my plea and You answered me. I spent the ending of 1994 and the beginning of 1995 at Mass at the Disciples of the Divine Master last night. It was like old times again. Thank You. Oh the joy to meet old friends again, and to be able to bring man suffering people to You for Your Love and consolation.*

Oh this day we join with you in honouring Your Holy Mother. Mary, You remained hidden in Your life on earth. Now Your Son desires to give You Your rightful place among men. You are His cohort and Mediatrix of graces here on earth. Jesus is present in the world, present to all people who seek Him. Wherever He is, You are also. As You reminded me when You told me 'go back to My Mother, She can do all I can do for you.' You remind us all of this again on the first day of each year. This feast-day was inspired by the Holy Spirit. Let us honour Your Mother, our Mother, for Your greater glory. Thank You Father, Son and Spirit for the gift of Mary to the human race, and specially to this land. Has She not come to us in our darkest hours to bless and comfort us, to warn us of impending dangers, to impede the forces of evil from destroying us. Truly She is our Queen of Peace and Mother of Reconciliation, Queen of Ireland, Queen of Glencree. Oh Mary, how grateful I

Mary, teach me to say the Rosary of Tears for Your intentions. Mary, sometimes Your tears are like ours, other times they are tears of blood. What is the difference and why?

"All tears are because of My Sons' sufferings in His people, but the tears of blood are when I see the sufferings of My Son for His priests."   2nd. Nov. 1995 *should be, how thankful to have been chosen to be one of the Five, to pray specially for the advancement of Your Shrine at Glencree, to bring peace and reconciliation to all peoples, families, communities, denominations throughout the land and the world. May we listen and answer Your call O Holy Mother.*

Later
Before The Blessed Sacrament:
Beloved, here I am

2ⁿᵈ January 1995: *Beloved, I have been neglecting You over the Christmas season. I haven't been making time for You before the Blessed Sacrament. But with Your help, I will try not to miss my daily Adoration.*

Beloved, so many I meet are broken and sad. I know You will not fail them. I do not have to mention all whom I promised to pray for and who asked my prayers. You know them all, and I know You will not fail them though I forget. These days are very stressful for N. and family specially. It is easy for outsiders to see the perfection of Your Love and Holy Will in the present situation. We can only pray that the family will find Your peace after the funeral takes place. This Christmas has been a very anxious and painful time for many, but You are Infinite Goodness, Infinite Love and will not fail anyone in their need.

3ʳᵈ January 1995
Before The Blessed Sacrament:
Oh Beloved the relief to be in Your Presence. I was afraid I wouldn't be able to make this morning. My breathing is becoming more laboured at times, but You told me to keep as far as possible to the routine.

Beloved, I keep annoying You as to what to do about the cough. Am I doing enough? I am waiting for Your direction. You know how indecisive I am about making decisions for myself! My little suffering is nothing in comparison to others. Do not listen to my complaints. Beloved, You bless me, You grace me. I cannot thank You enough. Mary, my Holy Mother, I depend on You to thank Him, to help me fulfil His need of me today and every day. Thank

You Mary for the peace I have again when I am awake at night. Now I can commune and pass the time with My Beloved instead of the previous anguish. I pray for love and gratitude in my heart for this great gift. I must go now. I hope to visit You for awhile later in the parish church. The Tuesday evening Adoration has been brought back as You asked. We rejoice in Your joy.

4th January 1995 - After the Eucharist
Before The Blessed Sacrament:

"Yes child, find comfort and solace here in My Presence.
Child, relate all to Me. Child, you suffer My pain now. You are My consolation and refuge also. Oh child, how I need My victim souls. Yes child, you are My victim soul now. The evil one will try and destroy all you hold dear. Do not falter. You will not falter because I am with you. Remember your Angel Guardian and above all My Holy Mother. She takes special care of you in your time of anguish."

I am reminded now of word of Our Lady to another -

'It is when you find no ground beneath your feet, you shall realise you are in flight to My embrace.'

Oh Holy Mother, I desire to consecrate myself to Your Immaculate Heart with all my family, my extended family, friends and all You have placed in my heart. Mary, help me in my weakness.

Beloved, am I boxing You in? Do I try to confine You within the limits of my own horizon. I am trying to follow the word You gave me in the early days -

'There are many paths and all paths that lead to Me are perfect.'

Are not the sightings of Mary, Her ways of bringing Her children back to repentance, part of Your plan for this land - part of Mary's plan to bring Your children back to You.

Mary, I would like to join the others at the Mass next Saturday at Glencree. Please give me the strength and health to go.
" Come to the waters,
Come to My Grotto
Come to My Son

He waits for you."

5th January 1995
During the night:
"Yes child, I called you. I need you My little one. Thank you for responding. Oh My pain - beyond your comprehension but again I must teach you of My thirst for souls. In the beginning it was too much, but over the years I have been preparing you to receive. Yes child, during this year I will prepare the soul. Be prepared to understand, to answer this call. I will come mostly in the quietness of the night as in the solitude of your nocturnal prayers. Do not let the distractions of the day disturb you, particularly these two days (Thursday and Friday) and every day.

I come to your home to receive and to comfort. Your home has become a haven of peace for many. Oh child, I thank you both for your faithfulness. Without Willie's agreement I couldn't use this home which has been given freely. It is a big commitment and your reward will be great. Rest My little one. I see all you carry in your heart these days. I take care of all."

Before The Blessed Sacrament:
Magnificat

'My soul glorifies the Lord
My spirit rejoices in God my Saviour
For He has blessed me lavishly
And makes me ready to respond.

He shatters my little world
And lets me be poor before Him
He takes from me all my plans
And gives me more than I can hope for or ask.

He gives me opportunities and the ability
To become free and burst through my boundaries
He gives me the strength to be daring
To build on Him alone for He shows
Himself as the ever greater One in my life.'
He has made known to me this :

See Rose, 'I will not forget you. I have carved you on the palm of

176

My hand. Is. 49:15. 'It is in my being servant that it becomes possible for God's Kingdom to break through here and now.'

(With regard to prayer imprimatur)
"Be obedient to whatever the Church decides."

6ᵗʰ **January 1995** - (First Friday)
Feast of the Epiphany:

Beloved, it is in pain and with a heavy heart I take my pen to write this day. I have suddenly realised - prompted by the Holy Spirit, how I have slipped back and taken so many graces and Your divine mercy for granted.

Firstly in my preparation for the Eucharist. Secondly as I sit in Your Presence, specially when You come in Your Eucharistic Presence to my home each Thursday and Friday. Truly the maxim 'familiarity breeds contempt' is so in me. Beloved, on my way to Mass this morning I was reminded that my speech impediment brought about great blessings in my life. I realise that now and I thank You. I thought of others with hearing problems, that when they give You their ears they hear You instead of listening to idle gossip etc.

My Beloved, please help to make reparation for all my sins of the past and to be open during this year, to receive a deeper awareness and true meaning of the Mass, and to be able to pray and live the Mass as You have taught me in my writings, and to love and have holy reverence for Your Presence in the Blessed Sacrament. Beloved, I need Your help and that of Your Holy Mother. Help me to be an example to others rather than a hindrance. Please forgive me dearly Beloved. Teach me to be silent, recollected in Your Presence and to keep my eyes on You always. Beloved, You are most merciful when we least deserve it. The Kings brought You gifts of incense, gold and myrrh this day. I have only my broken promises to offer You. Beloved, deliver me from my many miseries. Immaculate Heart of Mary, Spouse of the Holy Spirit, enclose me in Your Heart this day, that Your Son Jesus will see only You as You guide me into a spirit of loving adoration and reverence here in the Eucharistic Presence. Today is also the First Friday. It is surely a feast of feasts. Your Son comes laden with gifts for all, if only we had the openness of hearts to receive.

Thank You Lord for loving me as I am.
Thank You Lord for accepting me as I am.
Thank You Lord for trusting me as I am.
Thank You Lord for gifting me as I am.

8ᵗʰ January 1995:   *Beloved, thank You for all the graces and blessings of the past days, specially at Glencree yesterday.*

May Your Holy Will be done regarding the prayer. Thank You for Your word, Your peace and special reminder through another. Holy Mother Mary, thank You for the beautiful hymn we have received for Glencree. Mary, it truly spoke to all our hearts. Beloved, You created everyone to be a saint. Help us in our daily struggle to overcome all our weaknesses. The path to holiness is truly steep and rugged, impossible on our own, but with You all things are possible. You give us Your Holy Mother to protect and guide us along the way. May we respond with open hearts to the call of Her Immaculate Heart to find ourselves in You, Beloved.

9ᵗʰ January 1995:   *Abba Father, You will have to heal my cough if You want me to keep to my morning routine. I hope to be able to attend Mass.*

Later :
Abba Father, there are many questions I want to ask You. When I was thinking about the Conference on the Divine Mercy about to take place in Dublin in March next - will this be the last before Your time of judgement? If so, the Conference is most important and it behoves us all to pray fervently for it's success, to bring about a conversion in us all - a change of heart in the people of this land. Mary, we call on You, to speak, to guide out hearts, to prepare us for this great event about to take place. You never tire of giving us opportunities to amend our lives.

Bless all concerned in arranging this great event - Fr. Cathal and his group, the speakers and everyone called by You to be there.
(Afternoon)

Before The Blessed Sacrament:

"Child, dear child, I have been waiting for you. Child, I know you are not well. I will make you better here. Am I not your physician? Child, I will direct you later about your cough. Leave it to Me. An appointment will be cancelled and you will see the doctor at an earlier date than otherwise. Child, I will answer all your questions in time. Sit with Me child. I need loving hearts to share My Love. So many do not appreciate My Love.

My Mother has graced you in the past days. You received a healing yesterday and the day before at Her special shrine. Child, you will receive Her blessing each time you can make it - not only there, but I mention this place as it has a special significance for you. Your heart is there but you are unable to be there now on your own. As you lose certain faculties, I will supply your needs. Yes child, remember the little verse in the beginning. You see it in others. You will see it in yourself also. Child, I take and ask sacrifices in a very gentle way to prepare My little ones. You already know. You have guessed for yourself and you accept. It will not be for a while yet. It will never be as bad as you expect. Accept My Holy Will and all will be well. Now child, prepare for the Holy Sacrifice of the Mass and I will grace you with My Abundant Love. Thank you child. My Holy Mother leads and guides you now. Surrender to Her My little one."

Mary, help me to live in the perfection of the present moment to please Him. Thank You Mary for the blessings received by all at Glencree, on the First Saturday and Sunday 8th.

11ᵗʰ January 1995: *Beloved, I come to fulfil Your need of me, to find that Your need is to fulfil my need. I thank You. Oh Beloved, thank You, that I am able to come. Somehow You always find a way to fulfil Your need of us. Beloved, I pray for a listening heart, a loving heart, a heart that sees You in others. Oh Mary, I need Your Heart to change mine.*

Jesus, Mary and Joseph I love You, save souls, save the family, save this land of ours from the forces of evil that seek to destroy us. Thank You for all these churches that have facilitated and opened their doors to Eucharistic Adoration. Bless them all. Touch the hearts of all those who do not yet know Your need, poor misguided hearts.

12ᵗʰ January 1995
Before The Blessed Sacrament:
Mary, help me to make this day a day of reparation for all my sins of irreverence and indifference before the Blessed Sacrament. Help me to keep my mind on Jesus, to be present to His Presence. Direct me about the doctor.

"Make the phone call and I will do the rest."

Thank You.

Mary :
"Go ahead child with the other G.P."

13ᵗʰ January 1995
Before The Blessed Sacrament
Beloved, I feel that it is of the utmost importance that we pray for the media, first and foremost to print and expound in all areas 'truth in the news'. So much damage has been done to the church, state, individuals, through false printing, and programmes in television and radio. Beloved, what can we do? Beloved, what must we do? It is too powerful for us, beyond our capabilities, but not for You Lord. Give us the incentive to pray more and be constant in our prayer for a change of heart for those in control. The evil forces are in battle array, to destroy not only our youth but people of all ages. We beseech You now in the coming rosary to begin. We usually pray the sorrowful mysteries for peace and reconciliation in our own hearts, in our families, communities, country and the world. May a campaign for peace in all areas begin by a change of policy in the media, to put God into all areas of communication.

Beloved, there are so many lonely people in our midst. They hunger for love. Beloved, for many, You alone can fulfil this hunger. I see amongst the people who come here on these two days, the comfort and consolation each finds in Your Eucharistic Presence, and a peace the world cannot give.

Many churches have now opened their doors and expose Your

Presence, as You requested. Some say that there is no difference between adoring You in the Tabernacle and seeing You in the Host. Others preach good works doing and seeing You in others. I know that there is a place, a way of responding in every good thought, word or act, but are we not living in exceptional times, when so many evil forces are at work to take and destroy all that is good among us.

Beloved, increase our faith in the Word, that becomes Flesh in the Eucharist, to give us that boundless hope to overcome all evil, to respond to love, Your love for us all that guides us to work and serve You in others, and we will live to see Your Kingdom come on earth.

14th January 1995

My letter to parents and Bishops :

"The youth of this land is in great danger. They are being led astray. Their elders in Church and state must, make a stand before it is too late. Many are striving to guide their care according to the gospel but peer pressure is taking over. What will be the state of the next generation unless those in control will take a stand now. You have a department of education making the rules. What is the priority? Is it according to My teachings? I call on all parents, Bishops, people of good-will, people interested in the spiritual and moral upbringing of all, to stand up and be counted before it is too late to change the system. Look at other nations that are governed on the lines that now prevail and are being executed for future times (here). I tell you there are evil forces at work, insidious ways and means to take this present generation, to allow this present generation turn their back on all that was good, is good in your society. Parents take authority for your children, do not let go of your responsibilities. Demand, religious instruction for your children. This instruction should compliment the instruction and example in the home. Take heed, these are grave times."

14ᵗʰ January 1995   -   After The Eucharist
Before The Blessed Sacrament

O Lord, if I could only help one priest. You gave me all priests to be either my brothers, my children. I come now in intercession for one particularly. Beloved, nothing is impossible to You. Prayer is beyond all time and space. Listen to the cries of our hearts. Touch hearts now, specially those most in need. Take all self interest from my heart. 'Create in me a pure heart O Lord'. Thank You for all the graces and blessings You pour out on us all each day, everyday. Oh if only our hearts were open to receive all You seek to give us.

15ᵗʰ January 1995
Before The Blessed Sacrament

Beloved, I am depending on You, as to what to say, suggest, about the writings tomorrow. Do not let me think, say or do anything that is not according to Your will.

Take my self-will out of this situation. May the Holy Spirit lead and guide all now and in the days to come. The names of some come to my mind about the publication but I want only to suggest a name, inspired by the Holy Spirit.

Why do we worry about so many things. O Lord, how little trust we have in You. They are Your writings, written down by me. You alone know the end results. Teach me to pray. Send me Your Holy Spirit, without Him I am nothing. Thank You that I can still write. I realise now, having looked at the chart today, that my good eye has deteriorated a great deal and yet I can do most things. How good You are to me. My Holy One, oh how I wish I could respond more to Your Love in prayer. My mind has become so distracted of late. I give You what You take dearest One - that is all I have to offer now. Give me the stillness to have solitude of soul. Oh Lord, how I seek You and yet cannot give all You ask.

16ᵗʰ January 1995
Before The Blessed Sacrament:

"Yes child, the pain in your heart is Mine. Child, give Me all your attention now as We prepare for the Eucharist. Here I wait to give all. Make empty your soul to receive all I give."

'Abba I need Your Spirit to make room for my Beloved.'

17ᵗʰ January 1995: *Beloved, thank You for leading me to the doctor this day.* (Her first day back after being in hospital.)
'You do great things for us, O Lord, for You are Mighty, and Holy is Your name. And how we need Your care.' (Evening Prayer.)

18ᵗʰ January 1995: *Mary, thank You. Enclose me in Your Immaculate Heart. Help me to live my consecration.*

I miss not being able to go to Mass - and spend time before the Blessed Sacrament. I know I am not alone but it isn't the same. Mary, it increases my desire for The Eucharist.

19ᵗʰ January 1995
Before The Blessed Sacrament:
Beloved, thank You for today. How slow I am at times to accept the little trials. Now I am aware through my consecration to the Immaculate Heart of Your Holy Mother, Her sense of direction in my daily life. Truly it is amazing. I see it in every little happening of the day. How blind I have been. How deaf I have been, but today is another beginning. I am given a fresh opportunity to see and hear and believe. All honour, glory and praise to the Two Hearts of Love. How I need You Both to fulfil the needs of each Heart, each day.

Beloved, I know I try Your mercy at times, but I truly believe that is impossible! but it doesn't follow that we do not cause you pain and disappointment.

Later :
Beloved, thank You for the peace I received when I went for tests to the hospital. 'When You are with us, who can be against us?' Help me now to rest in You and give praise and thanks for all our goodness and loving kindness this day and everyday. Thank You also for answering my requests for others in writings, that comforted and encouraged them in their time of need.
20ᵗʰ January 1995: *Abba Father, now I can thank You, relate my sickness to my spiritual sickness. I pray now to allow the*

change I need, bring about a healing in both areas.

21ˢᵗ January 1995:   *Mary, my Immaculate Mother, fill my empty heart with Your love. I am so unsettled in mind and spirit.*

22ⁿᵈ January 1995
Before The Blessed Sacrament:
"Child, child, listen to Me, Let Love speak to your heart. Relate the anger to Mine. It is not misplaced. It is anger that was never dealt with, so it erupts at the least provocation. Yes child, I will help you to overcome it. Offer this pain to Me. How I am pained by disunity amongst My children. Today is Unity Sunday. Pray for unity amongst Christians. This is very close to My Heart.

Yes child, the spirit of dissension is everywhere dividing and causing havoc amongst My children. Call on My Mother who is caring for you. The temptations will increase as She draws you closer into Her Immaculate Heart. She prepares a special place for you. She has a special ministry for you in Glencree.

Child, dear child, I will Myself arrange the time to speak to your heart, to open your heart, that will bring about the healing you crave. In the meantime suffer all, offer all for love. Do not let the evil one take control. Remember We are present, more powerful, and will not allow him to overcome you. We will not fail you.

Child, as We continue to use you in your writing ministry, he will try every tactic to destroy and block Our word, from Our children, to thwart Our plans for this land.

Yes child, remember the writings before the cease-fire - they reached all participants in the talks. Now child, let Me enter your heart, speak to your heart. Thank you child. Be renewed in My Love."

Thank You Beloved for listening to the cry of my heart. Thank You also for the word You gave me for R. . . May I now listen to Your need of me.

27ᵗʰ January 1995   -   Praying for Glencree
Before The Blessed Sacrament:

"My children, I speak to your hearts now. Listen carefully, listen My dear, dear children .

Yes child, you have many questions on your mind. I will answer all in My time. I do not want to overburden you. You must take care of yourself. Your body and mind needs nursing for a while. Give the problems of others to Me. I will solve all also in My time. Offer Me your prayers and efforts.

Thank you child, thank you children. Oh the joy the Two Hearts of Love receive this night.

Children, oh children, it is not given to the hearts of mankind to see Our joy, the joys We receive through Our little ones. Continue dear children in your daily efforts, your daily struggles. We will not fail you. No pain, no suffering, related to Ours is ever wasted. It brings healings to others. Do not deprive Us of the joy We receive and the joy you give to others."
(Reading Is. 25:6-10. CT.)

On this mountain the LORD of hosts
Will provide for all peoples
A feast of rich food and choice wines.
On this mountain he will destroy
The veil that veils all peoples,
The web that is woven over all nations;
He will destroy death forever.
The Lord GOD will wipe away
The tears from all faces;
The reproach of his people he will remove
From the whole earth, for the LORD
Has spoken.

28ᵗʰ January 1995
Before The Blessed Sacrament:
Beloved, what is the little pain You ask me to suffer for love. All I ask dear Jesus is the strength here in Your Presence to be able to continue.

30ᵗʰ January 1995
Before The Blessed Sacrament:
Mary my Mother, teach me Your way of prayer for me. After the lecture on meditation prayer yesterday, I am confused. I am not familiar with using a mantra - but perhaps I need this to centre my thoughts and distractions in these times. I know You will help me to do what is right for me.

2ⁿᵈ February 1995 - Feast of the Presentation of Jesus in the Temple
Before The Blessed Sacrament:
"Yes child, this is a very important feast indeed. Truly it is a special day of grace in the Church, because of My Son, His Holy Mother and His foster-father Joseph. In presenting My Son, Mary and Joseph presents the whole human race, although this wasn't known to them at the time. Truly each of you was presented to Me on this day. Now children offer Me yourselves your hearts and wills and those who are praying the novena to the Immaculate Heart. Today is very special indeed. I call all My children to present themselves to the Immaculate Heart of Mary. She is Mother of My Son. Who else is so close to Me, who else deserves honour like Her. In honouring Her, you honour Me and My Son. I thank you dear children. I see and know your hearts, I see and know your needs, your pain, your joys. Give all to Me, specially during these two days and nights made holy down the ages through the saints and the first Saturday made holy through Our Lady of Fatima.

Yes child, about the question on your heart. I have already answered it. It is fitting that you be present. The other thoughts you keep in your heart. It was better that you didn't know too early. I always facilitate My little ones, especially when they surrender their wills to Mine. Now child, surrender yourself to the Immaculate Heart of Mary. She will lead you ever deeper into the Heart and Spirit of the Trinity."

3ʳᵈ February 1995 - Feast of St. Blaise. (First Friday)
Before The Blessed Sacrament:
"Yes child, to-day is the day of love, our love, My love for all hearts. Yes child, all Eucharistic Hearts. Here I call all on this day

of love. I cannot repeat this word too often. This is your calling My child. We now will concentrate on this area. I will call you at times to write on different situations (14th January) but this is not the main reason for these writings.

Child, I have given you over the years many insights into The Eucharist and The Eucharistic Presence. These I desire to be shared with others. These will comprise the first book. There is enough in the writings for a book on these alone. These are difficult and dangerous times. I will call you apart now to concentrate on these writings. Do not be fearful. I will prepare you for all I ask. My shield of peace will surround your soul. Yes child, do not be afraid of your human frailties. Cannot you see how I use all. Obedience is paramount now. My Spirit can penetrate all distractions, weaknesses, character traits, Do you not trust Me? How I have cared for you down the years, moulded you. Now child, My Holy Mother is caring for you in a special way. **You will be instrumental in Her plan for Glencree.** Do not be afraid. Remember the night in the past, I called you into intercession, the promises I made. You know now that I am always faithful to My promises. I take care now of the person on your mind (K.) Phone later, My Holy Mother is with her in her anxiety. Bring her into the rosary soon to be recited. Thank you My little one for listening. More later. Rest in Me now."

4ᵗʰ February 1995
1st Saturday:
Thank You Mary on this first Saturday of the month, to have been given such a simple form of prayer and available to all, from the youngest to the oldest, from the simplest to the most learned. Oh Mary, thank You. Truly it is the name of Your Son Jesus, when every thought, every time You pronounced His Name, every time You looked at Him from the beginning and never to end, was a prayer of Your Heart, mind and spirit, in unity with the Father and the Spirit.

You give me now on this day the fulfilment of my need, a way of prayer, simple prayer for my distracted mind, to fulfil His need of me and Your need of me. I am also one with the Trinity as I pronounce, repeat, ponder His Name to be our constant way of prayer - available to all, specially for these days of such evil influences the world over.

Mary, thank You again. I know You will teach me to develop this simple but most profound way of prayer to bring about all the healings I need in body, mind and spirit and for all I carry in my heart and the world - to bring about His Kingdom on earth as it is in Heaven.

Today the healing Mass of the Generations is celebrated again at Glencree. Mary, truly in the Name of Jesus and believing in His Divine Mercy, will bring about the healings of the past, present and future in our land, Surely the 'Jesus' prayer belongs to all, unites us all in our respective prayer and beliefs. Mary, Queen of Peace and Mother of Reconciliation, gather us all under Your mantle of love at Glencree today.

6ᵗʰ February 1995
Before The Blessed Sacrament:
Beloved, just a few words of thanks.

"Sit with Me child. That is all I ask of you now."

8ᵗʰ February 1995
Before The Blessed Sacrament:
Mary, teach me to pray with reverence in the Presence of Your Son. Mary, bless all who answer Your call for Glencree this night. Do You want me to go or bring the Blessed Sacrament to my home and unite with the others before the Blessed Sacrament. Thank You Mary for calling us to be part of Your plan for Glencree. Bless all for their dedication and faithfulness down the years. May peace prevail in their hearts, families, to bring peace and reconciliation to all in our land.

Later :
"Yes child, come to Glencree to-night. I need you. You will know why later."

9ᵗʰ February 1995
Before The Blessed Sacrament:

Beloved, I thank You for last night. Truly You never leave me in doubt. Surely You are my Wonder-Counsellor.

Now Beloved, direct me about our group prayer in Your Eucharistic Presence. The fifteen decades of the rosary as they are prayed during the day, Joyful in the morning for priests, Sorrowful for peace and reconciliation in the afternoons and the Glorious for all young people at night, pleases Your Holy Mother, but I need Your help to grow in silence and reverence in Your Presence and to be an example to others to encourage listening prayer of the heart - and yet not to offend. You did tell me on an occasion that You didn't want us to become too institutionalised and that all should feel at home I think.

Holy Mother Mary, we ask You to take control, to teach us how to please Jesus and to fulfil His need of us on these two days when He comes to visit us here.

9ᵗʰ February 1995 - During Gethsemane Hour - (Thurs. 9 -10 p.m.)
Before The Blessed Sacrament:
"Listen My child to My Heart, beating with Love this night. Thank you for your presence. Thank you for answering My call. Oh children, the comfort and solace We receive, the Two Hearts of Love on this night where We are welcomed and loved. Truly your reward will be great. You bring many souls back to repentance through your faithfulness to this hour, this Gethsemane Hour. It is difficult, but continue to make this effort. So many do not believe, do not respond to Our Love and many forces are at large to destroy Our little ones. Thank you dear children for your response and your love. We thank you for answering Our call to listen at this hour each week. We truly bless you all and all you carry in your hearts."

10ᵗʰ February 1995
Before The Blessed Sacrament:
"My child, My children, I am here. My Holy Mother also."

12ᵗʰ February 1995 (In bed): *Beloved, I thought that I would have had to call the doctor yesterday, but as You told me that You* *were caring for me, I didn't. I thank You for being much better today. Beloved, how I keep failing You when I do not trust You.*

13ᵗʰ February 1995:

(Still confined to the house and unable to go to Mass.)

"My child, My child, rest these days with Me. Give rest to your body and mind in Me. Do not waste these precious days and nights. Offer the discomfort for My chosen ones, so in need of prayer and sacrifice in these troubled times. I am your strength. Do not fail Me. Trust in Me, your Beloved."

Oh Holy Mother, help me to fulfil His need of me. I am so weak and so easily distracted.

16ᵗʰ February 1995
Before The Blessed Sacrament:

"Yes child, phone the doctor and she will confirm My wishes for you. Rest child in Me. I need you. I will answer your requests later.

My child, listen carefully now to all I speak to your heart. Many ask you for words of guidance. I will teach you to discern between those I choose to speak to your heart. This is a special gift, very powerful and yet can be misused. To protect you child, I will now limit such distractions for your sake. It is better that I do so, that the evil one will not try to disturb you.

I seek your mind free for My writings - the area that I have chosen you for. Child, the time is now ripe that I will use you to write again on the Holy Eucharist. This is the most profound of all writings. Do not be afraid nor worried about the state of your mind. Surrender yourself to Me My child. Little by little you will find peace of mind again, freed from distractions. Consecrate and allow your Holy Mother take over, take care and protect you. She, as I said before, can do all I can do. You will be guided by Her to let go of all that will not further My need of you. Yes child, be prepared for changes. Remember I am your Wonder-Counsellor, Mighty-God, Eternal-Father and Prince-of-Peace, who speaks now to you. My Holy Mother will teach you to attain the silence and solitude you now need for these coming writings. Do not be afraid of your health. I will sustain you for all I ask of you. Truly trust Me child,

My precious little child.

I will teach you to live in the present moment, not to waste one moment of time."

17ᵗʰ February 1995
Before The Blessed Sacrament:
Beloved, I give praise and thanks to You for all Your goodness to me this day. Thank You for the good news received about my health. Bless the doctor and may she receive the health and strength to carry out all her duties at home and in her surgery. I ask a special blessing for her daughter whose hearing was impaired through careless and dangerous practices and suffers much pain as a consequence. I believe dearly Beloved, You will find a way to relieve her and heal her. This family is very precious to You and an example to all.

Beloved, I bring before You this day, all those who have asked my prayers. Recently I have been very selfish, thinking of my own needs. And yet Beloved, I know You love me and accept me as I am. Help me to love You more each day. Mary, I am depending on You to guide and change me.

May The Two Hearts of Love be loved, praised and glorified throughout the world this day.

18ᵗʰ February 1995
Before The Eucharist:
Thank You Beloved for the word of encouragement received for another this morning. Thank You for the joy it gives me to share with her, and I realise it is nothing, just the barest reflection of the joy it gives You to give to Your little ones, who respond to Your Love. But I also realise the pain You suffer in our suffering. Thank You Beloved for Your Love and peace this day. May my receiving the Eucharist be a little reflection of this love You share with me. Thank You for coming to me in the Eucharist when I cannot go out to receive You.

21st February 1995
Before The Blessed Sacrament:

Abba Father, I am so in need of a change of heart.

"Be gentle with yourself My child. Rest in Me, rest on My Heart. All will be well My little one. There is no need to be afraid. I am always with you."

Thank You Abba, You are so kind, gentle and all tenderness with the least of us. Your Heart never changes. Your Love is unconditional - not like ours. While I had to remain indoors I have had more time to think. Help me to think of others, to die to self. How I miss the visits to the Eucharistic Presence. It is good to be back again. Thank You Abba Father.

"Do not force the mind to be quiet. Rest, let go. I am in control My child."

23rd February 1995: (In doctor's surgery)

Beloved, You are always close to me in such places, but perhaps because it is Thursday, I am in unity with the others at prayer at home before the Eucharistic Presence.

24th February 1995
Before The Blessed Sacrament:

Beloved, today is special. Today the "Five" are having Mass at our meeting tonight. May we truly enter into this great sacrifice in unity and love. May it be the beginning of a great stepping stone into the advancement of the needs of the Two Hearts of Love for Glencree. May the two great gifts of peace and reconciliation become manifested in our hearts to include one another, our families, our extended family, our country and the world.

Mary, our queen and Mother, wrap Your mantle of love around us all in preparation for this great honour. Bless the priest, the celebrant. May the Holy Spirit fill his heart, from his heart to receive, to share with us the humanity and divinity of Jesus, in this Holy Sacrament of Love, sacrifice and celebration.

25ᵗʰ February 1995: *Beloved, here I am. I hear distressing news today of another. We trust in You, because nothing is impossible to You.*

"Yes child, offer your little sufferings for this soul. Come to Me later. I wait for you."

26ᵗʰ February 1995
Before The Blessed Sacrament:

Beloved I didn't get back yesterday evening. I let the opportunity go. Forgive me for failing You again. Beloved, now that I am here, I thank You for the peace I receive in Your Presence. Oh how we fail to respond to Your ultimate calling, where You truly fulfil all Your promises, 'come to Me all you who are laboured and heavily burdened and I will refresh you......'

Beloved, You know all I carry in my heart - their needs, my needs. Trusting in You, all will be well. Help us all to die a little to ourselves each day and specially during lent, in preparation for Easter and the renewal of our consecration to the Immaculate Heart of Mary on 25th March, the feast of the Annunciation.

Later :
"Thank you child. Continue to pray for My chosen one. He is going through a great purification. He will rise again and be a pillar in My Church. Yes child, he is in need of your prayers and sacrifices. Trusting is loving and all will be well. Child, there will be a few obstacles yet to surmount before the format of the writings will be confirmed. More obstacles will be placed in the path before publication but My will, will be done. I will overcome all the blockages that will be placed against publication. Continue child to rest, pray, hope and give thanks for each day - the gift of life, of living. This is important child now."

28ᵗʰ February 1995: *Beloved, tomorrow lent begins. Help me to make a special effort to respond to Your Love and carry out Your Holy Will. You know my weaknesses and miseries. I depend on You to strengthen me and help me to fulfil Your need of me. I bring before You specially those You have given me - my family, my friends, my community. May we help and encourage one* *another to take that step nearer to You each day, that Easter will truly be a time of Resurrection as we try, with Your help to die a little to ourselves day by day.*

"Pray children, continue to pray for all My little ones. Give them to My Holy Mother to protect and care for. You will see, She will triumph over all evil, evil ways. Here in the Eucharistic Presence, she [G....] will find the peace she seeks, the peace she needs. Give all the little, little ones to Me and My Mother.

Rose, you will find the other writing. I will direct you to it.

It is evil and wicked to open up the emotions and curiosity of the little ones before they are ready to receive such instruction. Parents, you must take responsibility in these dangerous times for your children. Be watchful, protective, caring and loving. Gain the confidence of your children and above all, teach the little ones to pray by praying with them. It is My Mother's wish that all families pray the rosary together. It is paramount for these times.

My children, My little ones, I love you all, I seek you all. Oh how it hurts and pains Me to see the evil one devour My little ones."

7ᵗʰ March 1995
Before The Blessed Sacrament:
"Yes child, about the writings to D.... It is a call for prayer, more prayer, firstly for D.... himself. Through his answering the call, he will lead others to answer the call also. I will tell him later what to do. In the meantime I ask him to respond to My call for him - to be generous to My call. That is all I ask for now. He will be directed in the writings what he should do."

Oh Beloved, how unfaithful I have been to Your call to me. When I reread some of my own earlier writings last night, I realised how my previous fervour, and the time spent with You has lessened .

194

8ᵗʰ March 1995
At home:
Mary, my Holy Mother, I unite with the others at Glencree this night. They are so faithful whatever the weather. I know You will bless them all abundantly during this hour of Eucharistic Adoration, at this very cold and isolated church, on this freezing night.

10ᵗʰ March 1995
Before The Blessed Sacrament:
Mary, my Holy Mother, truly no one needs Your help as much as I do now. Oh Mary, please strengthen me to overcome this weakness that attacks me during the two days when Jesus is present in the Eucharist in my home.

Mary, how I must hurt Him when I neglect Him so much. Oh Mary, I need Your help to make these two days, days of silent retreat with My Beloved. It is different when I visit Him in other places. In my own home I am so easily distracted. Mary, You know why He comes here - why He favours us and gives us this honour each week. Oh Mary, take control of our minds, our hearts and our wills, to surrender ourselves to His needs. I remember once when I asked why the two prayer meetings that I attended at the time were so different and He told me that He came to each one for different reasons.

Mary, we pray to fulfil His need of us here during these two days. May I be more attentive to my own responsibilities.

Mary, one of my grandchildren is being confirmed tomorrow. We pray that it will bring a great blessing on all the family and a fresh outpouring of the Holy Spirit on the father, mother and other children.

11ᵗʰ March 1995:   *Come Holy Spirit, fill the hearts of all those being confirmed this day. May the Light of His Presence shine on all to make them soldiers for Christ in the days ahead. May they bring peace and consolation in their families and be pillars of hope in their schools and country.*

14ᵗʰ March 1995
After The Eucharist:

"Child, child, child, yes I call you to write. I need you My little one. I have much on My Mind and Heart to share with My little ones.

Yes child, I thank you for the little efforts you are making to come closer to Me. My Holy Mother is preparing you now for future times. She has her plans for Glencree already made. She has touched many hearts to answer Her call to have people visit Her at Glencree. There are many forces at work to destroy Her plans, because great the graces and blessings She has prepared for all who come. Come, you need not look to far off places to find My Mother (I looked at a video on Lourdes last night), She has taken up Her abode within you, in your home where She directs Her plans for Glencree. Yes children, I ask you to meet on Friday night as usual. I do not ask any special time. I leave it to yourselves.

Oh children, if you could only comprehend the graces of this night together, but then I do not want to overburden your bodies before you are ready. Yes child, I will see that you visit Glencree more often in the days ahead. You will see, you will have many opportunities to answer My call. Many will offer to take you. Oh children, dear children, you mustn't fear last Friday's word. You know We do not ask anything of Our little ones without the grace and strength to answer Our call. All will be well - you will see. Lent is a time for repentance. Your faults and weaknesses may be highlighted for your own purification. We prepare you for a glorious resurrection at Easter. Yes children, you will, each one, know and understand a little that is in Our Hearts this coming Easter.

We bless you now - always at the Holy Sacrifice of the Mass. Remember the Eucharist is the ultimate gift of love.
Give praise and thanks now little one."

16ᵗʰ March 1995
Before The Blessed Sacrament:

Beloved, thank You for allowing me to go to the Divine Masters last night to hear Debra speak. Truly it brought back old times and the joy and peace that was in my heart, I give praise and thanks.

Oh Mary, I give to You all the writings. It would appear that the first step towards publication has been taken today. Mary, do guide and lead me that anything I may suggest will be for the glory of Jesus.

17ᵗʰ March 1995
St. Patrick's Day:

"My child, My child, My Heart cries out this day to the people of Ireland and all Irish people throughout the world - to those who use, misuse, dishonour this feast-day in the name of St. Patrick.

Do you really believe that St. Patrick is honoured by your excesses everywhere on this day? My dear children, I call on you all to honour St. Patrick by giving thanks for the sufferings and hardship he endured to bring Christianity to your land. Remember it is a time of repentance taking place during the Lenten season. It was meant to be a day of special graces for all. How many are open, ready to receive all the blessings we have prepared for the people of this land.

My people, you are in need of much prayer. There are many forces at work because you leave doors open for evil to enter. The cease-fire rests on a pinhead. Children, it behoves you to come to Me in prayer. Truly prayer will add to your happiness on this day, the feast-day of your national Saint. But remember dear children, the many blessings this land and people have received down the ages, Because of the faithfulness of My little ones. I look at your land now - much is not to My liking. Oh children, take heed while there is still time. It is because of My little ones I hold back. My Holy Mother weeps tears of pain and sufferings to see you reject all you held worthily in the past.

Oh children, it gives Me such joy and happiness to see you joyful and happy on this day, but do not reject and destroy the God-given gifts I give you that bring true joy to your hearts. Thank you dear little one for inviting Me to your home this day. Many and rich will be graces and blessings I bring to all. How My Heart rejoices to come in the Blessed Sacrament this day and how all Heaven rejoices to join with you. Keep the flames alight and the fires burning throughout the land."

17ᵗʰ March 1995   -   (House)
Before The Blessed Sacrament:
Thank You Beloved for gracing us with Your Eucharistic Presence this day. Many came expecting You to be here. The joy and happiness is ours. I wish I could welcome You with more love and greater understanding, but then I think of my youngest grandchild of 14 months. When he comes, the joy he brings and he doesn't understand - and when You call us Your little ones I know You do not expect too much of us.

21ˢᵗ March 1995
Before The Blessed Sacrament:
Beloved, Mother, the feast of the Annunciation draws near and the Conference on Divine Mercy. Without Your "Yes" Mother, we wouldn't now be celebrating His Divine Mercy. We wouldn't know it. We thank You Mary for Your Yes. We beg You that our yes will be loud and clear and sincere on the 25ᵗʰ, also - Yes to You Mary, is yes to Jesus. Yes to Jesus is yes to His Divine Mercy, to share with others. This will need a transformation of no small proportions within my heart. Mary, my Mother, I believe that nothing is impossible to You. Are You not the Mediatrix of all graces? Mary, I know You will not fail me. I trust in You. I thank You.

Later
Before The Blessed Sacrament:
Mary, help me to separate the wheat from the chaff within my heart. Help me to concentrate on the things that are of God in the present circumstances - and direct us to do His Holy Will.

22ⁿᵈ March 1995
(Mass for Della):
Beloved, You know I wanted to go to You tonight. There was a hunger within my heart to be with You. Now I know it was right for me to stay at home, because You came to me.

Thank You for this day. I was able to do more than I expected - and may Your Holy Will be done in any arrangements made tonight regarding the writings. You relieve me of all responsibilities and place the burden on another - a burden of love on Your specially chosen one.

22ⁿᵈ March 1995
Before The Blessed Sacrament:
"My child, I missed you this day, but I know you were busy. Relax now with Me. I take care of all your cares, do I not? even down to the two doors. This is the car I have chosen for you. I will see that you will manage to drive it locally and small journeys - away from much traffic now. Your Angel Guardian will guide you and help you. My little one, give your heart to Mine now. I need your comfort and solace now and always."

Beloved, it is when we least deserve Your Love and mercy You bless us abundantly. Oh how I wish I could respond but You know I can only give what I receive from You. Of myself I am nothing, have nothing, can do nothing. As always all I have to offer You is the burden of my weaknesses and failings but I desire always to fulfil Your need of me. Thank You my Beloved. I wish I could be like others.

Oh Beloved, everything that concerns us concerns You. All aspects of our living here You make Your own. My Beloved, What I have just read disturbs me. I have got tickets for the conference this week-end. I neglected to ask first Your permission whether You desired that I should attend. I want to do Your Holy Will. Do tell me what I should do.

"Well child, if you weren't going W.. would not go. I want him there also."

25ᵗʰ March 1995: "My child, great were the blessings I poured out on all at this week-end at the Conference of Divine Mercy. Now child I invite you to return to your visitations to My Eucharistic Presence. There I need you. There you will find all the strength and graces you need for your daily living and above all at your daily Eucharist. Begin now to prepare for the week of My Passion and day of Resurrection by living the liturgy of the Church. Do not go beyond your own commitments nor calling. Thank you My little one. I am in control of writings now. My Will, will be done. You will see."

28ᵗʰ March 1995: (Indoors for the day)
Thank You Jesus - W.. is much improved. How good You are to us in times of anxiety. I didn't get to The Eucharist this day. I hope I appreciate You, welcome You and respond to Your love more fully tomorrow if You make it possible for me. Beloved, thank You for the peace of this day in spite of everything. Thank You Mary also.

30ᵗʰ March 1995
Before The Blessed Sacrament:

"Oh My dear, dear priests, I do not want to see you disheartened. Am I not your Spouse, your God, your Protector, your All? As you stand in My sandals at the Altar of Sacrifice, are you not aware, or at least believe that you are My Calvary, My Resurrection, My very all. My dear priests, how it pains Me to see you ridiculed, tormented, abused as I was. I know all are not perfect, but I didn't choose you because of your perfection. But dear priests, never doubt your special calling. Never doubt My Love. Do I not see all your efforts, know all your efforts in a world that no longer wants to listen, to hear My words through you. Do not be afraid of the ridicule. Relate all your sufferings, your rejections to Me and Mine. You stand in the way and behold the rejection of the world to Me. The more you suffer, the more you become like Me, the more I live in you, the more you become Me.

Take heart dear priests, the time is approaching when the rebuffs will be directed to those who rebuff you now. They will not be prepared for the onslaught that will come their way. The time is fast approaching when I will have My way, have the victory over such critics, inspired by evil, oh so subtle.

Wake up My people, wake up to the evil in your midst. Wake up before it is too late. I am ever ready, ever waiting like the prodigal Father for all My wayward children to return, to repent, to clasp you all to My ever merciful Heart while the time of mercy is here with you.

My child, (Rose) the time is coming when I will ask more of you. I

200

take into account your age, your state of health, but now I am asking you to sit with Me more often. I will make the time, you will see. I will be your strength. I have much for you to write yet. Give Me the space and time to quieten your mind, your spirit for these further writings. It will mean more Eucharistic Adoration. Your yes I ask and I will make the time, the place. My Holy Mother will be with you, will plan all for you. You will come to Glencree on Saturday. I will make it possible dear child. Come back to Me now with all your heart. I need you. I have need of you to write further on The Eucharist specially, My little one."

Mary, my Holy Mother, You know how weak I am, so easily distracted. Mary, without You my yes would mean nothing. I am depending on You now to make my yes sincere and meaningful, heartful and persevering. Immaculate Heart of Mary because I trust in Your faithfulness, in Your promises, I know You will not fail me to keep my promise to Your Son Jesus.

Let's pray the Magnificat together to seal my commitment.
Jer. 10: 23/24.

> Prayer of Jeremiah
> You know, O Lord,
> That man is not master of his way;
> Man's course is not within his choice,
> Nor is it for him to direct his step.
> Punish us, O Lord, but with equity,
> Not in anger, lest you have us dwindle away.

31ˢᵗ March 1995 - (House)
Before The Blessed Sacrament:

Beloved, here I am at last. Now I am on my own. You are so patient, so tolerant with me when I least deserve Your Love, Your mercy - You bless me with Your peace. Thank You Beloved for the beautiful, faithful little ones You send to comfort and console You when I neglect You. Perhaps You will find a way for the nun who called this morning to have You exposed for Adoration in her convent. So many hunger for Your Presence and those in control are bound by regulations. Because I can see no difficulties - tell me am I all wrong or do the others not know Your needs. Oh Beloved, because of the gift You give me do I pain You for taking

You so much for granted. Sometimes I doubt and yet I mustn't doubt what You give me to write. Beloved, do control me. Do not let me share or speak of to others if it displeases You. I am depending now on Your Holy Mother to guide and lead me in all I do, say and think to please You.

Beloved, I wasn't very loving and tolerant during the night and You didn't take away my peace. I wish I could love You, really love You like others. Perhaps I will learn some day.

Tomorrow, the First Saturday, we have the healing Mass of the Generations. How we all are in need of this healing in this land. The cease-fire is still precarious. You alone Lord can solve differences and divisions of centuries. Our Lady of Glencree, we call on You to help us be people of peace and reconciliation. May our prayer of intercession this night bring us a step nearer to solving our differences by dialogue. Oh Mary, how privileged we are to be called by You to help by our prayers, to make this little hamlet a place for peace and reconciliation for our land. We are just one of the little groups chosen by You to help to bring and share Your peace with others. How we need Your help and protection to be healed by ourselves first before we can help others.

Mary, we pray for a change of hearts, for unity within our little group to answer Your call. Do not let us fail You.

1ˢᵗ April 1995
Before The Blessed Sacrament:
Praise You Jesus, You are worthy of all praise. Such a beautiful day for our 'Healing Mass of the Generations' at Glencree. Truly it was a pet day after the long winter. How little we thank You for Your goodness. Thank You for the wonderful word we received last night at our meeting. If only we could have the faith of a mustard seed - how powerful, how rewarding - what blessings we receive at every Mass - if only we believed. No wonder You remind us to pray for all souls in purgatory, specially for our own family ties and the generations. You have to keep reminding us of the power of the Mass. Of late I have become very slack at my preparation. No wonder dearly Beloved I do not receive the same insights now. Mary, my Mother, help me to open my heart to

Yours. You were there, You are there. You will always be present. Keep reminding me, make me more attentive and faithful. One Mass could change my heart, my life, in preparation for the coming passion, death and resurrection of Your Son in 1995.

Beloved, W... is doubtful about message re. car. He wants confirmation. He thinks the setbacks are a sign that it isn't the right one. Give him Your peace - I believe.

"Oh child, he isn't well. It is difficult to make decisions or take decisions when one isn't well. He will be happy and grow to like this car."

3ʳᵈ April 1995
Before The Blessed Sacrament:
Oh Beloved, I take You so much for granted. You make Yourself so available to us in The Eucharistic Presence. You are exposed in many churches now and even at night in some.

Your thirst for souls is so great, so painful that You come, You give us Your living Presence to draw us all into Your Eucharistic Heart.

Truly Lord, we have the answer to all our needs here. Here You invite us to unburden our burdens unto You. Here You will strengthen us against all the evil forces that surround us, seek to enslave us against You.

Beloved, I give You now all those whom I know who are heavily burdened and seek Your comfort and consolation. I give praise and thanks to You for all the graces and blessings You pour out on me and my family now and always. Beloved, I am fearful to ask for a share in Your thirst but I know You will not fail to support me in all You give or ask of me.

Immaculate Heart of Mary, Spouse of the Holy Spirit, enclose me in Your Heart. Mary, help me to die to myself. Mary, I am so in need of Your help. I see all the virtues in others that I haven't got myself and yet I must accept myself as I am, and give praise and thanks for the burden of my weaknesses.

"Oh My child, My Child, you will experience again a taste of My thirst. I must prepare the body and soul to receive such a privilege. It is not possible to receive such an insight into My pain without much suffering oneself. Child, dear child, My Mother will teach you, prepare you, but first you must learn to receive the gift of silence. Spend more time with Me, allow Me speak to the soul. My Presence opens the heart and soul to My secrets, to those who suffer with Me."

Later :
"Child, do you not yet realise why I come seeking to be exposed on all altars and wherever I am accepted. Oh child, it is because of My thirst for souls. I come to touch souls, to gather souls to join with Me in My search for other lost souls. Each one is a part of Me - My very own. Look around, how few know of My Love, the pain of My Love for each one I create. Oh child, help Me. I call on all to open their hearts to the pain of My thirst for souls."

4ᵗʰ April 1995
Before The Blessed Sacrament:
Beloved, still my racing mind.

"My child, you mustn't worry about the format of the writings. Others will choose for Me, for you. Rest your mind, your body. Sit with Me. I will take care of you. All will be well. Go home now and take the opportunity of a little outing. Blessings little one."

5ᵗʰ April 1995
Before The Blessed Sacrament:
Thank You Beloved. You reveal to me that You are part of every little event in our daily lives - leading us, guiding us, protecting us if we allow You.

Holy Mother, You will confirm for us your plan for Glencree for the First Saturday of May. Truly it will he a very special day, but it would appear that it will not be possible for me to be there because of the wedding on that day. Do You ask for a Eucharistic procession on that day for a special blessing on the surrounding area?

"There is a core where all matters should be decided in agreement. Important matters should be referred to the

priests Fr. Cathal or Fr. Dan. Do not work independently of one another. Unity is paramount in the group.

Children, are you not the bearers and example for peace and reconciliation for this little hamlet or shrine. Be an example to all who visit this place of holiness. Much depends on you, Our five little hearts.

Rose, later I will direct you about the First Saturday."

Mary, You told me before that it was alright to leave 'message' with my name on it. I think Jesus wants me to take a more hidden role now. It would appear that Satan is succeeding in dividing many little groups now. Mary, do not let it happen to us. I know You will not.

Thank You oh Holy Mother for everything.

6ᵗʰ April 1995
Before the Blessed Sacrament:
My Beloved, I find it so difficult to be quiet in Your Presence. Is it alright to help another, by sharing writings when we are alone.
I know these two days, 1st Thursday and 1st Friday are very special days each month. I want to give You all You ask, and need of me. Mary, Mediatrix of all graces, open our hearts to receive all You seek to give us. Bless all, specially those who do the vigil. How privileged we are to have You in our home.

Beloved, this day week (13th) is Holy Thursday. How it behoves us all to make reparation for all the times we have received You in the Eucharist with indifference and coldness.

Later :
Beloved, I know You await now those who come to the night vigil.

7ᵗʰ April 1995 - First Friday
Before The Blessed Sacrament:
Beloved, how easily my anger is aroused because of another's actions. Let my decision be according to Your Holy Will. Oh Beloved, how often we provoke You, always You show us mercy. Direct me in the present situation O Dearest One.

10ᵗʰ April 1995
Before The Blessed Sacrament:
Holy Mother, after the word received the other day (5/4) about our group meeting for Glencree, would You rather that a small gazette be brought out monthly to let people know the events that are taking place and that others may be free to write in, making suggestions etc. We pray that we be open to Your plan alone and not some human interests of our own. Mary, wrap Your mantle of unity around us and protect us from the wiles of the evil one.

13ᵗʰ April 1995 - Holy Thursday
Before The Blessed Sacrament:
Beloved, You satisfy the hungry heart. Today You welcome back Your friends. Thank You. We pray to be one in Your joy this day to commemorate the institution of The Sacrament of Love. We believe, increase our faith in boundless hope for perfect love to satisfy Your hungry Heart.

"My child, My child, pray for My other child. She needs much love. You can give it to her. Do not exclude her altogether. Speak to her when you meet her. Speak in a loving way, as a mother. She needs a mothers love and care. I will help you. Do not be discouraged yourself. I understand.

About your other prayer dear child - do not get involved. It doesn't concern you. Give all to your little group where I receive much love and consolation. More later My little one.

Oh the pleasure dear child, it gives Me to be in this house today. So few churches now allow Me to be present to My people this day, above all days and how I long to be amongst My little ones, specially those who hunger for My Presence."

17th April 1995
Before The Blessed Sacrament:

Beloved, Resurrected Christ, I come to love You, praise You and thank You. You are truly with Your people during these days. There is much on my heart but I haven't the words to write. There is much on my heart that I haven't the answers to, but I have so much to give thanks for. I pray for the graces I need to fulfil Your need of me now, and I know that these graces are available to me in the daily Eucharist. Oh Beloved, would that I had the faith of a mustard seed, to trust You to live in the sacrament of the present moment, and discard all that does not pertain to the spiritual life, my daily walk with You.

I thank You dearly Beloved for Your infinite patience with me, for my neglect recently, but I trust my Holy Mother to lead and guide me through the days ahead.

"Child, come back later and I will speak to your heart. I wait for you, always I wait. We have much work yet to accomplish together. Do not fear the restlessness and confusion at times. As I reminded you before, My Spirit can penetrate the mind anytime, all times, whatever the confusion, and child, to write the most profound of writings. Go in peace now My little one, all is well. Trust Me, trust Me."

Later :

Thank You Beloved for making it possible for me to visit You again. I haven't learned to drive the new car yet. I mustn't delay, because when I do I will be able to answer Your call without always depending on others to bring me.

18th April 1995
Before The Blessed Sacrament:

Beloved, I see now Your ways are not our ways. Mary, my Holy Mother, guide me and lead me into the ways of Your Son, along the path He has prepared for me, to share with others and to see You in everybody who comes to my home to visit You in the Blessed Sacrament. You alone are the One who heals bodies, minds and spirits. You alone are 'The Wonder-Counsellor, Mighty-God, Eternal-Father, Prince-of-Peace'.

"Child, you remember rightly. Now you know My plan for you. I choose who I will - the most unlikely. You know and will know the work is Mine. You are and will be My instrument in this ministry. Give Me your whole co-operation. The work is Mine. The calling is Mine. The fruits are Mine, Mine alone."

Beloved, with the help of Your Holy Mother I surrender my whole being to You now. Your will not my will, be done.

19ᵗʰ April 1995
Before The Blessed Sacrament:
Beloved, here I am, ready to write for You, in answer to Your call.

"Yes child, I have much on My Heart this day - much for you to write. Remember My Spirit is in control, always in control. Your obedience pleases Me. Yes child, I have accepted your surrender to My Holy Will. I will be your strength, I will lead you all day, every day. Tomorrow begins your ministry - another ministry.

These people come in faith. I will acknowledge their faith. I touch hearts where I will, when I will. You will not be aware of your tiredness when you spend your wakefulness at night with Me. I will suffice, My strength will be with you throughout the day. I prepare W... also for the work ahead. It will be a double ministry. His approval is all I ask of him. He will safeguard you from the dangers and any excessiveness. I will direct him also. You have nothing to fear. Was I not in control on that day in Galway many years ago?

Yes child, I have sent you many helpers now to work on the writings. You will have very little work to see to yourself. Do not worry about the delay, everything is according to My plan now. The blockages and hassle will be hidden from you, not to disturb your peace. Come back later My little one. I need you. It is time to go now."

20ᵗʰ April 1995
Before The Blessed Sacrament:
Beloved, bless us this day, to do Your Holy Will in all things. Open our hearts to Your Holy Spirit.

20th April 1995
Before The Blessed Sacrament:
Oh Beloved, thank You. Surely You have shown us that Your ways are above our ways. How could we ever doubt Your love.

Thank You for allowing us to see the faith of others. How we limit You, limit others and above all limit ourselves in our acceptance of others. Oh Beloved, forgive me. How lovingly and tenderly You show me my weaknesses and help me to correct myself - not by myself but through Your grace.

21st April 1995
Before The Blessed Sacrament:
Oh Beloved, how distracted I have been this day when I should be ever prayerful and grateful for all Your goodness to us. How You have blessed us and our home. Truly You overlook our weaknesses and use the most unlikely. Beloved, I trust in You to change all that displeases You in me. I know all are sinful and weak but I am most in need of Your mercy. I often think I take Your mercy for granted. I have no understanding yet of the cost of our salvation, and all the pain I cause You at times. I wish I could have a little of Your mercy for others, specially at times of testing.

Beloved, we have made no plans yet for Divine Mercy Sunday. May Your will be ours. Thank You Beloved for Your goodness to me all the days of my life. Help me to practise the sacrament of the present moment, now and always.

Later : (for meeting)
"My child, yes I have a word for My faithful little ones. Children, We welcome you here to Our night of love - the love of the Two Hearts. How We look forward to this night each week. It isn't always possible for the five to be together, but you unite in spirit. We thank you for answering Our call. Sometimes it doesn't suit, you are tired and We thank you for your efforts. You are truly rewarded a hundred-fold. Children, it is beyond your comprehension to understand and realise the commitment you have made. So much depends on your yes. Yes is most important to any call. You understand now Rose. It may cost you much in the days ahead but remember We are your strength always. This

you will see to be a part of the Glencree commitment - when Glencree will become a meeting place for all. You will see it to be as a consequence to the healing Masses of the Generations. I need you all to be a part of the renewed Church We are preparing for Our people.

Child, children, We cannot let you see the complete plan yet, but We let you see enough to encourage you to continue. We see your sufferings, your efforts. We bless you. Your reward will be great. You carry many souls in your hearts and many more you do not know, but your day will come when all will be revealed. Thank you dear children. Give praise and thanks for all the blessings We pour out on you on this night of love from the Two Hearts of Love."

22ⁿᵈ April 1995
Before The Blessed Sacrament:

Thank You Beloved.
You alone I need
You alone I want.
Oh the hunger that fills my heart
A hunger not for food for the body, nor for the goods of the world.

You alone can fulfil this
Hunger I carry within me.
How can I be Your disciple
How can I fulfil Your call
How can I fulfil Your need of me.

Without Your strength
My heart is empty in it's emptiness
But You take me, accept me in my nothingness.
Oh Lord, oh Holy One, how merciful You are to me a sinner
Can I not? I cannot share Your mercy on my own.

Mary, Mother of Mercy
I call on You this day
To prepare me for tomorrow
The feast of Divine Mercy
To receive, to share with others a touch of the Divine.

Oh Lord, how we hurt You, pain You, reject You by our attitude -

210

often buried deep, to surface when we least expect, and unable to control in our human weakness. Oh Two Hearts of Love, You share all You are, all You have with each of us. Let us respond with Your shared love to share with others the Two Hearts of Love.

23rd April 1995 - Feast of Divine Mercy
Before The Blessed Sacrament:
Beloved, I join with Your little ones everywhere in loving adoration. By myself I have nothing to offer You but the burden of my weaknesses. I carry another specially in my heart this day - one who is suffering greatly. May Your peace reign in her heart in her heart these last days. How quickly the limitations of old age come upon us. Help us to live every day as if it were our last - how our attitudes would change and changes take place. How helpless we are on our own.

'Holy God, Holy Mighty One, Holy Immortal One, have mercy on us and on the whole world.'

24th April 1995
Before the Blessed Sacrament:
Beloved, there are times when You call on us to accompany You at night and later we know why. Last night was one such night. If I had known perhaps I would have been more generous in my response to Your request.

I bring all You place on my heart to You now in the Blessed Sacrament. Beloved, I thank You for the gentle and tender way You are teaching me humility. I see Your words coming to pass in the daily happenings of my life now. I try not to think of the mountains of changes that have yet to take place within me. Here I find the strength and perseverance to go on believing and hoping for that love You implanted in me from the beginning. I trust in You my Beloved, not to allow me fail You in Your quest for my soul, to fill the vacuum I leave within You.

25ᵗʰ April 1995 - In bed:
"My child"

My Beloved, You call me. Here I am.

"Yes child, My Heart overflows with love this day and every day. I weep with My children who weep this day. My Heart breaks to see My little ones sad. But believe Me My dear little ones, I hold you all close to My Heart. You are part of Me. Your heart beats with Mine and My Holy Mother. Come to Me this day. Let Me be your comfort and consolation. My Heart bleeds to see you distraught. Listen My dear children, you carry your cross now, but see it as the **ILLUMINOUS CROSS** (I spoke to you in your writings). It is the cross that saves, redeems other souls. My Heart thirsts for souls. Oh My pain for souls these days. Evil is everywhere but My victim-souls will have the victory. See My little ones, My light shines in the midst of darkness to allow your light be victorious. How I wait for all My little ones - always waiting at the threshold, beyond the threshold. Yes children, I wait for each one, all My little ones. I wait."

Thank You My Beloved. Many of Your little ones will find comfort in these words. Oh how good You are to me. Help me to be Your comfort for others.

28ᵗʰ April 1995
<u>Before The Blessed Sacrament:</u>
Abba Father, never before have I been more truly aware that You are and have been always my Wonder-Counsellor, Mighty-God, Eternal-Father, Prince-of-Peace. You have surrounded me with helpers preparing the writings for publication. You are protecting me from all the hassle as You said You would, and yet there are times I try to involve myself when I shouldn't.

Help me now to allow those to whom You have given this work to take full control and to the writer of the foreword.

Mary, my Mother, help me to carry out the instructions of the 17th April. Mary, I depend on You now not to let me fail Him. He asks so little of me and blesses me a hundred-fold. Mary, teach me

212

how to rest in Him before the Eucharistic Presence. He needs me more than I need Him. This is so difficult to grasp in our human understanding.

29ᵗʰ April 1995
After The Eucharist:

Beloved, today I learn, is the feast of St. Catherine of Sienna. Perhaps it is of no insignificance that the people You send me to prepare the writings for publication meet this morning. May we have the blessings and intercession of St. Catherine on our work and particularly that Sr. Kathleen who has been given this task is a member of the Order of Dominicans. Beloved, as there is no coincidences in Your planning, I believe today is an important day for us all.

Today is confirmation day in our parish. May the children being confirmed be open to receive the graces and gifts of the Holy Spirit, to prevail against the peer pressure of today's world.

Mary, Mother of all, wrap Your mantle of love and protection around all Your children, our children, our children's children, to lead them to Jesus.

Thank You Mary, Spouse of the Holy Spirit. Enclose us all in Your Immaculate Heart.

4ᵗʰ May 1995
Before The Blessed Sacrament:

"Thank you child for this day. Thank you for inviting Me here for these two days and night. How My Mother and I look forward to these days each month. Oh the comfort and solace We receive here from all who visit Us. Truly Our Hearts rejoice to have you with Us.

Oh children, let Us carry your burdens. Relate all pain and suffering to Ours. We will help you to carry all for Our sakes. Yes there is much sufferings in the world because there is much evil about and Our little ones suffer. Reread often the word We gave you on 25/4/95. It will lift your hearts above the cross. We ask that you know it as the **ILLUMINOUS CROSS**. Yes children, We carry you in Our Hearts always. The blessings We pour out on these days are beyond your comprehension, but believe dear children in the word. This is important. Pray for the living and the dead.

(R. & T.)
As you cannot attend the Healing Mass of the generations on this coming first Saturday child, children, you will be in Our Hearts and share in the fruits. You will be used where you are on this day. We extend the invitation to you both for Monday. Yes children, you are part - a very important part of this group, this place. We need you both. Do not fail Us."

Beloved, thank You for Your beautiful words of appreciation and consolation, and the way You prepared me beforehand for the disappointments concerning the writings. You spoil me and how little I appreciate all Your goodness to me.

5ᵗʰ May 1995 - (At my breakfast)
First Friday:
"Rose, yes I call you. Thank you for your quick response. I have much to speak to you this day. Truly today is a day of much graces for each and everyone who answers My call. I call, so many do not hear, they are so engrossed in the world. Many are so obsessed by cares and anxieties and fail to listen. And am I not the One who relieves and takes upon Myself their burdens.

Child, do you not see the way I relieve you of all your anxieties, listen to your cries for help. Is not My yoke easy and burden light when you rest in Me? Child, dear child, My Mother will help you to obtain the quiet I need of you now. I do not blame you. It is something you are not capable now of achieving on your own. You will know it is My doing, My grace. Beloved child, I am doing great and wonderful things now in your life, in your way of life. Everybody, everyone has a different calling and a need to fulfil in Me. Each is unique. I gather together My little ones to be a support to one another in their hours of need - do I not?

Child, remember Paray-Le-Monial, all I taught you in that holy place, blessed by Me. Here I brought about the devotion to My Sacred Heart through St. Margaret Mary. Through you and others I now bring about, I ask to be adored and worshipped through My Eucharistic Heart. Yes child, this is the calling I have prepared for

214

you from the beginning, now to be added, The Immaculate Heart of My Mother. Child, many graces are coming about now through the healing Masses of the Generations. Some you are aware of, many more you are not. You wonder about Glencree. Write child. Do not be afraid. I have My reason for calling you to this place. You were here as a child. You do not remember. I remember, and the prayers of your parents. I answer. Child, did I not make a promise about your own children and grandchildren. All young people need much prayer, and I answer all prayers. Do not doubt My little one. Have I not brought to fruition the deepest desires of your heart?

Child, do not worry about this day. Make the phone call in obedience. You will see.

You have much to do this day. Much for Me and much for others. Come child, give Me your heart. I wait. Am I not always waiting on My little child to bring Me comfort and solace before My Eucharistic Presence. Remember My need, My need of you particularly this day."

After The Eucharist:
Oh Sacred and Merciful Heart of Jesus and Immaculate Heart of Mary, I trust in You to enable me to do Your Holy Will, to be one in Your Oneness.

Today, with trust in Your promises I speak with my heart. Do with me as You please. I subject myself to Your will. As of today, Your Holy Will shall be my nourishment and I will be faithful to Your commands, with the help of Your grace. Do with me as You please. I beg You O Lord, be with me every moment of my life.

Beloved, thank You for the pain in my heart I experienced today for my youngest grandchild after his little accident. Oh how we must pain You when we turn our backs on You, specially today. I realise we must suffer to realise the pain You suffer because of us.

How gentle You are with me as You let me see into Your Heart. Oh Mary, no wonder You weep so much these days because of the pain and suffering we cause Your Son.

Thank You Mary for the peace and reconciliation that You have brought about between E. and I, and between .... and her son. Truly You are the Mediatrix of all graces. I regret not being able to go to Glencree tomorrow. I pray that all will be well for S. and P. The blessings of her family passes from generation to generation.

"Children of the Two Hearts, We pour out Our blessings on you this night. We rejoice in your presence, we rejoice with you. All Heaven rejoices on this special day now dedicated to the Eucharistic Heart and the Immaculate Heart of Mary.

Oh children, thank you for answering Our call, as you prepare for tomorrow's Mass of the Generations. Your country is in need of much healing. Nights such as this bring great graces on your land and peace to the hearts of your people. Pray children, continue to pray for peace. Many hearts are in need of healing - oh so many. Anger is just below the surface and it takes very little for this anger to erupt. Children, you hold back My anger at the rejection of many of My children. Look to Bosnia. Oh the turmoil and suffering, not only there but throughout the world. Children, you truly hold back the arm of the Father.

The Two Hearts of Love thank you again and bless you and yours."

7ᵗʰ May 1995: "Yes child, take rest. Better to take it easy now for awhile. Do not overtax the mind. Come to Me tonight. Spend some time in My Presence. I will rest your body and mind. Yes child, take it easy."

8ᵗʰ May 1995: *Today we celebrate the ending in Europe of the second world war. Peace and reconciliation is being prayed for all over the world.*

Beloved, change my heart, change all our hearts to allow our prayers to be fulfilled.

Saturday, 1st Saturday and Glencree was consecrated to the Two Hearts at the Grotto, fulfilling a word we received over twelve months ago and recently. Beloved, in Your wisdom, T. and myself weren't present at the ceremony but our hearts were united with the others.

Today's Gospel reading John 10:1-10 has much significance for me.

"Amen, amen, I say to you, whoever does not enter a sheepfold through the gate but climbs over elsewhere is a thief and a robber. But whoever enters through the gate is the shepherd of the sheep. The gatekeeper opens it for him, and the sheep hear his voice, as he calls his own sheep by name and leads them out. When he has driven out all his own, he walks ahead of them, and the sheep follow him, because they recognize his voice. But they will not follow a stranger; they will run away from him, because they do not recognize the voice of strangers."

Although Jesus used this figure of speech, they did not realise what he was trying to tell them.

So Jesus said again, "Amen, amen, I say to you, I am the gate for the sheep. All who came [before me] are thieves and robbers, but the sheep did not listen to them. I am the gate. Whoever enters through me will be saved, and will come in and go out, and find pasture. A thief comes only to steal and slaughter and destroy, I came so that they might have life and have it more abundantly."

9ᵗʰ May 1995
Before The Blessed Sacrament:
Beloved, thank You for now. Thank You for yesterday. Oh I have so much to thank You for. You take care of all my needs. Help me to find You everywhere, to see You everywhere and to know You everywhere, in everyone I encounter in my daily life, that I may be open to share Your graces, Your goodness with others, while I have the health, the strength and understanding.

11ᵗʰ May 1995
Before The Blessed Sacrament:
"I call on all political leaders to allow your members have a free vote in the forthcoming legislation on divorce.

Let the people see that democracy still prevails in this land. Let the people speak. Let the people proclaim their views, their desires. Priests, I ask you to speak out. Do not be afraid. Look to other lands where divorce is part of the ethos. See the results. It cannot be controlled. It will become the norm if the family is not upheld. The country will lose it's foundation. There are sad cases, sad circumstances. To follow Me is difficult, was always difficult.

I ask leaders of the Church, My Church, to uphold the sanctity of the Sacrament of marriage. Do not fail My people. You do not have to have a pluralistic society. Who controls? Who is in control of events? Other nations are already learning to their regret the dangers, the consequences of this legislation. It doesn't matter how you try to control, it spreads like forest fires to destroy, to bring destruction within families, specially amongst the youth."

Abba Father - what do You want me to do with today's writing? Help me to listen. I am so distracted at the present time. Mary, enclose me in Your Immaculate Heart.

"Child, there is more to come later. I will direct you."

13ᵗʰ May 1995
Before The Blessed Sacrament:
Today we celebrate the first apparition of Mary to the children of Fatima.

Oh Mary, Your messages of these times are happening now. Oh Mary, the world is so in need of Your protection and care, perhaps more today than ever in history.

Mary:
"Yes My child, I come, I make Myself known to My children as never before. Evil is rampant throughout the world, but My Father and Son have given Me the victory over evil. I am conquering. I will conquer. Never lose hope in the power of My intercession in the world, for the world. My shrines are proof of this. All is for My Son to lead all My children to My Son. I come to touch the hearts of all, to follow My Son, to turn their backs on the world and all its attachments. Yes child, I come to be your advocate. I cannot rest until I see My children, all My children return to the Heart of My Son.

I use you My little one to direct others to the Eucharistic Presence. Here you found My Son. Here you must lead others. Symbols and signs are only a help to return to Him who is the Way, the Truth and the Life. I come to gather all My little ones who are lost and need the shepherd.

Trust Me My little one. Have I not always answered your prayers, cared for you and protected you down the years. A mother always seeks all that is best for her child, and I know. You carry many people, many souls in your heart. Give them all to Me. Give yourself to My Son who waits for you. I will help you find the peace you need, the peace you seek, as the mind becomes more distracted and confused. Do not be afraid My little one. Offer all for the One who thirsts for souls, all souls.

Yes child, I will use you to bring the Eucharistic Presence to Glencree more often. Yes child, during the coming months you will take the monstrance to Glencree on Friday evenings for your meetings, excluding the First Fridays, where you will continue this period of Adoration in your own home for the present. We will prepare the way for you."

Beloved, are we to have the adoration in the church or in the room we have been promised.

"Yes child, you will have the Adoration in the room. I will arrange this for you. Always have five - even if one or more of you cannot come yourselves."

15ᵗʰ May 1995
Before The Blessed Sacrament:

Thank You Beloved for giving me the strength to make it. I so wanted to give thanks this day for Your beautiful plan of yesterday. I couldn't even think or wish better. I was so glad to have visited E…. while she was still conscious. I pray for a peaceful death for her and reconciliation within all the family.

Oh Beloved, Your ways are so above ours - and also to have had the opportunity to visit Fr. E…. on the way down. Surely he is at peace and on the way home to his reward. I thank You for the privilege of being a friend. And he always gave me such encouragement about the writings down the years. These two souls I place specially on the altar of all graces at the coming Mass.

16ᵗʰ May 1995
Before The Blessed Sacrament:

Truly these days are days to give thanks. I trust in You and my

Holy Mother, to fulfil Your need of me each day. I find it difficult to carry out my daily chores, or am I just making excuses for my laziness.

Perhaps when I return home now I will have the energy to cover the essentials. Beloved, I thank You. Help me to visit You again in the afternoon at the Parish church where You are released from Your prison for a few hours.

Later :
"Stay where you are child. I ask you to write in response to the letter you have just written (not included in writings). I thank you, I thank you. I see all your efforts and T... also. Do not fail Me little ones. Do continue to pray together. I understand. I make allowances. Children you pray as one together. Do I not answer you, confirm you, teach you and comfort you through each other.
I will disclose My plans for you both through one another. Yes child, I will give you the strength to share the writings. Wait until Sr. K. returns to discuss publication. Ring Fr. C. re recent writings, to receive his blessing on further undertaking. Later you can give him past writings. The others must confirm the room first and make ready for My coming.

Yes child, you will open many doors to My Eucharistic Presence. I ask much of you. You trust Me. You do not make difficulties as others do. You will be My instrument to open many more Tabernacle doors. You know, first and foremost I desire to be with My people. Others are afraid. They make many difficulties. They do not see that I am in control - all events are under My control. When I am taken out of the Tabernacle I become as a magnet to My people. I place a hunger in their hearts.

"When I am taken out of the Tabernacle I become as a magnet to My people. I place a hunger in their hearts."

They come to Me to be comforted and consoled in a living and personal way. I am more present to them, I am more present. I come in the pinnacle of My humility in The Host, and only because I cannot reveal Myself in My reality. Oh children, I repeat again and again - do not be afraid. Open Tabernacle doors. Let Me be present to My children - to see Me, My living Presence in The

Host."

17ᵗʰ May 1995
Before The Blessed Sacrament:
Beloved, my mind is very distracted this morning. Make it possible for me to call again. I have so much to do this day and so little energy. I offer all for E…. in her last agony. May she rest in peace with her family and in You.

18ᵗʰ May 1995
Before The Blessed Sacrament:
E…. died during the night. May she rest in peace.

21ˢᵗ May 1995: "My child, I need you to spend much time with Me tomorrow. You may go to the cemetery - return early for more Adoration and Mass.

Pray for all who seek your prayers by being present to My Eucharistic Presence."

22ⁿᵈ May 1995 - (40 hours in parish church)
Before The Blessed Sacrament:
Thank You Beloved for Your direction last night.
Beloved, so many people are in need of Your help. Please listen to the cries of our hearts. Give all peace, the peace the world cannot give You know the needs of all who have asked my prayers.

23ʳᵈ May 1995
Before The Blessed Sacrament:
"Do not be afraid My son, My faithful son. I take care of you. You are in My Immaculate Heart. You suffer for others, do you not know? Relate all to My sufferings, My sufferings for others. Son of Mine, learn to eat again. I hold your hand. All will be well as you trust in Me to restore the body. It is difficult to make decisions. When the body is weak, the mind becomes weak also. The darkness is not of Me. I need you whole to complete the work I

have given you. Take heart My son. Begin today. My joy seeks to fill your heart. See the light, Our light, in the darkness and oppression. All is not dark. See Our victory beyond the darkness. We are in control of the Church. You are in the time of purification but purification is not darkness. It prepares the fruits for the next phase and next generation.

Oh children (T. & R.) give Me all you carry in your hearts. Your hearts are too little to carry the burdens of others. We control, We conquer, We have the victory. Take no part in gossip. Keep the minds free and open. We have much work for you both. Learn to live one day at a time. It is easier for you Rose to do this and more vital at your stage. Remember T...'s work will be more public and needs your prayer to protect her. Yes children, you compliment one another. It is vital, this hour together each day, Our faithful little friends, Children, We bless you both this day. We cover you with Our love. Thank you, thank you, for being so faithful to Our calling."

Later
Before The Blessed Sacrament:
Beloved, how is it that when I fail You, You bless me. Yesterday I failed to carry out Your word for me. Today You answer my requests. How merciful You are to me, who fails You so often. Oh if only I could accept others just a little of the way You accept my weakness, how much joy I could give others. Although I spent a little while with You yesterday morning, I only arrived back in time for the closing Mass of the 40 hours at 8 p.m.

"Oh child, dear child, I am not a task master. Do I not accept all My little ones with love, specially when their heart is centred on Me. Yes child, you spent your time well yesterday. Do not think of the failures but the good you achieved. So many doubt My Love. This Is more painful than all the little failures due to human weakness. Yes child, do spread this message of My Love, My mercy. How I wait for all My children to accept My forgiveness, My Love. How I wait for all My lost sheep. Oh the pain they cause Me by doubting My Love."

My Beloved, words of thanks fail me. Beloved, I believe that my soul may be at peace and at prayer even though my mind may be confused. You are so good to me always.

25th May 1995
Before The Blessed Sacrament:
Beloved, today we celebrate with You Your ascension into Heaven. Let our hearts be filled with Your joy as You return to Your Father. Prepare our hearts to receive You on this special day.

27th May 1995
After The Eucharist:
Beloved, You spoke to my heart earlier about the writings. Am I to direct Sr. R. to Fr. H. ? I know You will tell me later. Thank You.

29th May 1995
Before The Blessed Sacrament:
Beloved, as I listen to the downpour of rain outside I am reminded that even the elements are angry because of the inhumanity of man in the world, to one another. Beloved, may we bring comfort to Your Holy Presence in our presence here with You.

We bring before You all that is not of You in the world this day. We can only pray : 'May Your Kingdom come on earth as it is in Heaven.' You are The All Powerful God, who sustains us with the hope You place within us that 'all is well, all will be well' especially when we come into Your Eucharistic Presence. Beloved, so many young people now face exams and oh the stress and pain they inflict on most. Beloved, You alone can change the present state of education and preparation for adult life. Help us by our prayers to help change the present pressures on our young people to give them a more spiritual and healthy outlook on life to be able to praise and thank You in their joys and sorrows, to see the perfection of Your Love and Holy Will in all the circumstances and situations they encounter and will encounter on their journey.

We their elders, haven't made life easier for them by our attitudes. Forgive us for our failures and have mercy on all who come after us.

"My child, My dear child, the youth of this day are under great temptations. Evil is all around them. Evil is idolised through evil men. Child, children, come before My Eucharistic Presence often. I speak to those who can make the time. Many have time to spare, mean well, but do not think it necessary. Many churches are empty during the daytime. Many are depressed because they have no jobs. Come to Me and I will help to change their hearts. I will give them the incentive to spend their time fruitfully and bring peace and joy into their hearts.

Think of My demented children in Yugoslavia, distorted in mind and spirit. Children, pray. Pray for My children in all war-torn situations. I do not ask you to carry the burden. Give the burden to Me. Believe and trust in Me, that I have the power to conquer all evil, will have the victory over all evil."

"Come back later child. I need you."

31ˢᵗ May 1995 - Feast of the Visitation of Mary to Her cousin Elizabeth
Before The Blessed Sacrament:
Mary, You always bless me on Your feast-days. Today You tell me to give Jesus all He takes. As my concentration is deteriorating, my prayer seems to be full of distraction because of my inability to be silent. As all prayer is gift - with Your help I surrender my poor weak efforts to be embellished by You, before offering to my Beloved. Thank You Mary. Help me to make my prayer of consecration from a loving heart.

2ⁿᵈ June 1995 - First Friday
Before The Blessed Sacrament:
Beloved, I have been reading the diaries of others lately and I become so discouraged because of the way I treat You - my lack of response to Your Everlasting Love. My Beloved, I pray that this Pentecost I will be open to receive a fresh outpouring of Your Holy Spirit. How I need Him to ignite the fire of love within me. My heart is so empty of love these times. I know this darkness is not of You. I have allowed the depression and oppression of the world to overcome me, and You continue to gift me with Your Eucharistic Presence in my home. Were it not that I believe Your Love for me is unconditional, I would despair of myself. Beloved, on this day that You have made specially holy over the years, I offer the pain

of my ungrateful and indifferent heart for others.

Mary, help me in my quest and hunger for His Love, to be able to respond again to His overwhelming Love and need of me. So many others are starved to know Him and experience His Love, and I seem to have thrown away the beautiful gifts He bestowed on me in the past. Oh Beloved, You have not hidden Yourself but it is my lack of response that pains me. You know I am nothing without You. I cannot help myself and as Pentecost Sunday is only two days away and the Healing Mass for the Generations is tomorrow, the first Saturday at Glencree, I look forward for a fresh outpouring of the Fire of the Spirit on us all, our families, our country and throughout the world. May the Fire of the Spirit dispel the evil in our midst and throughout the world, Amen.

3ʳᵈ June 1995: *Beloved, there is a glimpse of hope in the Bosnian situation this morning, with the return of 120 of the UN prisoners. Beloved, merciful One, have pity on all the innocent victims of this war and all other wars throughout the world. Surely they suffer with You. I am reminded of the poem You gave me about El Salvador in the throes of their sufferings. What pain You suffer because of us, what pain we inflict on You.*

May the peoples of the world stop, think, listen for the breath of the Holy Spirit and allow the Spirit of Hope enter our hearts to strengthen and change our hearts of the evil influences of our times.

4ᵗʰ June 1995 - Pentecost Sunday
Before The Blessed Sacrament:
"Child, I told you it would not be always easy sitting here in My Eucharistic Presence. Child, you are overwrought. The publishing of the writings is not part of your work. Leave it to others. I will direct them. It is all working according to My plan now. Each step will fall into place in My time child. Leave all to Me. Rest little one in My Heart. Leave all to Us. Your Holy Mother is taking over."

7th June 1995
Before The Blessed Sacrament:

Thank You Beloved for this day. Again and again I make arrangements without asking You beforehand. Should I have settled on tomorrow to go to the publishers about the writings - leaving You when You visit my home tomorrow. I know many others will be with You, but I want Your blessing before I go. Oh Beloved, check my impulsiveness when I seek to take control.

"Oh My child, My dear child, you are a child to Me. You are My child. I see your efforts, I see your weaknesses. Do I not accept you as you are? I use you in your weakness. Thank you child. You will see My Holy Will come to pass in the availability of others. All will be well, yes My child, all is well. Rest in Me now My little one. Rest in Me."

Mary, teach me to pray as my Beloved asks. Give rest to my restless spirit.

"My beloved child, do I not know that you do not doubt My Love in all circumstances. Now I will bring you into an understanding of My great mercy. See the way I taught Blessed Faustina. Now I will use you to bring My Mercy to all My little ones. You say you will never become a daughter - I do not want to make you My daughter. I called you to be a little child, totally dependent on Me and My Holy Mother from moment to moment, minute to minute, day by day. I seek to teach the very ordinary, the very humble of My great mercy. Not the theologians, those of great intellect, but those of lesser understanding, those who live in faith, and all My little ones.

These writings in one respect will be a sequence to the writings of Sr. Faustina. Simple and yet profound for simple and humble people. It is fitting child that these writings will be published by the publishers of the diaries of Sr. Faustina. Now child, I have disclosed My plan for you. I do not want to see My little ones anxious. (Sr. K. and yourself)

See the ways My plans knit together. Oh child, lift up your heart in love, praise and thanksgiving for My Divine and Infinite Mercy for one and all My little ones."

8ᵗʰ June 1995
Before The Blessed Sacrament:
(Today Sr. Kath. and myself bring the writings from beginning to 1990 incl. to the Publishers for examination.)

Thank You Jesus and Mary for these days. You make me so aware of the wonder of Your ways in all my distractions and failures. What a comfort and consolation to know that You have taken over the writings. Now I pray and hope to detach myself completely. Truly I cannot repeat often enough - You are for all - our Wonder-Counsellor, Mighty-God. Eternal-Father, Prince-of-Peace. 'How great Thou art. How great Thou art.'

Later :
Oh Mary, save me from the coldness and indifference that I carry in my heart in the Presence of Jesus in the Eucharist. Do not let me be a cause of pain to Him again. Please help me Mary, my Mother. I unite with the others at Glencree tonight at Adoration.

9ᵗʰ June 1995
Before The Blessed Sacrament:
Truly Beloved, when You instituted the Eucharist at the last supper, You bequeathed to mankind the pinnacle of Your humility and vulnerability. You put Yourself under the control of mankind, to receive glory or profanity. You allowed Yourself to be at the mercy of man in the Eucharist, and a servant at the service of others. In the past Your Presence in the Eucharist was protected to the extent that seldom were You allowed to be exposed to Your people - shut away from the gaze of mankind in case of disrespect, injury and even theft.

"All the while I yearned to be present to My people. Now that the world is in the state of greater evil since the time of Noah, I desire and seek to be allowed be where I will be seen so that all may be prepared in faith to be healed in body, mind and spirit in preparation for My second coming in the world.

Pray, believe, with boundless hope for the fulfilment of that day."

Later :

Beloved, the thought came to me this morning here in Your Eucharistic Presence that parts of the writing received on 7/6/95 could be used as a foreword to the writings. I know You will direct us about this at the appropriate time. I keep forgetting You are in control. Help me to surrender all to You.

"My child, My little one, I like to hear your thoughts, to write as you wish. Remember the joy I receive reading all your little letters even though I know all in advance.

I give you this day, a day of quiet, to sit with Me, listen to Me, talk with Me. Thank you My little one. Prepare also for this night of prayer together. It is a new venture, a stepping out in faith. I will bless you, protect you. Great joy will greet you. My faithful little ones, come in unity, come in love to give all of yourselves to the Two Hearts of Love. Repercussions of this night will be far and wide in this place. It is a beginning. You will comprehend at a later date. Pray child now. Be present to My Presence is all I ask."

10ᵗʰ June 1995   -   After The Eucharist
Before The Blessed Sacrament:
"Yes My child, My beloved child, I have much to share with you this day. Yes children, I brought you together last night in the upper room. Oh the joy in Our Two Hearts (last night) that welcomed you together here.

Now child, you ask Me to open more homes to My Eucharistic Presence, to open more tabernacle doors in My churches. These requests will be answered in time.

The prayers of My Eucharistic Adorers will bring these about. Truly then I will bring to fruition the desires of Our Heart and the hunger placed in the hearts of Our little ones.

I ask you dear child to spend much time with Me in the days before the Feast of Corpus Christi. This is truly Our feast-day. Dear child do not dwell on your inadequacies, weaknesses. I use the weak to confound the strong - do I not? Yes children, do not be disappointed about the mistake about Glencree. I can turn all to My advantage. It will help to speed up the development of this shrine so close to My Holy Mother, so necessary in these times. I am, We are rebuilding and replacing the shrines destroyed by evil men over the centuries. **My people will know My Mother as Mother of My Church in this land again. I cannot fail Her intercession for this land, nor disappoint Her**.

My little one, you have much on your mind these days. Forget about all but the essentials. I will bring about the healings you seek, and I think necessary. Surrender all to Me and trust My Mother and I. We take care of all. All is well My dear, dear child. My Mother encloses you and your care in Her mantle of love. Rest now dear child in the Two Hearts of Love."

11th June 1995:   "What hurts child is a source of grace. Child, come to Me this day. I have much again for you to write. Yes child you will collect ...   I will bless you both. It will be a new outlook on home for her. Take her to your heart. She needs love, assurance and praise. Yes child, she is very sensitive about beginnings. Be a Nanna, a loving Nanna. I need your comfort and consolation this day.

The Eucharist will never change - always The Ultimate."

13th June 1995
Before The Blessed Sacrament:
"Yes child, in answering your prayers for a change of heart - it is only through pain and sufferings you grow - grace and response to grace. Oh child, the blessings brought about through little efforts and sacrifices are the makings of Sainthood. I created all to be living saints on earth - glorified saints in My Eternal Kingdom."

14th June 1995
Before The Blessed Sacrament:
Abba Father, You remind me that sometimes You send a little child to deliver a message You do not want to deliver Yourself.

Abba Father, in the name of Jesus, open my heart to receive Your Holy Spirit.

I pray to prepare for this special feast-day of Your Son tomorrow the feast of Corpus Christi. Make it possible for me to return later.

Mary, bless all travellers today, specially those I carry in my heart.

14ᵗʰ June 1995
Eve of Corpus Christi:
Beloved, I wish I could visit You again in the Blessed Sacrament. You know my dilemma. I do not know what to do, but You are the God who waits. Mary, prepare me for His feast-day tomorrow. I pray to be able to fulfil His need of me. How must those who really seek You suffer, not being able to fulfil this hunger You place within their souls.

15ᵗʰ June 1995: "Yes, stay at home child. - (Sat. 17th) It is a time for spiritual fasting. Others (R.& M.) should do the same. They mean well but it is not My design for them. Do not worry about T.. You judge rightly. It is a time of great suffering but much will be born during these days. Yes child, she could and should take the prayer Magnificat to her heart. It is already there. Yes child, she needs a change at the present time. It will relieve the pressures on her. She needs your support in prayer."

Oh Beloved, I can only give what I receive from You on Your feast-day, our feast-day.

"Later child, I will speak to your heart. Give Me all your attention now. I wait."

15ᵗʰ June 1995: *Dear Holy Mother, I bring all I carry in my heart into this rosary, specially priests and religious who most need our prayers and Your mercy. Mother of Mercy and Merciful Mother, how You must suffer to see Your Son suffer.*

Mary, I need Your guidance and help now as to what I should do about the 'word' given to me yesterday. I know Jesus and You will give me a word in writing to give to the priests. May His will be done to bring about His Kingdom on earth. Thank You Mary. I give You all You give me.

My Beloved, it pains my heart when it is touched by Your love and mercy and the way I respond to Your graces. Then I remember the prayer - 'Praise and thank Me for the burden of your weaknesses.' Oh Beloved, how often I pain You, fail You while I sit here in Your Eucharistic Presence. Teach me how to be present to Your Presence at all times. I keep forgetting. Other times I take You so much for granted. Help me in my continuous struggle to fulfil Your need of me.

Later :
Mary, tonight we go to Glencree. We ask Your blessing and protection on us. May our hearts be one with the Two hearts of Love to fulfil Your need of us, that Your plan for this place will be fulfilled by our prayers to bring others to peace and reconciliation. Mary, help us to begin with ourselves. Root out all that keeps us apart.

18th June 1995
Before The Blessed Sacrament:
Beloved, I find You here on my doorstep exposed in the Eucharistic Presence. You make it so easy for me to respond to Your call.

Beloved, I must remember that each time I come into Your Presence, it is a call to pray specially for Your priests.

Beloved, I know You will direct me as to what I am to do about the word received from Patricia on Corpus Christi. Many thoughts are racing through my mind these days. I need the light of the Holy Spirit to lead and guide me Yet I know - all is well, all will be well, and I must have no anxiety about it or it would be a lack of trust in You. The coming Friday is the feast of the Sacred Heart. How better to please You than to have complete trust in You, in Your Love for all - Love that is infinite, constant and everlasting. Already dearest Beloved, we both are finding benefit from the change. May it bring us closer together in You.

Later :
Mary, thank You for confirming my prayer, my need. Oh what a loving Mother You are to us, how full of tenderness and mercy. Mary, my tears are tears of joy but, Yours are tears of pain and suffering to see the sufferings of Your Son.

19ᵗʰ June 1995
Before The Blessed Sacrament:

Thank You Beloved for making yourself so available to us. You make it so simple for priests to answer Your call for Eucharistic Adoration when You place this hunger in the hearts of Your people.

I haven't responded as I should but always You allow for my weaknesses and failures. You bless our weak, weak efforts to answer Your call for Eucharistic Adoration throughout our land. Do listen to our cries for the cease-fire to continue. Mary, Queen of Peace and Mother of Reconciliation, touch the hearts of all sections of the community to turn to You. We see now the consequences of the war in Bosnia. Mary, we can never thank You enough for Your intercession for our people.

Mary, I would like to visit Your shrine in Knock before I return home, if it is in Your plan. I leave all to You to arrange, against all the odds. I hope to come back later if possible.

23ʳᵈ June 1995   -   Feast of the Sacred Heart
Before The Blessed Sacrament:

"Child, you did not think that I would let this day pass without a word of encouragement for My little child.

My beloved child, I look at you this day. My gaze never leaves you whether you are present in the room or not. You never venture far from Me. Oh My dear child how happy I am to be present here today. You and others have served Me well, very well over the years. Be appreciative as I am appreciative of all your efforts to satisfy My hungry Heart. Today I wish to pour out on all My faithful friends everywhere, torrents of love and mercy from a Heart tormented by love for each and everyone I create. And so many do not know of this Love I carry for each one. Oh the longing and hunger I suffer for all in My Heart.

Oh child, oh children, it takes so little to satisfy Me. Oh so little, remember the crumbs from the rich man's table, so I hunger for the love of all.

Oh children of My Sacred Heart, I wait with great expectation on each First Friday specially for each one and so few answer My call. Now do I not humble Myself to be present to all in My Eucharistic Presence in as many churches and oratories as will allow Me. There are still many churches in this land do not think it fitting nor necessary to have exposition.

My priests, My dear priests wake up. I am calling all to return to Eucharistic Adoration of My Sacred Heart before the evil one will destroy you. My dear, dear priests I need you, I wait for you, to strengthen you, to protect you against the onslaught of evil. Here you will learn the power of the Eucharist, to make the sacrifice and celebration of your daily Mass the centre of your life, the praying and the living of the Eucharist the most important part of your daily exercises, the centre and the ultimate.

Why have I called you, chosen you? To be spiritual fathers and providers to My little ones, to feed their souls with My Body and Blood. When I created the world, mankind, I created the fruits to fulfil the needs of mankind for their bodies and the capabilities for all their necessities to be developed by man over the centuries, perhaps not always to be developed for their betterment but that was to be part of the freedom I gave to all.

Now child, I know you have many questions and directions you ask of Me and asked for by others. These I will disclose later. Prepare now for your hour of prayer. I need your full attention."

25ᵗʰ June 1995:   *Mary, our Holy Mother, thank You for last night to celebrate with the Two Hearts of Love. May this day be a continuation of the two feast-days.*

2ⁿᵈ July 1995
Before The Blessed Sacrament:
Beloved, do not let the anger within me thwart my judgement. Recently Lord, I have been asking You for the grace of repentance - truly I need it.

I thank You for all the blessings received at Glencree yesterday at the Healing Mass of the Generations and the realisation of the very many areas that need healing specially in my own life. May it help me to be more compassionate to others and non-judgemental. Beloved, I have failed You in so many ways in the past, today and everyday. Do not let me lose heart. I know You wouldn't want this and

I am reminded of when You told me that the spiritual journey was like the pendulum of a clock. When we move too much to one or other side, the evil one waits with the sin of pride and the other with the sin of despair. Help us Dear One to keep the balance.

May the Spirit of truth and holiness invade our hearts with His light at all times, to keep us ever vigilant of the subtleness of the attacks of the evil one to destroy us.

Beloved, You know the needs of all those who have asked my prayers. Do not disappoint them because of me. Oh if they only knew how much You love them, they wouldn't have to ask anybody but You and Your Holy Mother.

Beloved, I see now that the only way You can bring about the change of heart I need is through pain, suffering and repentance in a moment to moment struggle. Help me. I place my trust in the Two Hearts of Love.

4ᵗʰ July 1995
Before The Blessed Sacrament:
Beloved, the news this day in our land is very disheartening, even frightening. Beloved, You alone can save and preserve the cease-fire. We had become too complacent even though You told us that the cease-fire rested on a pinhead.

Oh Mary, Queen of Peace and Mother of Reconciliation, listen to the cries of our hearts for peace to prevail in our land and throughout the world. Even though our Church and country are in a state of confusion at the present time, we trust in You. We trust in You. Lead and guide the leaders of Church and state to listen, to pray, to allow the Holy Spirit control their lives through these turbulent times. We stand on Your promises. We trust in You.

"Oh My dear child, how I suffer to see and perceive all that is happening in this land. I see the faithfulness of My faithful few. I listen to the cries of My little ones that keep the sparks of faith alive in this land. Yes child, I see and perceive. My Heart is torn apart, pierced through by the sinfulness and rejection of mankind of My commandments. How easy for the evil one to entice away My own, My children. Pray, pray, pray. I call you My child, to open your home to My Eucharistic Presence on 10th July in response to the word I sent you through another. I assemble My intercessors to this day of prayer for Church and State, to make amends, to appease My broken and tormented Heart.

Oh children : Abide in Me. Abide with Me. Abide through Me, in intercession with My Holy Mother to stay His hand, the hand of justice on this land so dear to all Our Hearts.

Children, come to appease Our broken Hearts."

Beloved, I believe, I know nothing is impossible to You and You are always faithful to Your promises. Remember Nineveh. Beloved, do I have to do any more about this word? Beloved, You never ask anything of us unless You want to answer our prayers. Our hope is in You because of the gift of faith that came to us through our ancestors. You have called for the Healing Masses of the Generations to heal and cement the virtues of Faith, Hope and Love in our hearts. Have You not?

Later
Before The Blessed Sacrament:
Beloved, thank You for the trust You place in me by making me Your little messenger. How unworthy and weak I am for such an awesome work. Were it not for the beautiful people You place around me to keep me faithful I would be lost forever. Beloved, during these coming days may I be open to the urgings of the Holy Spirit and Mary His Beloved Spouse, to protect me from the evil I carry within me and is about me to destroy me and fail You.

May Your Holy Will be accomplished in Church and state in our country. Praise and thank You for all Your goodness and kindness to me now and always.

6ᵗʰ July 1995 - Feast of St. Maria Goretti

Before The Blessed Sacrament:

Truly the message from today's reading : Gen. 22. 1-19 is that the Lord provides when we give Him what He asks.

The Testing of Abraham

'Some time after these events, God put Abraham to the test. He called to him, "Abraham!" "Ready!" he replied. Then God said: "Take your son Isaac, your only one, whom you love, and go to the land of Moriah. There you shall offer him up as a holocaust on a height that I will point out to you." Early the next morning Abraham saddled his donkey, took with him his son Isaac, and two of his servants as well, and with the wood that he had cut for the holocaust, set out for the place of which God had told him.

On the third day Abraham got sight of the place from afar. Then he said to his servants: "Both of you stay here with the donkey, while the boy and I go on over yonder. We will worship and then come back to you." Thereupon Abraham took the wood for the holocaust and laid it on his son Isaac's shoulders, while he himself carried the fire and the knife. As the two walked on together, Isaac spoke to his father Abraham: "Father!" he said. "Yes, son," he replied. Isaac continued, "Here are the fire and the wood, but where is the sheep for the holocaust?" "Son," Abraham answered, "God himself will provide the sheep for the holocaust." Then the two continued going forward.

When they came to the place of which God had told him, Abraham built an altar there and arranged the wood on it. Next he tied up his son Isaac, and put him on top of the wood on the altar. Then he reached out and took the knife to slaughter his son. "But the LORD's messenger called to him from heaven, "Abraham, Abraham!" "Yes, Lord," he answered. "Do not lay your hand on the boy," said the messenger. "Do not do the least thing to him. I know now how devoted you are to God, since you did not withhold from me your own beloved son." As Abraham looked about, he spied a ram caught by its horns in the thicket. So he went and took the ram and offered it up as a holocaust in place of his son. Abraham named the site Yahweh-yireh; hence people now say, "On the mountain the LORD will see."

Again the LORD'S messenger called to Abraham from heaven and said: "I swear by myself, declares the LORD, that because you acted as you did in not withholding from me your beloved son, I will bless you abundantly and make your descendants as countless as the stars of the sky and the sands of the seashore; your descendants shall take possession of the gates of their enemies, and in your descendants all the nations of the earth shall find blessing - all this because you obeyed my

236

command."

Abraham then returned to his servants, and they set out together for Beer-sheba, where Abraham made his home.

Thinking of the state of the Church in our land and the trouble in the North again I am reminded of the words of Julian of Norwich : 'All is well. All will be well'. *Where is my trust ?*

"Oh child, I will speak to your heart. Child I am very much troubled. I seek places, churches, oratories, homes to rest My troubled Heart in hearts open to receive Me. Of late child, you have felt detached from Me. This was all part of My plan for you. You will understand the pain of others who never know Me nor come close to Me.

Child, dear child, I prepare you now for the most profound of writings for My Church, My Hierarchy. I always choose little children for My most sublime works to confound those of great intellect. There are many reasons for this My child. I will explain to you later, at a later date. Do not worry My little one about the state of your mind, the little set-backs. Give Me all. Surrender all to Me. Let Me be in control now. I need your full co-operation for your future. Child, you have been experiencing of late the confusion in My Church. Truly it is confused. There are many in authority not fit to be leaders, directing My little ones. They bring disgrace and disunity within My Church and confusion on all. The days ahead will become darker but child, I give you the light to see beyond the darkness. The insight I gave you this morning into the day's reading was a preparation for the days ahead. Child, hold on to this faith. Truly it will strengthen you and sustain you as I unfold My plans. Do not be afraid My little one. There is much evil about but evil has no power unto Mine.

The prophecies for these times will be fulfilled. Child, I will be your Wonder-Counsellor, Mighty-God, Eternal-Father, Prince-of-Peace.

My Spirit will lead you into the truth and not fail you. Trust Us. I give you My Holy Mother to care for you, protect you against the evil forces that will try and destroy you.

Child, remember, I am your Abba always."

7ᵗʰ July 1995
First Friday:
Beloved, I feel that You have been waiting for me all morning to receive my full attention, to speak to my heart again. Oh Beloved, I wonder at You using the likes of me to be a messenger. Such a sublime calling for the likes of me. Oh Beloved, You will have to give me graces I need to fulfil Your need of me - not alone by the day, but moment by moment. Truly Your calling into the spiritual life is a moment to moment existence as You told me in the early days of these writings. Beloved, oh how often I fail in one day alone and how often You have to lift me up again and again. And You remind me that this You delight in, if we keep trying - and I remember when You told me that 'trying is success in Your eyes'. Beloved, it is now nearing the hour of three o'clock in the afternoon. Help me at least to give You my full attention during this hour in reparation for all my failures on this special day, today and in the past.

Beloved, like Sr. Faustina, You have shown me infinite mercy over the years and perhaps I have taken advantage of Your infinite love and not understood nor accepted the cost of my redemption. But then, no little child realises the pain and suffering we cause our parents while we are still a child.

8ᵗʰ July 1995: *Today is a new beginning. Beloved, I thank You for the opportunity to make amends for yesterday and all my yesterdays. Today we are called to visit Glencree. Mary, Queen of Peace and Mother of Reconciliation, we pray, we hope, to be open to the graces You have prepared for us at the Eucharistic Presence of Your Son. Mary, we need Your guidance for the leaflet proposed for information on Glencree. May unity and peace reign in the hearts of all who pray for Glencree.*

9ᵗʰ July 1995
Before The Blessed Sacrament:
My Beloved Spouse - truly I can call You my Spouse also. You call me to abide in You as You abide in me - no such intimate relationship within humans on earth. You came to give us everything of Yourself - to be fulfilled in the Eucharist, when the

238

Word - You, second person of the Trinity becomes flesh. Now I sit in Your Eucharistic Presence - the Presence that is both human and divine. Our human intellect cannot perceive nor understand this great mystery that will always remain mystery to our human understanding. Beloved, I am trying to understand Your words of 6th July to comprehend such a calling that is beyond my capacity to fulfil, but with You and through You I will succeed, and with the help of Your Holy Mother, I will overcome all the obstacles and weaknesses I inherited and collected during my life. You prepare me and make me aware through the Healing Masses of the Generations, the spiritual, physical, emotional, that I carry within me in lesser or greater proportions than others - but which You took upon Yourself to redeem through Your passion and death, and now to be claimed by all in so far as we respond through the graces You make available to us in our daily lives.

11ᵗʰ July 1995
Before The Blessed Sacrament:
Thank You Beloved for visiting my home again yesterday to spend the day with us in the Blessed Sacrament. Thank You Beloved that today's march went off peacefully. Tomorrow is the twelfth. Truly as You said, the cease-fire rests on a pinhead but I know You will listen to the cries of Your little ones - for peace to be maintained in the North. Oh Beloved, we do not deserve it. There is so much hatred and resentment still in our hearts, but You have always shown such mercy to us. You will listen to our feeble cries again. Mary, intercede for Your children on this island. 'They do not know what they are doing.'

We have been and would be but for Your grace. Help us all dearest One during these coming days.

Oh how the people of Bosnia suffer and so much prayer in Medjugorje.

13ᵗʰ July 1995
Before The Blessed Sacrament:
Beloved, thank You for listening to the prayers of Your little one. The 12th past without too much violence. The cease-fire is still preserved, but as You reminded us - 'it still rests on a pinhead.'

Here I am dear, dear Lord. My heart is listening.

14ᵗʰ July 1995
Before The Blessed Sacrament:
"Beloved child, rest in Me this day, rest with Me. I need you My little one. Many ask much of you. I will take care of all. Do I not know the needs of those you carry in your heart.

Much greater needs I ask of you now My child. You carry a reflection of My burden for Bosnia. Truly child, My Mother weeps also to see this land torn apart by hatred. Child, do not worry. Many have the same question in their hearts. Your mission today is to pray for peace in the hearts of all in this land, so dear to the Heart of My Holy Mother. Later in the day I will direct you about this evening. All will work out according to My plan. Rest My little one. I will touch the hearts of all you carry in your heart. What greater blessing can I offer them My little one."

Beloved, thank You. With Your holy help I will try and give You this day. Mary Immaculate, enclose me in Your Heart. I relate my tears to Yours oh Holy Mother.

15ᵗʰ July 1995   - Eve of Feast of Our Lady of Mt. Carmel
Before The Blessed Sacrament
Holy Mother, I await a reply for guidance about the week-end.

Do You call me to this vigil here tonight, spend tomorrow as usual, or go to Knock? Mary, You know I only want to do His Will and I can never make up my mind. I do feel an urgent plea to pray for Bosnia. All the anger of the past that is below the surface arises within me. It cannot be right and yet is it part of the evil in the world today.

Mary, no wonder You weep. No wonder You suffer to see the sufferings of Your Son by man's inhumanity to man and yet we are all to blame. We are all part of the greed of mankind for power and possessions in today's world. Oh Mary, listen to the cries of our hearts for peace and reconciliation within ourselves, families, communities, our own country, Bosnia and throughout the world. Mary, be our strength and companion in the dark days ahead.

Keep us ever hopeful and to look beyond all the happenings not to our liking in the days ahead - knowing that Jesus Your Son is in control, will have the victory over evil to bring good out of all to those who love Him. Mary, Queen of Hope, pray for the world.

"Come back later My child and I will tell you My plan for this week-end."

Later
Before The Blessed Sacrament:
"Yes child, I call you to spend as much time as possible this day in prayer. Child, I will help you to concentrate and quieten the mind. I have much for you to write. Relax now. Let Me rest in you and I will speak to your heart.

My child, it is not by way of a dark overgrown path. This is not My plan. Child, the evil one will try to keep you in darkness. I am your light. Keep turned towards the light - the light of the Spirit."

16ᵗʰ July 1995   - Feast of Our Lady of Mt. Carmel
Before The Blessed Sacrament:
Immaculate Heart of Mary, enclose me in Your Heart.

Mary, lead and guide me along the path of righteousness this day and help me to fulfil His need of me.

Mary:
"My child, it is coming near your time to leave. I cannot let you go without a few words on this day, My feast-day. It pleases My Heart to see so many in this land remember. Yes child, My Heart overflows with gratitude to be remembered. Child, you will come to Me later - at home or here. I will speak to your heart again. Child, I will help you to pray. It mustn't be forced. Prayer is meant to be an intimate communication or conversation with My Son and Me. Remember always, I am your loving, holy Mother, always concerned for the plans of My Son for you. I know the need of My Son, the plans of My Son for you now and forever.

Turn to Me. I am ever with you, waiting to answer every cry for help. Trust Me My little one. I expect you later. May the blessings of My Son, the Holy Trinity be with you now, and all you carry in your heart. Give all to Us. Trust Us to fulfil your deepest desires for each and everyone."

18ᵗʰ July 1995: *Are we not all being asked now, and given this same opportunity, to pray and live the prayer You gave another :*

"Go out to the nations and teach them to pray to the Father this prayer :

Father all Merciful,
let those who hear and hear again
yet never understand,
hear Your Voice this time
and understand that it is You
the Holy of Holies;
open the eyes of those who see and see,
yet never perceive,
to see with their eyes this time
Your Holy Face and Your Glory.
Place Your Finger on their heart
so that their heart may open
and understand Your Faithfulness,
I pray and ask You all these things,
Righteous Father,
so that all the nations
be converted and be healed
through the Wounds of Your Beloved Son,
Jesus Christ; Amen."   Message of 6th July 1990.

God Our Father, we press our open wounds to the precious wounds of Jesus Your Son, that Your Will and ours be one.

Through these shared wounds may we be healed and bring Your healing love to others, that all may be enriched in the fullness of love, through Jesus, the Divine Humanity.

18ᵗʰ July 1995: *My Beloved, thank You for the beautiful insight You gave me at the Consecration at the Mass this morning. How I wish to retain such moments for myself and others. Oh so selfish of me, but Beloved You understand. So many times of late I am so forgetful and indifferent to these precious moments - that I try*

242

to remember them to make my daily Eucharist more meaningful and reverent for Your sake, and for others. I do so want the daily Eucharist to be the centre and ultimate of my prayer each day where I will fulfil Your need of me, and I will receive the strength and nourishment to take that step nearer to You each day that I am able to fulfil this commitment. I desire above all else to live the remainder of my days like the priests who received the grace to persevere to the end.

Oh Beloved, each day now the media highlight some weakness or another in a member of the priesthood. Truly our Church, all churches are under attack, but we must see it as the best purification of all Your struggling people that makes way for the new renewed Church of the future.

And Beloved, if the darkness within ourselves were to be revealed - would it? should not the words be repeated to each of us - 'who is without sin throw the first stone'. Beloved, merciful Father, You speak this prayer. Was it ever more necessary and important than in these times?

Merciful Father, only You can solve the war in Bosnia and put an end to the slaughter. Mary, Queen of Peace and Mother of Consolation and Reconciliation, pray for the world.

18th July 1995:   "Oh My child, My little child, My Heart bleeds to see man's inhumanity to man. Continue to pray. Continue to gather all My little ones to pray - if possible before The Blessed Sacrament. Here My Heart is comforted. Here I find refuge in the hearts of My little ones - those who are prepared to sacrifice time when possible to sit with Me. I know many do not see this as the answer, but I assure you My little one - here I hear the cries of My little ones - their cries pierce My Heart to touch other hearts. Here I wait for My chosen ones, always waiting to strengthen and sustain them against the snares of evil. Do I not know of the battle waged against them. Was I not tempted also. The continuous intimate prayer and relationship with My Father sustained Me. Did I not suffer all your sufferings My own dear chosen ones, chosen by Me to sustain My little lambs.

Thank you for answering My call My little one. Come - pray, pray child. My Holy Mother will be your teacher and the Holy Spirit will lead and guide you."

Oh Holy Spirit - Spirit of truth and holiness, invade my heart with Your light.

19ᵗʰ July 1995
Before The Blessed Sacrament:
Jesus and Mary, You are always on the side of the oppressed. Listen to the cries of our hearts for the people of Bosnia.

"Child, as I explained to you on a previous occasion in another country (in El Salvador) all are My children. I desire the hearts of all. But always it is the little ones who suffer in the hands of the oppressors. My child, give Me your burden. I will have the victory over the evil that prevails over this country. Man is helpless. Let the nations call on Me for the solution to their problems. Otherwise their solutions are built on straw."

20ᵗʰ July 1995
Before The Blessed Sacrament:
My Beloved, my heart bleeds with Yours to see the atrocities that are taking place in Bosnia.

"Do not worry My little one. I have all under My control. My time will come. Pray little one, pray."

My Beloved, as I listened to the debate last night on TV about the present position in our Church, I realise how easy for me to be led astray. Oh how I need the Holy Spirit to lead and guide me into the truth and trust in the faithfulness of Your promises.

21ˢᵗ July 1995
Before The Blessed Sacrament:
"Yes My little one, I do ask you to write. Do I not gather you together here before My Eucharistic Presence each Friday night to take upon Myself your cares, your problems, your anxieties - to refresh you for the coming week and the days ahead. Yes My little ones, the evil one will try and cause differences wherever and

whenever he will get a foothold. He will attempt this between yourselves, between each one's own family and outside. Be prepared little ones, be prepared. You are My special chosen ones to bring the gift of peace and reconciliation to Glencree. More and more you will be aware of this in the days ahead. Many groups, many sections will find this peace when they visit this chosen haven and know it to be a place of peace and reconciliation. Members of My Church, who are now confused and be more so in the future, will come to Me and My Holy Mother to find peace of mind at this place made holy by your concentrated efforts and prayers. Children, be prepared for attacks of all sorts. But remember, I am a God, always faithful to My promises.

I promise you My dear little ones that I will not allow the evil one overcome you. Trust in Me My dear, dear children. All I spoke to T... this day will come about. Trust Me. I will lift you above and beyond what others may suffer in the dark days ahead."

22ⁿᵈ July 1995
Feast of St. Mary Magdalene:

Oh the emptiness that fills my heart.
The pain of loving
Love unfulfilled.
You seek me, You wait for me
For my response
My only response - my emptiness.

Oh how I need a change of heart
A heart of flesh not stone
Today we celebrate the heart of one
Once dead in sin
Sin repented when she received Your touch
How she suffered because You allowed it thus
And healing was complete.

Though she sinned much You forgave.
The warmth of her response wiped the scars away
Only love remained.
Repentance must be soaked in love

To wipe away the tears
And leave no scars.
The circle is then complete.
No breaks, no missing links
To break the bond of true love.

St. Mary Magdalene, remember us to-day
You rest now with Him at peace in love.

22ⁿᵈ July 1995 - Feast of St. Mary Magdalene
Before The Blessed Sacrament:
"Child, why do you think I share My secrets with you. It is My child, because you have found favour with Me. I look into your heart. There is much there you cannot express. Your stammer curtailed you in the past. Your stammer curtails you now. All is well My little one. Come often that I might speak to your heart. Thank you child. Thank you for answering My call this night."

23ʳᵈ July 1995: *Beloved., You know that it is my desire to answer Your call more often, but I am curtailed. I would give thanks for as it is said, 'absence makes the heart grow fonder'.*

Sometimes I wonder is it an escape from duty, from love of my neighbour. Yet I know You wait - always waiting to welcome the visitor, no matter how we feel - whether we have anything to give or not - but always we carry within us the burden of our weaknesses to offer You. Perhaps this is the greatest gift of all. It is all of ourselves we have to offer.

Before The Blessed Sacrament:
More and more I am realising the blessings I received because of my speech impediment, down the years. Surely it put a brake on my words of anger many times, to allow peace to reign. And truly the blessings outweighed the pain and sufferings it caused me.

25ᵗʰ July 1995 - Feast of St. James
Before The Blessed Sacrament:
"My child, My need is so great this day. Everywhere the evil one rises up against My little ones. Yes the battle is raging now. And

how he disturbs My very little ones. Keep praying for the youth, young people everywhere. The draw of evil is upon them.

Wars are a result of evil. Evil draws more evil. Yes child, what you see and hear is part of a raging battle upon the earth. But child, remember to look beyond. My time will come. My victory will overcome. Keep your mind, heart and spirit fixed on Me."

27ᵗʰ July 1995
Before The Blessed Sacrament:
Beloved, may I never lose the wonderment of Your goodness. Too often I am negative. Too often we allow ourselves to be oppressed by the state of the world. The media never allows us rest. Help me to depend less and less on the media for news, discussions etc. - only sufficient to increase my prayer for others in need.

28ᵗʰ July 1995
Before The Blessed Sacrament:
'Lord Jesus, come to us today' (from morning prayer)

> " I have come, I have come.
> I am here, I am here."

"Yes child, I need your attention, your co-operation this day. I have much on My Heart. I wish you to write. You pray the rosary now. Prepare. My Holy Mother prays it with you."

Mary, we have much on our hearts. Firstly we need Your guidance about tonight and I am wondering about going to Achill on my own for the week-end.

"Children, you will come together as usual at Glencree tonight. I will answer many questions for you there. Yes child, I will take care of you on this trip. On your own it will be more of a retreat. There We will speak to your heart. Do not be fearful. We will arrange all."

"About the writings child, do not worry. All will be well. We told you that there will be many set-backs. Any writings for the Church on the Eucharist are much attacked by the evil one. It is Our problem. Do not worry. Let Sr. Kathleen be at peace."

29ᵗʰ July 1995

<u>**On the train:**</u>

Thank You Jesus and Mary. I am on my way. All is perfect because of Your goodness and love. I pray that my heart will be open and my spirit responsive to Your Holy Will.

(At the House of Prayer in Achill)
Before The Blessed Sacrament:

Here I am dearest Jesus and Mary, with my accommodation secured and trip arranged direct to Knock on Monday. Only You dearest Ones could have arranged all in Your perfect way. How faithful You are to Your promises.

We have been told that Christina is quite ill and suffering much and in the state of great abandonment - perhaps for our sinfulness and the graces You have prepared for us during these days. Help us in our own little way to help other souls in need and in response for Your continual goodness to us.

Truly Lord, You are present in the Blessed Sacrament and in the beauty of Your creation in nature outside, to prepare us for the coming of Your Holy Spirit in our hearts. How our Holy Mother chooses places of great natural beauty to reveal Herself to Her little ones. May we allow Her capture and possess our hearts during these days in this holy place, made holy by the presence of many and much prayer and the deep suffering of Christina.

How blessed we are. We thank You for Your loving kindness to us now and always. Thank You oh The Two Hearts of Love.

"Oh child, I have seen that all is well for you on this weekend. It will give you the confidence that you need to be more independent of others and to depend on Us - to strengthen your faith, to increase your hope, to share with others. See the way We gather Our little ones to be in the right places at the right times, to confirm that there is no such thing as coincidences in Our plans! Open hearts are all that We ask and are needed in the spiritual walk with Us."

30th July 1995 - At the House of Prayer

Before The Blessed Sacrament:

Beloved, truly You have shown me Your love this week-end. You have made it truly special and very peaceful. I remember I have been cut off from the media. How peaceful our lives could be without the distractions of horrid accounts of human degradation. Being in the atmosphere where Your Eucharistic Presence is exposed. daily, I realise that if only our hearts and minds were centred on You instead of being under the influence of TV and daily newspapers, now part of the necessary furniture in most homes now. We hope and pray that other channels will not be added to our present overloaded channels on TV to corrupt further our little ones. Beloved., unless we pray more, unless we can turn the tide of evil in our midst, You will not be able to stave off the purge that will be necessary to change the chain of events that are destroying our people, particularly our children. Lord, as we listen to the reading of the day, can we not help to stave off the chastisement that is our due. Oh Beloved, I have surely seen and met with many who are an example to me - who truly make me feel so inadequate and I think that because of the gift You give me that I am better in Your eyes than they are. Beloved, You know all and. see all, and the last gift that came my way makes me feel so unworthy and highlights my weaknesses. My Beloved, I realise the wonderful gift You have left me, beyond the diagnosis of the doctors - my eyesight. When I look around. at the beauty of nature around me, I thank You for this opportunity to have been able to visit and see again. Perhaps I may come again, if it be Your Holy Will.

Mary, my Holy Mother, You have truly made this little holiday more memorable and I look forward. to meeting Jesus and. Yourself again tomorrow at Knock. Bless all my care at home. I wish they were here also. Perhaps one day You will arrange such a holiday for them.

Bless everybody I encountered on this trip. We have all been blessed by Christine's sufferings. May her health be restored to continue Your work - we pray.

1ˢᵗ August 1995
Before The Blessed Sacrament:
Beloved, another feast-day of blessings at Knock yesterday. Mary, my Holy Mother, You certainly took care of me during the past days. All my needs were fulfilled. Mary, bless all I encountered on this trip. Truly all radiated the light of the Spirit. Mary, there is still hope for our country - to see the crowds at Knock yesterday and specially all the priests who attended. We can be proud of our priests and may the conference for priests held each year in All Hallows during the month of August, bring very many blessings on the Church in our country and the world.

Later :
"My child, I call you back. I do not overburden you with My sufferings but, I ask of you to write of My pain in these times - this day and everyday. My Church is falling apart. My people are not listening. Yes child, I know many do, but you meet and associate and go places where My little ones gather. Outside child, in your neighbourhood, city, country, My Heart breaks to see the state of the hearts of My people. See how few visit Me here. See, the newspapers this day. Listen to the news. See My torment, see My suffering. Yes child, My Mother sees and weeps. Yes child, children, She weeps tears of blood to see the state of men's souls.

Child, I do not want you to hold in your heart any confusion nor division. I need an open heart, freed from the influences of all the evil forces that seek to confuse and divide all My little ones. No one from the more learned and influential to the lowliest escapes the snares of evil now. But, I do not want to see you fearful. Continue to trust in Me - in Us. Were Our plans not apparent, Our care of you not apparent moment by moment throughout the past days? Yes child, continue to see the perfection of Our Love, and Holy Will in all the circumstances of your life now. Child, you will be tested, tested. I am not telling you this to frighten you but to prepare you.

Yes child, I give you these words to write because of the love I hold in My Heart. You are now one with Us, united to Us in your daily consecration. Yes child, because I choose you to write for My Church in the days ahead, you will suffer much, be tormented by evil, but My Holy Mother will be with you at all times to protect you. I tell you this to give you confidence and hope. Turn to Us in all your difficulties. Look to Us in all your endeavours. We will not fail you."

Beloved, I know now that this has to be all Your work. I have nothing of myself to offer You to undertake anything You ask of me. I will need Your grace to surrender all to You, to make this work possible. (I see the old discarded watering can in the shed again). Nothing is impossible to You dearest One.

3ʳᵈ August 1995
<u>Before The Blessed Sacrament:</u>
Thank You for this day. You were all giving. I was all taking. Oh Beloved, help me to rest in You, to let You rest in me.

Bless the little boy who came here this day for healing of his cancer condition. You alone are the healer. Comfort his parents and sisters.

(After another writing to my Beloved)
"Don't worry My little one. You are trying and that is sufficient. Rest now. Let Me rest in you. Keep reminding yourself 'All is well, all will be well'".

4ᵗʰ August 1995   -   First Friday
<u>Before The Blessed Sacrament:</u>
Beloved, today war breaks out between Croatia and Bosnian Serbs, and as always it is the little ones suffer, like You.

Oh Beloved, Is this the beginning of something much greater, much, much greater that You have been warning us about - but because of the writings You have given me recently, I have much hope in my heart.

My Beloved, I pray that I may fulfil Your need of me today and everyday and that the warring hearts of many in our land, including my own, will be touched by You to restore peace, the peace that has come about through You alone, in response to prayers.

6ᵗʰ August 1995 - Feast of The Transfiguration
Before The Blessed Sacrament:
Beloved, may I realise that I am on Mount Tabor also when I am in Your Eucharistic Presence.

Oh Beloved, I do not want to be in the state that I am. Total irreverence, indifferent - lack of reverence.

Beloved, how I must hurt You, pain You, when I am like this. But, this is all I have to offer You now. I know it would be easier for me if I could feel the light and majesty of Your Presence - so Beloved, I take this to be a penance that I can offer to You.

I have just been given this beautiful thought 'Faith is vision in darkness'. If that is what I am experiencing - I give praise and thanks to You for my present suffering - but at the same time I realise that I need so much spiritual healing that I would despair of myself and I know that this would wound You infinitely more.

Beloved, it pains me at times to see and know Your infinite mercy and never doubt Your Love. Beloved, on this very special feast-day of Your Transfiguration I trust in You to change all that displeases You in Your time, in Your way, if I allow You.

Oh Beloved, open my heart to Your Holy Spirit and the Immaculate Heart of Your Most Holy Mother, to allow You make a home of peace in silence in my soul.

7ᵗʰ August 1995 - (Monday)
After The Eucharist:
Oh Mary Queen of Peace, let's pray for the country specially chosen by You to speak to Your children for these times :

Oh Bosnia, oh Bosnia
Do you not hear; do you not heed
The pleas of your Mother
Calling on you to make peace in your land
With prayer in your hearts
And praise on your lips.

People travel from near and far away places
To receive healing and peace where your Mother appears.
Pray for your leaders for a change of heart.

Think of the little one, think of their sufferings
Suffering with Him.
God created enough for all
But man in his greed has never enough
And make war the answer.

"Beloved child, it is only in the darkness of faith I can touch and heal the soul. Yes child, you will experience the darkness of the days ahead. It will be a testing of faith but you must remember and share with others, the hope I have placed in your heart in the writings. Be prepared, be aware. Continue to look beyond always. Am I not in control. Have I not the victory? Never doubt the words and instructions I give you, no matter how others will judge them. Yes child, later I will give you a further writing as I promised on 11th May last. Remember I do not give you instructions in advance. I have My plans made. I will let them be known to you later. Thank you My little one. I will lead you into silence again. Offer your sufferings for My priests who are being led astray. Oh My poor priests. Offer all for them. Keep them ever in your heart, especially those I give you and those most in need of My mercy. Be at peace now My little one."

10ᵗʰ August 1995
Before The Blessed Sacrament:
"My child, My dear child, I have been waiting for you. I have much on My Heart to share with you.

You will hear much, to make confusion, to bring confusion in the days ahead. Try My little one not to become involved. I am with you always to direct you and guide you. I will not allow the evil one lead you astray. That is not to say that you will not suffer the darkness in My Church, in My people in the days ahead. Already the spirit of division and confusion are rampant everywhere. Child, about the writing of 11/5 last. Do not move for the present. Already there is confusion within the parties. I use all to bring My plans to fruition. Remember the writing specially chosen by Sr. Kathleen. Take heed of this. It is important for you My little one. Little by little Our little one, We will lead you back to the silence you seek. Try and keep sitting at Our feet in the Eucharistic Presence. This child is your ministry. Here you will be safe. Yes child, here the evil one cannot take over. I do not say you cannot be tempted as I said before - he will try, but he is powerless.

Dear child, I know the difficulties in your own family. I see all, and the comfort you bring to others. Many are led to Eucharistic Adoration through your faithfulness and example. Never forget this. I will show you a way to exclude the non-essentials without hurting anyone. I ask you My little one to cut down on outside activities. Remember I want you free and fit to carry out My needs of you."

Holy Spirit, Spirit of Truth and Holiness, invade my heart with Your light.

"Child, remember that there are times when only the flimsiest of veils separate the manifestations of the Holy Spirit and evil spirits. Child, be careful. Call on Us whenever you are in difficulties. Pray for the gift of discernment daily at the Holy Eucharist. We answer all prayer from the heart."

Beloved, I keep forgetting all You tell me. How can I remember?

"Child, I see into your heart. I cover your desires and your needs."

Beloved, You know the needs of my family better than I do. Please help them, teach them to know Your Love. I give them to You and Your Holy Mother to protect and care for them. Beloved, forgive me for always thinking of myself and my needs. Help me to keep my mind, heart and spirit focused on You here in Your Eucharistic presence.

12th August 1995
Before The Blessed Sacrament:
"Now child, listen carefully. You see now why I ask more Eucharistic Adoration from you. You will form this Movement in your home. I place the souls of all your family and extended family in your heart this day. Child, I stand by you, give you the strength to intercede now for the souls of your family."

Later
Before The Eucharistic Presence:
Beloved, thank You for this day - and the wonder of Your ways. I was nonplussed at first at Your word. Now I thank You for the

peace. I depend on You now Jesus and Mary to lead and guide me every step of the way in the 'Magnificat Meal Movement International.' What next Beloved?

I forgot to thank You both for the extraordinary night last night - the Healing Mass of the Generations at Glencree. Truly the word received (T...) is already being seen to happen. May we continue to grow in peace and unity together. God bless all Your holy priests and make them holier.

13ᵗʰ August 1995
Before The Blessed Sacrament:
Beloved, I bring before You all You place on my heart this day. Now Beloved I realise why You gave me the writing on how good and kind You are to me. Always You tell me of impending trouble. How can I thank You? - never.

You know all my miseries and failures and yet You continue to give me writings. How patient and tolerant You are with me.

Beloved, I give You all now. Lead and direct me through Your Holy Mother. May my consecration to Her Immaculate Heart on the feast-day of the Assumption come from a sincere and loving heart.

Mary, help me to fulfil His need of me and carry out His Holy Will in my daily living.

15ᵗʰ August 1995
Feast of The Assumption:
Happy and Holy feast-day dear Mother. May we help to wipe a tear from Your Immaculate Heart this day by our renewed consecration. May our Eucharist bring a renewed commitment of love to the Two Hearts of Love in our hearts, in the hearts of all Your children, on the feast of Your Assumption into Heaven.

Before The Blessed Sacrament:
Mother of the Apostles, Co-Redemptrix, Mediatrix of all graces, Advocate.

Mary, my mind, my spirit cannot comprehend the significance of this day. Look into my heart, read my desires, read my needs.

255

You alone can guide and lead me to bring to fruition the needs for me of the Two Hearts of Love.

16th August 1995
After The Eucharist:
Beloved, You speak the same words to me now as You spoke to Martha. Mary, teach me how to sit at His feet like Mary Magdalene when He needs me.

Mary, about the beads - what should I do? But first Mary - should I have hurried to make Mass again last night? I was on edge, I couldn't rest. Please help me in my discernment. I give myself to You. I am all Yours now. Help me.

Mary :
"Yes child, be at peace about last night. You were overwrought and the book later didn't help. Child of My Immaculate Heart, keep the beads. Use them to pray with the sick. It will bring comfort to each one in their sickness. Yes child - accept them as a gift from Me to you through My precious child, Kathleen. There is a close bond between you now because of the writings. Her heart was open to receive. So it will be with all who read them with open hearts, specially My own. Child, be at ease. Rest more. I take care of you."

Before The Blessed Sacrament:
Beloved, accompany Sr. K. on her long journey back to the missions. May we learn from her and follow her example in her faith, hope and love of the Holy Eucharist.

17th August 1995
Before The Blessed Sacrament:
"Yes child, I did not give you a spirit of timidity but of power. You speak in My power against the evil of the Toronto Blessing. You will cut no corners. I will speak through you My little one. I will protect you against the dangers of speaking out. Look to Me child and My Holy Mother. She has Her mantle around you, that will guard you.

Child, I will send others to you who are being influenced by this so called blessing. Your protection is My Eucharistic Presence. Remember this each day. Here you will receive writings to counteract this force in My elect. Do not be afraid Our little one. We have been preparing you for these times. Yes child, I will give you a writing for the Conference of Priests in All Hallows, to be prepared to be warned of the dangers for themselves, for My Church. Pray much My little one. Do not let anyone curtail you, frighten you. It is My work. You are surrounded by My angels - to overcome. Rest now My little one. Prepare for the coming rosary."

18ᵗʰ August 1995
Before The Eucharistic Presence:
"Child, dear child, no pressures, no anxiety. I will supply all that is needed. Rest in peace now. Do not let the evil one disturb your peace. All is well. All will be well. I am in control."

About this evening Beloved, where will we have our meeting?

"In your home My little one.   I will cover all."

19th August 1995   - Feast of St. Eudes.
Before The Blessed Sacrament:
Beloved, I write through my tears. I write with Your tears and the tears of Your Holy Mother, because of the evil that is penetrating the Holy Church. Beloved, You know my weaknesses. And yet I believe and know that You must be leading and carrying me these days wherever I go and those to whom I am led. Each day I learn something new about this movement that is entering all the churches - the Toronto Blessing - so powerful and yet so evil. Oh Mary my Holy Mother, take me over this day and everyday. Protect me. Help me. Do not let me fail Him, my Beloved, in anything He asks of me. The battle has begun, is now waging.

"My child, you will hear of many more priests who have been taken in by this movement. Do not worry. I will guide and protect you. Fear not, you are My little instrument. I will send many to support you in this great battle against evil forces."

Later
Before The Blessed Sacrament:
Beloved - back again to my haven of peace. Beloved, I have

nothing to offer You but the burden of my weaknesses and my very weak efforts at prayer. Mary, embellish all, before offering to Jesus.

"Child, be prepared. I will send you forth to speak in My Name. My angels will accompany you. You will speak in My Name. Do not be afraid. I will put My words in your mouth.

I am preparing Glencree for the many who will come to find peace and reconciliation, who have been taken in by this false blessing."

22ⁿᵈ August 1995 - Feast of the Queenship of Mary
Before The Blessed Sacrament:
Oh Mary, thank You. This day I learn that the words received on the 17th and 18th of the month for All Hallows were lost so the book was not delivered as requested on 18th. Today I pray that all will be delivered. Oh Mary, thank You for bringing into the light for us the wiles and snares of evil forces. Mary, thank You for Your protection and care. Mary, I hope to come back later. I join with all Your little ones at Knock this day. May our country be blessed by the prayers of all, to bring about further peace in the North.

Mary:
"My child, My little one, I have heard your hearts desire. Child, I love you, I protect you. Today is the favoured day for these papers to arrive at All Hallows, through the priest who can vouch for their authenticity.

Now child, We take over. You have done well. You have carried out the instructions of My Son. He will speak to the hearts of those concerned. Much prayer is needed in your land to stave off the evil forces bent on destroying the cease-fire.

Yes child, to be forewarned is to be forearmed. That is why I need My priests to be aware of the danger before it takes hold in this land. Here in All Hallows where My priests gather this month, I want your writing of 17th August, this and the booklet to be shared. Through this booklet of Debra's, they will be prepared for this evil before it spreads. It is insidious and evil - made attractive for all who seek Me through My Holy Spirit.

Yes child, there is much at stake. I take care of your family. Let them commence the rosary. The family rosary will bring the peace and settlement so dear to their hearts. Child, do not fear."

Beloved, thank You. Without Your strength I couldn't have survived this day. Beloved, I thank You for those You send to help to carry out Your need of me.

Bless our meeting this night. Thank You for one another. Mary, Queen of Peace and Mother of Reconciliation, pray for us.

"Yes child, all will be well."
Your prayers are being answered."

24ᵗʰ August 1995 - Feast of St. Bartholomew
Before The Blessed Sacrament:
Beloved, thank You. All went according to Your plan. I ask a special blessing on J... this morning. Cover him with Your Precious Blood at this important meeting. May it be the beginning of conversion for many. Much is at stake. Thank You Jesus and Mary.

'Lord hold him in the palm of Your hand.'

Later :
"Child, My precious child, listen to My Heart beating with love, as I await My little ones this night. How I look forward to this night of love - the hour you accompany Me in Gethsemane.

My Holy Mother prepares you in the Holy Rosary. How united We are in the presence of My Angels and Saints who are in adoration now in your midst.

Children of My Heart, My Eucharistic Heart, I pour out My Love on each one this night and always - My army of Adorers everywhere. I saw this hour with you in the garden of Gethsemane. It gave Me such joy in the midst of all My sufferings, to see My faithful followers in the years and centuries ahead.

Children, dear children, I call on all, I plead with all for your perseverance in the days ahead, dark days, but remember, beyond the clouds, the silver linings. Keep hope always in your hearts. My children, My dear precious children, My Heart, Our Hearts, leap with joy to welcome you as you enter Our Presence - and all others who spend time with Us.

Thus I speak - a little reminder to encourage and fortify you to persevere. Unite with all My little ones, My army of Eucharistic Adorers in this land and throughout the world, wherever you are."

25ᵗʰ August 1995
Before The Blessed Sacrament:
Beloved, we desire to desire all You desire for us. May this day bring more joy to the Two Hearts of Love than yesterday, so that each day that passes may bring to each one, that step nearer to You and into eternity.

26ᵗʰ August 1995 - After the Eucharist
Before The Blessed Sacrament:
Beloved, I prayed that You would set my heart on fire with the Holy Spirit. Beloved, I do not understand, the emotions that are within me since I received the words about the Toronto Blessing. Is it my anger, Your anger - the evil one taking over to make me so dogmatic. Beloved, I ask for Your discernment this day. I know You will not fail and Mary will not cease to take care of me always.

"Oh child, dear child, you mustn't worry. Many will speak out against you. The word that was given you by another many years ago will come to pass. Anyone who speaks out as you will, for My sake, will suffer much rejection and abuse. Spend much time with Me, here in My Eucharistic Presence. I send you many to support you in prayer. Fear not My little one. I will guide and lead you to those I choose. Pray for the misguided amongst My very own. These cause Me the most pain. Bless you, bless you. You have Our blessings - the fire of the Spirit in this walk with Us."

Ps. 91/92. Our Protector.

PSALM 91 - GOD OUR PROTECTOR

Whoever goes to the LORD for safety,
whoever remains under the protection of
the Almighty,
can say to him,
"You are my defender and protector.
You are my God; in you I trust."
He will keep you safe from all hidden
dangers
and from all deadly diseases.
He will cover you with his wings;
you will be safe in his care;
his faithfulness will protect and defend you.
You need not fear any dangers at night
or sudden attacks during the day
or the plagues that strike in the dark
or the evils that kill in daylight.
A thousand may fall dead beside you,
ten thousand all round you,
but you will not be harmed.
You will look and see
how the wicked are punished.

You have made the Lord your defender,
the Most High your protector,
and so no disaster will strike you,
no violence will come near your home.
God will put his angels in charge of you
to protect you wherever you go.
They will hold you up with their hands,
to keep you from hurting your feet on the
stones.
You will trample down lions and snakes,
fierce lions and poisonous snakes.

God says, "I will save those who love me
and will protect those who know me as
LORD.
When they call to me, I will answer them;
When they are in trouble, I will be with
them.
I will rescue them and honour them.
I will reward them with long life;
I will save them."

PSALM 92 - A SONG OF PRAISE

How good it is to give thanks to you,
LORD,
To sing in your honour, O Most High God,
To proclaim your constant love every
morning
and your faithfulness every night,
with the music of stringed instruments
and with melody on the harp.
Your mighty deeds, O Lord, make me
glad;
because of what you have done, I sing for
joy.

How great are your actions, Lord!
How deep are your thoughts!
There is something a fool cannot know;
a stupid man cannot understand:
the wicked may grow like weeds,
those who do wrong may prosper;
yet they will be totally destroyed,
because you, Lord, are supreme for ever.
We know that your enemies will die,
and all the wicked will be defeated.
You have made me as strong as a wild
ox;
you have blessed me with happiness.
I have seen the defeat of my enemies
and heard the cries of the wicked.

The righteous will flourish like palm-trees;
they will grow like the cedars of Lebanon.
They are like trees planted in the house
of the Lord,
that flourish in the Temple of our God,
that still bear fruit in old age
and are always green and strong.
This shows that the LORD is just,
that there is no wrong in my protector.

"This is My work, My little one. I use the very little for these dangerous missions."

29ᵗʰ August 1995   -   Beheading of John the Baptist
Before The Blessed Sacrament:
The first Martyr for You Beloved. May he be an example to us for the present times. He received the Spirit through Your Presence in the womb of Mary at the Visitation.

Mary :
"My child, take care, take care. I care for your physical and spiritual welfare. You have much on your mind. Give all to Me, My precious child. Rest your little mind. Pray in your heart through My Immaculate Heart. I will embellish all before offering to My Son.

Much will be answered at tomorrow night's meeting. Come all united in love, and Our peace will prevail. It pleases Us to see you all at oneness in one another. Yes child, the evil one will try and divide those specially chosen to promote unity and reconciliation. Be loving and tolerant of one another. We come, We bring you together to unite you in love, to listen to the needs of each one and to bring peace to the hearts of all."

30ᵗʰ August 1995
Before The Blessed Sacrament:
Abba Father, here I am. Speak Lord, Your servant is listening.

"Yes child, you do not have to worry. I guide you now every step of the way during these days. I do not want you to strain your mind about what you should do or not do. I will choose the people to whom you will send the booklet and your instructions. This is My work, My little one. I use the very little for these dangerous missions. The battle is raging now between good and evil. The wars are an indication. The evil spirits are parading around seeking to devour My own, My little ones. Everyone is in danger of being caught in this net - My Church, My elect, My peoples of all nations. **Child, you have no conception yet of the extent of your writing mission.** My Mother, My angels will protect you - and above all The Eucharist and Eucharistic Adoration. Do not worry child, The Eucharist will be made available in times of need.

Child, you will receive hassle. Learn to accept all, relate all to Our sufferings in the present climate in the world. We will teach you silence in prayer, in living. You worry about many things and people now. Give all to Us and We will relieve you, free you of these anxieties, to be open for the writings We are about to ask of you. We do not want this to be a burden on you. The contents are Our responsibilities. You are too small to carry them yourself."

31ˢᵗ August 1995:
Before The Blessed Sacrament:
(in answer to request of 29/8/'95)
"Yes child, We must draw the people together first. People nowadays have got used to so much luxury and human comforts that they are not prepared for much hardship. Yes child, I will also prepare the way for the central heating as offered and suggested by another. (D.) He does it out of the goodness of his heart. Accept his offer as coming from Us."

"Child, do not let the requests of so many worry you. We will answer in Our own time, at Our own pace. Bring all before Us here in The Eucharistic Presence."

Mary, I know You are like Jesus. You will ask Him for a word of direction for ... He is appealing to Your Heart to touch the Heart of Your Son for an answer.

1ˢᵗ September 1995
Before The Blessed Sacrament:
"Yes child, I wait for you. My child, I thank you for this home, this house. I have made it My own. Now I gather all My little broken ones to find comfort and a place of rest here in My Eucharistic Presence. Yes child, your commitment, your perseverance over the years is being rewarded. Child, it is true, I hold you in the palm of My Hand. Have no fear, I am with you in the new found mission I place upon your little shoulders and I hide from you all the dangers. Take My word My little one. He will try all areas. The evil one will try in every possible way to destroy your peace, My peace within you. Think back dear child to the day I made you aware of the shield I placed around you. Believe Me My child, he will try and penetrate this shield, but trust Me, trust Me My child always.

You are not aware now, nor will I allow you see the many attempts and areas he will try to destroy. Keep hope in your heart. Today you celebrate the day specially dedicated to My Sacred Heart. Here in My Eucharistic Presence I pour out My blessings on all, who remember.

Child, I will use you to counteract the other false blessing that is bent on destroying My blessing. It is the most evil force ever to destroy My Eucharistic Blessing. Many in this land have answered My call for Eucharistic Adoration. This is the greatest thorn to his success in all he seeks to conquer.

My child, I will take care Myself of The Eucharist in your home. I will bring, continue to fulfil My plan for your home. You will see. You will see. Little one rest in My Heart, My Eucharistic Heart this day. Prepare for the fulfilment of Our oneness in the Eucharist later. My child, build your life, your living on the daily Eucharist. Here you will draw My own chosen ones by your faithfulness. Do not worry about the wiles of the evil one. He will try your spirit. Your spirit is Mine. My Spirit is yours. Bless you My little one. Bless all My faithful little ones who never fail to comfort Me in My Eucharistic Presence.

Others may down this calling. I am the solid reality of today, this day and always. Child, I need you simple, unaware of the depths of your calling.

I bless you."

Beloved, I haven't the words to answer You, to thank You. Oh I take You so much for granted. Mary help me.

We are nothing O Lord, save us from ourselves.

1ˢᵗ September 1995:

Beloved, I thank You for the hope that fills my heart this day
Truly it is a blessing of the Holy Spirit
And yet it must be rooted in reality.
There are times when hope alone keeps us going
Amongst the dangers of the unseen
That seek to trap us.

We must believe that You O Lord are in control of all
Upon this earth in which we live

In our human existence and beyond.
Our souls never die
That part of You that lives to eternity
Whether for our salvation or damnation.

We dare not think of the latter
Our will is our own.
You gave us this freedom
To decide for ourselves.
And yet O Lord it does not depend on us entirely
Without Your touch how could we survive
The onslaught of the wicked
Who condemned themselves to never ending darkness
Now desperately trying to set snares for all to follow in their paths.

You give us the ways and means
To accept Your way, Your truth, Your life
To bring others with us
As we struggle within
Ourselves to keep to the narrow path that leads to You
And avoid the easy path of least resistance that leads nowhere.

1ˢᵗ September 1995: *Beloved, they use Your children as pawns, as in a game of chess, to barter with in war. Oh Beloved, heal our warring hearts. Save us from ourselves - when our own are caught up in this exchange.*

Beloved, these incidents give us just a glimpse of Your sufferings, Your fears, before Your own passion. Truly we all carry much anger that is ready to erupt at the slightest provocation.

Beloved, have mercy on us all. How glib we are at times to think we can decide for You, direct You, in Your plans for a solution. We are nothing - save us from ourselves O Lord.

4ᵗʰ September 1995
Before The Blessed Sacrament:
Beloved, I want to write all that is on my mind, but I am so tired. You know all. I wish I could do only what You ask of me, but I am so impulsive. I must depend on the guidance of the Holy Spirit at all times.

Already I am aware of the toll on my mind when I write or speak on the other's blessing. I know I will find the strength and comfort I need here with You. Thank You Beloved.

5th September 1995
Before the Blessed Sacrament:

"My child, My little child, await My instructions. I do not want to burden your weak mind with too much at the present time. You will write more before We ask you to distribute more. Take outdoor exercise little one. Do household chores. We will give you the strength. Listen to the cares of others. Remember your family. We will provide for your present needs. Lean on Us for strength for body, mind and spirit. We are your support and consolation.

Prepare for the 8th when I will speak to you further. Bless you My little one."

8th September 1995 - Feast the Birthday of Mary
Before The Blessed Sacrament:

"Yes My child, My precious, I have a writing for you on this day. Do I not always grace you specially on My feast-days? This day is specially dear to you. Do not worry about the attacks this day. We see into your heart. The evil one is trying desperately now to take away your peace because you have been called into special ministry. Yes child, all My little ones gather as one this day. All bring comfort and solace to our broken Hearts, so much suffering and torment amongst all Our little ones and especially in the warring areas throughout the world - evidence of the wiles of the evil one. Today wherever We are remembered and glorified truly We pour out Our blessing on all. Oh children, your perseverance in prayer stays the hand of the

Father. Oh, the power of prayer, prayer of the heart, prayer of intercession for the stray, for your country, for all nations."

"My Holy Mother does not receive the glory of Her solemnity amongst many, oh how impoverished because of this. My Mother has the victory over evil given to Her. How few understand this. Yes child, My Mother's power will be made known soon. Everywhere She chooses, appears, will receive a sign, a permanent sign of Her presence. Children, you prepare Glencree by your prayers and faithfulness for times ahead. As I said before, My little one, here many will find refuge in the days ahead. She is preparing all for the dark days in which Our light will never be extinguished. Have no fear Our little ones, Keep hope ever present in your hearts. The good news is always full of hope. There is a dark side and a bright side to all situations. Look to Me. Relate all to Me and I will lift you beyond, from the human to the divine in all circumstances. Remember child, to pray to see the perfection of My Love and Holy Will in all the circumstances of your life, so different at times yet so profound. One of the great truths of living in this world is that it is the preparation for life eternal."

Mary, we visit Your shrine at Glencree this night. May we bring joy and solace to the Two Hearts of Love. Bless all. May we be at oneness with all who recognise Your glory as daughter of the Father, Mother of the Son, Spouse of the Holy Spirit. You who are now about to be proclaimed Co-Redemptrix, Mediatrix of All Graces and Advocate, pray for us that Jesus may reign in all hearts.

9th September 1995
Before The Blessed Sacrament:
Thank You Jesus and Mary for all the graces and blessings received at Glencree last night. The unity was apparent and peace and joy prevailed within all hearts. Thank You.

10th September 1995
Before The Blessed Sacrament:
Thank You my Beloved. Here You change my desolation into consolation. I kept wondering earlier whether I had done the right

thing this morning - my impulsiveness again I seem not to be able to control. And yet Beloved, sometimes I think You use it. I like to think so at times - because I had been disturbed since, makes me think You used me. I bring all those You place on my heart to You now for Your blessing and comfort.

Later :
O Beloved, how time flies in Your company. I am expected home now. I must go. Thank You. I love You. I give so little and receive so much.

12ᵗʰ September 1995: *Mary, help me to make this day a more pleasing one for my Beloved.*

Later
Before The Blessed Sacrament:
Beloved, many suffer Your sufferings of the present times - in the Church, in the world. I was about to go early.

"Stay a little longer child. I am so in need of company. When you go, I go back into My prison again."

16ᵗʰ September 1995: *Oh Mary, thank You for the very many graces You poured out on the group yesterday. In all Your sufferings You ministered to ours, showing us an example through one of the Five, the power of the healing Masses of the Generations. Mary, You only allow us see a little at a time of Your plans for this little hamlet chosen by You to be a refuge, a place of peace and reconciliation for all who come seeking consolation.*

Oh Mary, I cannot give all of myself like the others. Oh Mary, I keep holding back when suffering is mentioned. My heart cannot really say 'fiat'. The others are prepared. Help me to speak these words in deeds, in answer to Your call, when You call. Mary, I give You myself. You know His need of me. Help me to fulfil His need today.

"Child, precious child, prepare yourself for the coming Eucharist. I will speak to your heart then."

> "The day is not far off when I will speak to all hearts. Many will not like what I say, reveal, but all will receive the opportunity to repent, convert. Yes child, before the great purification and chastisement I will reveal Myself to all hearts. Many will believe through love, some in fear, and My word will be proclaimed."

Later

Before The Blessed Sacrament:

"Yes child, thank you for answering My call. Yes child, I leave you in no doubt about the writings. You mustn't worry. Soon I will arrange their printing. You will follow My instructions. No longer will they be blocked, delayed. You may pass this word to Sr. K. Continue dear child to answer My call. I wait for you. Here I will direct you. I have much for you to write for My Church, for your land. You will write and do as I ask. Afterwards they are no longer your responsibility. If others do not listen to me take heed, the onus will be on them.

Yes child, there is much not to My liking in this land. My gospel is not heeded. They no longer listen to My word. The day is not far off when I will speak to all hearts. Many will not like what I say, reveal, but all will receive the opportunity to repent, convert. Yes child, before the great purification and chastisement I will reveal Myself to all hearts. Many will believe through love, some in fear, and My word will be proclaimed.

Child, dear child, I take care of your health in body, mind and spirit. Come to Me for all your needs. Am I not always your Wonder-Counsellor, Mighty-God, Eternal-Father, Prince-of-Peace

270

and Physician? Bless you. bless you."

Beloved, thank You. I wish I could listen to You. You always listen to me and answer all my needs. Beloved, I bring You all those who asked my prayers recently and all I promised to pray for. Perhaps I will be able to call back later.

19ᵗʰ September 1995
<u>Before The Blessed Sacrament:</u>

Thank You Beloved for answering my doubts through another this morning. Beloved, we fail You so often. We do not listen to Your cries for comfort and consolation. I am so miserable because I have nothing to offer You but the burden of my weaknesses. 'Great is my sin but greater still is Your love.' I know this, because of the mercy You have shown me down the years - and I must never, never doubt Your Love.

Beloved, I pray that I do not take this Love too much for granted. Mary, embellish my weak, weak efforts at responding with Your love. Mary, thank You. I give all who have asked for prayers into Your safe keeping. I prepare to leave now. May I carry the Two Hearts of Love within me to share with others.

21ˢᵗ September 1995   -   Feast of St. Matthew
<u>Before The Blessed Sacrament:</u>

Truly Lord, as it is said of St. Matthew, You call the unlikely ones. Oh Beloved, we cannot open our hearts like he did to Your Holy Spirit without Your help. We prepare for the graces for all to answer Your call this day.

22ⁿᵈ September 1995
<u>Before The Blessed Sacrament:</u>

Abba, Abba, when my heart is full of requests I remember just to repeat Your Name and call on You. You know - I have written all in a letter to Jesus and Mary. Now I give all to You. May Your Holy Will be done in all situations.

"My child, My child, My little child, how can I not answer your cries for help. Your trust, your surrender - yes."

Oh Beloved, so much is happening these days in our land. Truly the Church is being battered by the media and the people who are struggling to be Your disciples, by the government.

Oh Beloved, people are confused, young people are confused. Is it any wonder the evil one has found such a footing in our land - and with the cease-fire being threatened, surely we are in need, in great need. You alone Beloved can fulfil this need.

Beloved, we pray that You will continue to sustain us in hope - Your hope that all is well, all will be well in our land.

We thank You for all the words of encouragement You give us, all Your promises. Let us believe and hope that You will never fail us. About the coming referendum, You promised me another word. You know I haven't the ability now to explain myself. I am very forgetful and confused at times. It makes me angry to see the hold of evil over many of our legislators. How they can brow-beat the people, confuse and fool them in their approach.

Beloved, we believe You alone have the victory over all evil. We thank You for Fr. Kennedy. He was not afraid to speak out. He did a great favour for the mothers and youths of our land. We pray for his protection. We thank You for the BBC production. They allowed all to speak and share their views but the light and truth of the Holy Spirit in Fr. Kennedy couldn't be extinguished. Oh Beloved, we pray that all bishops and priests will not be afraid to preach the gospels. The people are hungry for direction. Beloved, Beloved, another area that troubles me - more so because it effects my own - the area of drugs in schools. Beloved, I pray for protection in all schools. I pray for protection for my son in Skerries because of the drug problem there. Beloved, thank You for Your loving kindness to me always. How we all need You in these troubled times to discern the wood from the chaff.

Beloved, I forget to pray for the gift of discernment each day as You told me. Mary, my Holy Mother, I pray for the gift of silence. Mary, I need You. We need You, specially the Five. Bless our prayer meeting this night. I know the Two Hearts will speak to our hearts again. We love You. We need You.

24th September 1995
Before The Blessed Sacrament:

Beloved, forgive me for gossiping and all the while You were waiting for me here. Mary, my Holy Mother, help me to ignore as far as possible all the scandal of these times within the Church. The media and all who are against You and seeking to discredit all its members specially the hierarchy - Mary we know You are suffering the sufferings of Your Divine Son. Mary, with Your help, we really desire to be a comfort and solace to The Two Hearts of Love in these turbulent times. We believe if the coming referendum allows divorce in our land, it will bring us all deeper into the clutches of the evil one. May Your holy will be done.

Beloved, it worries me to hear that the Toronto Blessing is spreading within our Church members primarily through the Charismatic Prayer groups. We bring all to You here in Your Eucharistic Presence. Many good God-fearing people are being influenced by the emotionalism at these gatherings. Protect them all in Your Eucharistic Presence.

"My child, My child, take it easy. I will direct you when to go public on this. In the meantime, I use many now to sow the seeds of danger to counteract the evil influences about. Pray child, rest in Me. Abide in Me as I abide in you, My little one."

26th September 1995
Before The Blessed Sacrament:

Mary, our Holy Mother, we need You. The world needs You. Mary, Queen of Peace and Mother of Reconciliation, be specially present with all parties at the peace conference on Bosnia in New York this day.

28th September 1995
Before The Blessed Sacrament:

Beloved, we bring to You our political leaders who are debating legislation for divorce in our country this day. They place a whip on their members. Beloved, You control, You are in control. Nothing is impossible to You. The media plan, they think they have put a blockage on the Church to speak out because of all the

recent scandals and that there would be no vote in the Dail to change the constitution. Beloved, touch the hearts of those who are not happy with this legislation to speak out.
Jesus, we place our trust in You.

29ᵗʰ September 1995
Feast of the Archangels, Michael, Gabriel and Raphael.
Before The Blessed Sacrament:
"My child, My child, My Heart bleeds with My Church, for My Church in these times. Yes child, I want you to have a balanced outlook on the happenings these days. My Church is now going through the purification that had to come. This will now become the renewed Church I spoke about to you many years ago. Remember a thousand years is as one day to the Lord and one day as a thousand years. Yes child, you now live in a very important and glorious time, the beginnings of a new era. As I said before, keep looking beyond the happenings of these days to the times beyond. My Spirit is about to pour out His blessings anew on the Church. You see why the evil one is trying to usurp his power by a blessing of his own. (Toronto blessing).

I want you to see it as a very insidious evil trying to destroy My Church in it's time of purification.

My child, My children, I want you all to be aware of the power of prayer during these troubled times. I do not want you to be overcome by the oppression the evil one is trying to pin on all My little ones, My children everywhere throughout the world.

It would appear he is having the victory over goodness. Let Me assure you My dear children, nothing is further from the truth. I am allowing him now to hang himself. You will see. You will see. My child, have faith in all My promises. Have faith little one. I choose you because of your littleness. The high and mighty he can more easily destroy.

Trust little children in the Two Hearts of Love. We will lead you, guide you along the path of holiness, the narrow path, the way to eternal happiness."

30ᵗʰ September 1995 - After The Eucharist
<u>Before The Blessed Sacrament:</u>

Mary :
"My child, My little one, the Father desires to speak to your heart. Truly He blessed you during the Eucharist. He recalled past favours to strengthen you for the days ahead."

Abba Father:
"Yes My little one, the thoughts come from Me. I have cared for you down the years. Now I prepare you for your last mission, as I said, the most dangerous. As little children are not aware of the dangers that surround them, neither will you because you are protected by My angels. You will enter where angels fear to tread. Yes child, fear not. I am always with you in the battle now raging against My people, against My Church, against establishments, against all institutions in need of healing. I am about to sweep away all that is not to My liking. Great will be the repercussions but My little ones will see, will see and accept through My grace, will perceive with My grace the necessity of these changes about to happen. The proud and powerful will be brought down. All must be humbled to be brought to salvation.

Yes child, I will teach you to listen, I will teach you to pray. I will teach and direct you to act, yes child, through suffering. I have given you the holiest of Mothers to care for you. Turn to Her who led you to Her Son, who led you to know Me. Child, I have kept the promise I made to you here (Consolata) many years ago, did I not? Now that you cannot come as you would wish, offer all in sacrifice to Me. Remember the writings on spiritual fasting that leads one into the purification of the soul. Yes child, the tears help to wash the windows of the soul that you might all the better look in at yourself and let Me look out.

Remember dear child, you have been truly blessed over the years. Continue to give praise and thanksgiving for all the graces received and see the perfection of My Holy Will in all the circumstances of your life now and always.

I ask you dear child to rest your mind this week-end. Do not feel prayer is the fulfilment of all commitments. Listen to the urgings of the Spirit and respond. That is all I ask of you. I will be with you to care for your grandchildren. Yes child, the youth need much prayer in this present age. They are bombarded with much distraction by the evil one and the present state of society doesn't help their immortal souls. You must go now child. I go with you. I bless you. I bless your care."

1st October 1995
Before The Blessed Sacrament:
Most Holy Trinity, I haven't the words to speak, write my thanksgiving for all the graces received from You from the beginning of time to the end. Look to my heart, my soul - I depend on You to change me - to be able to respond. Truly I know the blessings of these days - who could be more unworthy than I to be chosen as Your little messenger - who will listen? I pray for The strength not to fail You. You know my weakness. You know my miseries. 'Great is my sin, but greater still is Your love and mercy'.
3rd October 1995   - After the Eucharist
Before the Tabernacle:
Beloved, we return home today. I thank You for the change, the rest. I need Your strength to fulfil Your need of me. Direct me whether I should now take the writings from ------. I await Your instructions. I know that I can trust in You.

4th October 1995   -   Feast of St. Francis of Assisi
After The Eucharist:
St. Francis, many years ago we made You caretaker of our home. Intercede for the family and extended family, specially this day. Help us all to renew our lives to renew our Church and that the youth of the day will not be deprived of a Christian education in our present pluralistic society. St. Francis, Your intercession and influence was never more needed than in the present state of the world. Hear our appeals, our cries for change. Help us begin with ourselves.

5th October 1995
Before The Blessed Sacrament:
Beloved, all who love You and are trying to be Your disciples are suffering with You these days. We know Your Church, Your

people, our country, the world, are in great need of purification.

Beloved, we weep for You. We weep with You. We are all guilty. We are all in need of Your mercy. Each and everyone of us needs purifying. During these days of adoration (Thursday morning to Friday night) may we be of some consolation to the Two Hearts of Love in Your desolation. Beloved, You are our consolation always but how often, how seldom are our hearts centred on Your need of us? Beloved, my eyes and heart have been opened in the past days to see the effects of the present state of Church and government on our youth. Oh Beloved, truly they need our prayers. Forgive us for failing them. We have allowed our country be taken over, to become a pluralist society. However we mustn't allow these situations to take us over. We believe You are in control, have control over all. We trust in Your mercy and victory.

May Your Will be done in the coming referendum. Whatever the results of the recent poll, nothing is impossible to You. We remember 1986. Much can happen in the next eight weeks.

"Have patience My little one. I will answer your questions one by one in My time. Come little one. I need you now. Rest in Me, as I abide in you, here in My Eucharistic Presence - no more have I to offer you - no more, no greater."

6ᵗʰ October 1995 - First Friday
Before The Blessed Sacrament:
"My child, My little one, this is a special day in your home ever since you were in Paray-Le-Monial, the birth place of this feast (1st Friday) now to be celebrated as the feast of My Eucharistic Heart. We have come a long way together since the writings of those days. Yes child, I have made My Home in your home. Much and great have been the comfort and consolation We, the Two Hearts of Love have received in your home. Yes child, yes children, you have both been faithful to your commitment down the years, and all the others who have come to pray here also. I recommend specially all partakers in the vigils. Oh such comfort and consolation they have brought Us down the years.

Yes child, your home has been a haven of rest for all. Prayers have been answered. Healings of body, mind and spirits have taken place. Truly it has been a haven of peace and safety and a place of comfort and consolation for all who come in expectant faith and love.

Yes child, remember your country, your government specially at prayer. Yes child, you see and suffer My dissatisfaction with the legislators and perpetrators of schemes not to My liking. I will have My way. Child, I do not want you to carry My burdens on your little shoulders. Try again to live one day at a time, and each day as if it was your last. Keep trying little one. We will help you. Child, as We promised We will take care of your family. You take care of My messages, My mission for you in these times. My strength goes with you to carry out My designs and My Holy Mother cares for you and protects you, also My angels.

Child, the most important gift of the day is your daily Eucharist. Prepare again as in the past. It is a very special blessing to be able to attend Mass daily at your age. I will remind you of all the insights you received in the past to make it very special and the most important exercise of the day."

7ᵗʰ October 1995
Feast of Our Lady of the Rosary - First Saturday
After the Eucharist:
Mary, thank You for this day and the blessings at Holy Mass.

All Your children honour You this day and bless You for all the graces received through the Holy Rosary. May it become the family prayer in all homes again as it was in the past. Mary, we need You so much but we also know that Your need of us is infinitely greater. Help us not to fail You today. And as we gather at Glencree for the Mass of the Generations this afternoon, may we be united with all Your children everywhere in honouring Your solemnity as Co-Redemptrix, Mediatrix of all Graces and Advocate. Immaculate Heart of Mary, Spouse of the Holy Spirit, enclose us all in Your Heart.

"My child, My precious little one, I hear your prayer, I see into your heart, I enclose you in Mine. Great will be the blessings of this afternoon on all who come in love and faith. I see all. You are all part of My army who gather everywhere throughout the world this day. It is a special day of pilgrimage to honour My Son. You have My prayers of intercession for all your needs, spiritual and temporal. I am one with each one in your joys, in your sufferings. I rejoice and console. I comfort and condole. I strengthen and give hope. I am present to each one to fulfil all the needs of all My children throughout the world.

Pray a rosary on the journey in preparation and as part of the pilgrimage."

8ᵗʰ October 1995:

From morning prayer :
> 'Praise Father, Son and Holy Spirit Blest
> Trinity and source of grace,
> Who call us out of nothingness,
> To find in You our resting-place.'

"Child, you are still anxious about the word I promised. Do not worry My little one. Polls do not determine the results. I am in control. They will be surprised by the results. You will see My little one. Wait and see, all will be well. The legislators will be crushed by the results."

Beloved, do You still ask the priests to speak out ?

"Yes, and Bishops."

Beloved, can I spread this word ?

"Yes My child."

11ᵗʰ October 1995
Before The Blessed Sacrament:

"I call on all political leaders to allow your members have a free vote in the forthcoming legislation on divorce.

Let the people see that democracy still prevails in this land. Let the people speak. Let the people proclaim their views, their desires. Priests, I ask you to speak out. Do not be afraid. Look to other lands where divorce is part of the ethos. See the results. It cannot be controlled. It will become the norm if the family is not upheld. The country will lose it's foundation. There are sad cases, sad circumstances. To follow Me is difficult, was always difficult.

I ask leaders of the Church, My Church, to uphold the sanctity of the Sacrament of marriage. Do not fail My people. You do not have to have a pluralistic society. Who controls? Who is in control of events? Other nations are already learning to their regret, the dangers, the consequences of this legislation.

It doesn't matter how you try to control, it spreads like forest fires to destroy, to bring destruction within families, specially amongst the youth."

Abba Father - what do You want me to do with today's writing? Help me to listen. I am so distracted at the present time. Mary, enclose me in Your Immaculate Heart.

"Child, there is more to come later. I will direct you."

15ᵗʰ October 1995
Before The Blessed Sacrament:
May Your will be done in the coming referendum. Whatever the results of the recent poll, nothing is impossible to You. We remember 1986. Much can happen in the next eight weeks.

"Have patience My little one. I will answer your questions one by one in My time. Come little one. I need you now. Rest in Me, as I abide in you, here in My Eucharistic Presence - no more have I to offer you - no more, no greater."

9ᵗʰ October 1995
Before The Blessed Sacrament:
Abba Father, Abba Father, I come in thanksgiving for all the graces and blessings of this day and every day. I come in intercession for all who have asked my prayers. Still my restless mind to give You all, my Triune God.

Beloved, You do not ask me to suffer as is my due - but ask others to offer theirs for me.

Beloved, You know the three whom I carry in my heart specially now. May Your peace be upon them.

"Oh My beloved child, I take care of all. Each one will receive the peace they seek. You will see."

10th October 1995
Before The Blessed Sacrament:

Beloved, thank You for Your peace - how disturbed I was this morning. Again You come to my rescue. I await Your instructions - so much crowds my mind. I pray for Fr. Tim, for his safety these days, who is on pilgrimage to Mexico city. I read again the extracts he sent me. Your ways are truly wonderful. The Spirit pierces all my confusion. I never thank You enough - and You answer my prayers of yesterday. May I treasure Your Presence today and everyday, the Presence that casts out all fear.

Later
Before The Blessed Sacrament:

Holy Spirit, Spirit of truth and holiness, invade our hearts with Your light. How often I jump to false conclusions because I do not pray before thinking, before acting.

12th October 1995
Before The Blessed Sacrament:

'The Lord is coming in power. The prize of His victory is with Him. ' (from morning prayer.)

Yes Lord, I believe You are always faithful to Your promises. What an awesome word You speak to my heart, Beloved, namely that the word (8th Oct.) You gave me about the coming referendum could be compared to the word You gave Mary concerning Elizabeth at the Annunciation, that is that it would confirm the writings You give me on the Toronto blessing. When they see the fulfilment of Your Word in the Church, they will be more ready to accept the writings.

"Yes My child, I do not leave you in darkness. I give you the sign that others will be convinced. Now your writings will be accepted more freely by My priests who will in turn be more ready to fulfil My needs of them. The writings regarding The Eucharist and priests, will be much sought after now and listened to and put into practice."

Abba Father, am I like the man in today's gospel (Luke 11. 5-13) who keeps bothering You?

Further Teachings on Prayer

And he said to them, "Suppose one of you has a friend to whom he goes at midnight and says, 'Friend, lend me three loaves of bread, for a friend of mine has arrived at my house from a journey and I have nothing to offer him,' and he says in reply from within, 'Do not bother me, the door has already been locked and my children and I are already in bed. I cannot get up to give you anything.' I tell you, if he does not get up to give him the loaves because of their friendship, he will get up to give him whatever he needs because of his persistence.

The Answer to Prayer

"And I tell you, ask and you will receive; seek and you will find; knock and the door will be opened to you. 'For everyone who asks, receives; and the one who seeks, finds; and to the one who knocks, the door will be opened. "What father among you would hand his son a snake when he asks for a fish? Or hand him a scorpion when he asks for an egg? If you then, who are wicked, know how to give good gifts to your children, how much more will the Father in heaven give the holy Spirit to those who ask him?"

"No My child, certainly not. I have specially chosen you for the mission I place upon you. I have prepared you over the years, good and faithful little one. Your reward will be great. Child, be prepared for many remarks like the one this day. I will be your shield, and you come between the arrows and Me, and give hope to others while your faith is being tested."

[You remind me Lord of the faith of Abram.]

13ᵗʰ October 1995
Before The Blessed Sacrament:

"My child, I have read your letter. I take all you say and ask to My Heart, Our Hearts. We set in motion a further solution now. We answer your prayers of this night. Already We plan a peaceful solution and way of healing for D. Yes child, trust Us. We will not fail you. Be united in your prayers and intercession. Bring all to the Throne of the Most High, The Triune God, Father of all, Spouse of all, Sanctifier of all, and Mary, Daughter, Mother and Spouse. Believe all will be well. All is well."

We ask Beloved, here in Your Eucharistic Presence for light, that her heart will be made aware of Your power in a situation beyond her power to solve nor his to respond in his present state of mind and physical condition. We praise and thank You for answering our prayers.

16th October 1995
Feast of St. Margaret Mary:
Beloved, I had forgotten this day's feast - and it always meant so much to me since my visits to Paray-Le-Monial, where I received so many blessings and met many others that brought me closer to You. I expect that I will never visit this holy place again but who knows?

St. Margaret Mary, intercede for us this day before the Throne of the Most High. You know our needs and the needs of all those we carry in our hearts. We unite with all who unite with you in prayer this day.

19th October 1995
Before The Blessed Sacrament:
"I missed you this morning My little one. I need your attention now. You have done all you could about tonight's meeting. Much prayer is needed to foil the evil influences around. Keep faith My little one in the word I gave you on the referendum. All will be well My little one. I take care of your health. I give you the strength for each day at the Eucharist. It was no accident this morning the breaking of the thermometer. Believe in Me. I am your physician. Yes child, I take care of you."

20th October 1995
Before The Blessed Sacrament:
Beloved, forgive me for neglecting You this day. I have been very disturbed about the meeting in All Hallows last night. Though I wasn't present I do not like all I hear. If I am disturbed - how about Your Holy Spirit whose power is being usurped by the spirit of evil! and above all by Your own elect whom You warned me about. Beloved, I know You protect me because without Your guidance where would I be?

Beloved, direct me about the M.M.M. hour of adoration. I was thinking of 3-4 p.m. on Fridays - to begin on the 1st Friday in November. Is that alright? I pray that this is in accordance with Your Holy Will and Your word on 12th August last. You know I only want what pleases You now.

21ˢᵗ October 1995: "Yes child, I call you to write. All you rehearsed in your mind (this morning) will come to pass. Yes child, you will have to speak out. I will give you the words when the time comes. How in a Christian country, no one felt they could pronounce My Name, quote My word (Late, late show last night) Oh how far the media has progressed backwards, specially at these chat-shows that are so popular. Oh My children, I could have been more angry in My word to you (for the five) I could have spoken thus to you - children, I do not want - I will not allow the evil one enter your little group but, dear, dear children, be careful, be careful. Your Holy Mother has you gathered under Her cloak. Let Her be your guide, your protector, your image. Yes children, last night was truly a night of love. Each one has been blessed to give to the other. Do not let the sharp edges grate on one another. I am moulding you remember, for the days ahead. My plans are already made. Know Our touch, always. I remind you of the verse of the poem on the Eucharist :

'When Jesus comes I will know that He is living
A person within me, abiding in me
Loving me, fulfilling me, strengthening me
Listening always for my response
I am never alone, always touching God.'

"The fire of the Holy Spirit I create within you, can also be a burden."

22ⁿᵈ October 1995 - Mission Sunday
Before The Blessed Sacrament:
My Beloved, give me the grace to fulfil my mission this day. Truly You do not ask of me the sufferings I see in others but help me to see the perfection of Your Love and Holy Will in all the circumstances of my life today. If only I could practise this, it would suffice. I foresee many ways I could die to myself in the

coming week. I await Your directions - my Wonder-Counsellor! Please help me not to be so impulsive. Oh how I need Your Holy Spirit and His loving Spouse, Mary.

22ⁿᵈ October 1995: "Yes My child, I do need you to write. Your little mind is not able to receive much these days. It needs resting. Rest in Me My child. Do not try to achieve too much. A little at a time. I will lead and guide you. Rome was not built in a day. I am in control remember."

23ʳᵈ October 1995
<u>Before The Blessed Sacrament:</u>
Abba, I pray I do Your Holy Will to glorify You not myself.

"No My dear child, you go and speak in My Name. I cover you. You must confront My priests. This is most important. Did I not give you a promise. Stand on My promises. They are your pillar of strength. Step out in faith My little one. You are surrounded and protected by My Holy Mother and the angels."

26ᵗʰ October 1995
<u>Before The Blessed Sacrament:</u>
From morning prayer :
'The priests will again feed with plenty
And My people will be filled with My blessings.'

Beloved, what a consoling word for these times when the evil one is trying to usurp the blessing of the Holy Spirit. How confused we all feel. On Beloved, help us to keep our eyes on You at all times. I remember the time You told me that I could so easily get lost. Please do not let this happen. Mary, my Holy Mother, keep me safe in Your Immaculate Heart.

27ᵗʰ October 1995
<u>Before The Blessed Sacrament:</u>
"My child, My child, I need you before you run off again. I understand you have much on your mind and much to do this day to please everyone. Child, you mustn't be anxious. You must keep

trusting in Me by the day, by the present moment. I will not fail you. I will direct you as I need you in the coming days. Find Me in the ordinary things, with your family, in walking by the sea. Am I not everywhere and above all within you - when you cannot visit Me in the Blessed Sacrament. Child, you need this change, this rest. I have much more work for you to do."

"You could not keep going at the present pace. I do not ask this of you. I want you to rest in Me, to quieten the spirit to be one with Me. Let each day unfold, let My Spirit lead and guide you, let My peace prevail in the family. Love accomplishes much with young people. Be patient and tolerant. I will support you both."

29ᵗʰ October 1995
Before The Blessed Sacrament:

Beloved, I missed You. I thank You for this day. You were right - a great tiredness is upon me, but I find my rest in You, and Your strength revives me. I know I fail You in the little You ask of me and this mornings gospel (Luke 18. 9-14) speaks to my heart. I have so much to learn and only You can change me.

'Jesus Lord, have mercy on me a sinner.'

"Yes child, I am working through the problems of those you carry in your heart. You mustn't carry the problems of others now. I ask you to trust in Me, as I ask of them. It is not as fearful as one expects. I am in control. Each one I carry in My Heart. My Church is being exposed. Previous faults and lack of discernment are being brought out into the limelight where only healings can take place. The Church is the people. All move together in the Holy Spirit. No suffering is wasted. Each one who suffers for My sake, I use in the process. The Church is changing through the present purification. I am taking care of both victors and victims. All are My children. I seek all. The Church has seen dark, dark days before and survived. My Church will rise again through the prayers and sufferings of My people. All My little ones suffer in one way or another to bring about the healings, the changes necessary in the institutional Church. It has to die to self to rise again under the power of the Holy Spirit. As I said before, I am preparing all My little ones to be the seeds of My new Church, My renewed Church. All must suffer to bring this about. But, be assured all, that I am your strength, I will be your strength in these times. Have no fear. I carry you all - all who look to Me, depend on Me - live for Me now and in the days ahead."

(I speak specially child to the one who suffers much these days. Give her the hope she needs. All will be well. I ask much, the reward is great. She has a place in the renewal of My Church.)

"There's so much good in the worst of us and so much bad in the best of us, that it isn't right for any of us to criticise the rest of us."

31st October 1995 - (Hallow Eve)
After the Eucharist:
"Child, dear child, give Me your anxieties. Am I not a well of comfort and consolations for all parents, grandparents, guardians of children, this night of revelry. The dangers are great I know, Much prayer is needed for the youth. Remember to trust Me with your care. I take care and I protect them against all evil. Yes child, there is much evil about on this night - insidious evil that tries to destroy My innocents. Also dangerous customs that continue to increase by the year and there is a greed for profit at any price, but I will hold those responsible in My own way. I am in control. Let go My child. Give your care to Me. I am in control. I will protect."

1st November 1995
Feast of All Saints:
Beloved, thank You for this beautiful feast-day. We rejoice with all the saints in Heaven, many of whom we knew and are part of our family tree. We rejoice and praise Your glory together.

Thank You for caring for our care these days. What a wonderful provider and faithful God You are to all who call on You and more often we forget and neglect You - our God whose love is infinite, constant and everlasting. The veil has been lifted for the saints in Heaven. May our faith increase in boundless hope each day, to find this perfect love in You when You call us to Yourself.

2ⁿᵈ November 1995   -   Feast of All Saints
Before The Blessed Sacrament:
Beloved, You wanted to speak to my heart earlier and I was called away. You have infinite patience with me. I wish I could be attentive like others. I have as much concentration now as my little grandchildren. Please help me. I really want to fulfil Your need of me each day. I seem to always fail You. I have nothing but interruptions when You visit my home. At least I hope to be able to help others at times.

Beloved, the family are not here tonight, the vigil night. Would I be able to spend part of the night with You? I haven't tried for a long time now. Tell me what I should do. I know You have much on Your Heart and I think only about my own needs. I forget all You suffer because of our sinfulness and I must think and pray for all the souls in purgatory this night, specially any priests and bishops whom people forget to pray for.

Mary, teach me to say the Rosary of Tears for Your intentions. Mary. sometimes Your tears are like ours, other times they are tears of blood. What is the difference and why?

"All tears are because of My Sons' sufferings in His people, but the tears of blood are when I see the sufferings of My Son for His priests."

3ʳᵈ November 1995   -   First Friday
Before The Blessed Sacrament:
"Now child, I need you. Others who mean well can often be a distraction. Do not let messages take over before My Eucharistic Presence. I feel rejected at times. I am not a God of condemnation but if one could only understand the power of My Eucharistic Presence one would not be able to speak, hear another, read. I do not want to overburden anyone. I love and welcome each one beyond your human understanding, but resting in Me, resting in My Spirit give Me the most comfort and consolation. Oh child, the power of Eucharistic prayer. Today I want you to honour My Eucharistic Heart as far as possible in silence. Yes child, it is difficult for you. All want to speak to you and hear My latest words I speak to your heart. But, all these are not important. I ask prayer of the heart, intimate prayer, My Heart,

your heart in unity, in love.

Oh child, your mission is now dangerous. Here you will find the strength necessary to go forth in My Name. I ask all who come now, as far as possible to give Me the silence of soul that I might find the comfort and solace I seek in all hearts, in the hearts of all My little ones. Many find this very difficult. I will build on the efforts of all. These times are dangerous times. But, here in My Eucharistic Presence the evil one is powerless. He is trying to usurp My power ever here. Child, be forearmed to his insidious ways of trying to destroy. Here in Me, with Me, We will destroy together the power of evil in your midst, in your country and in the world. Yes child, I have challenged the other. He means well but try My little one to dissuade and not allow these distractions to continue. I bless all who come during the day and night. Truly they have My blessing, My true blessing, not that of those received from the evil one who is trying to usurp Mine." (Toronto blessing)

Beloved, You answer my prayer of yesterday. I am sorry for having offended You and hurt You. Teach me to be firm in my resolve in the future and give me a listening heart, a heart that will be centred on You and You alone. Holy Mother, please help me.

"Child, you do not have to be rude to anyone but gentle and kind in a loving way, that touches the heart."

3ʳᵈ November 1995
Later :
From evening prayer :
'Turn back my soul to Your rest.'

Beloved, You pour out more love and mercy when we least deserve it. Oh what beautiful people came to visit You in our home this evening. Truly You bless us with Your loving kindness to-day and everyday. And I wanted to stay tonight and You arranged it all in Your own wondrous way. Thank You my Beloved. Beloved, I bring all who asked my prayers this day, specially those who suffer much. The good suffer the most. They are the salt of the earth.

5th November 1995
Before The Blessed Sacrament:

Mary, thank You for the wonderful day of graces at Glencree yesterday. Truly these masses for the healings of the generations, are opening up for us all, the need for repentance in our own lives and the lives of our ancestors. The Church is surely being challenged in these times. And as we are all part of the Church, we are all in need of purification to be converted. Unless our sinfulness and weaknesses are brought out in the open, we cannot repent and receive the love and mercy of the Lord that changes us.

Now that the Eucharistic Presence has been exposed in our midst, may our hearts be opened to receive the healing light of Your Spirit to lead us further into the Truth.

Beloved, turn back my soul in silence to Your need of me and my need of You.

6th November 1995:

Beloved, Beloved.
(J. & M. came back from holiday - J. very ill)
"Yes My child, all will be well. The strain is a little too much for you. Take care, detach yourself. I am in control. Visit Me. I will give you the strength for tonight. Remember a day at a time. Your presence will help the others. It is part of living now My child. I take care of all. I will use the situation to reach all. Child, do not worry. Relate all to Me, relate all. Pray, pray, pray child."

8th November 1995
Before The Blessed Sacrament:

"Beloved child, I leave you in no doubt. I want you to come to Glencree to-night. Here as I told you, you will find refuge in times of need. It is not necessary to go away on retreat this week-end. Spend much time with Me in My Eucharistic Presence. You need a rest child, more rest. Do not take on the cares and burdens now. Pray for all who ask prayers. I will bring to your mind the writings that are to be brought forward for these times. My child, I need you for these times. I will help you to concentrate and be more attentive in My Presence. Children, I have bonded you together.

Pray much together. You will both go through trying times together. Prayer will mould you and cement you in My love, to be faithful in these times of confusion and division. Pray for the five, Glencree and the priests involved specially. All is well. All will be well. This must be your spiritual motto. I speak to your two hearts now. You are one in Our Two Hearts of Love. Remember this always."

Later :
"Beloved child, I call you to pray for this night at Glencree. I have much to offer My little ones this night. The Two Hearts of Love are full of Our Goodness. We are here to share Our bountiful blessings with all who make this journey, this pilgrimage this night."

"Oh children, pray for all, your country, so in need of your prayers. The evil one is bent on destroying, deafening Our little ones to Our Word in these times. Pray that he will not succeed. Pray much. We protect you, We love you, We are your strength in the days ahead. The power of the Eucharist is over this land, this area. Nothing will prevail against this power, but We need your prayer to foil the evil, your prayer of intercession that many forces seek to destroy.

Remember We are in control. We will have the victory. Prepare now - now. Pray continually, pray always. We are always listening, waiting. We bless you children."

9th November 1995:   "My child, there is no need to write. I cover that person in My Heart. She has suffered much. All is well, all will be well now. Let this be her motto also now and always. The result of her sufferings has now been put into motion. I take over. Let her rest now, her well earned rest. Time of suffering is now past in this matter. The fruits of her sufferings will be manifested later."

10th November 1995
Before The Blessed Sacrament:
"Beloved child, spend this day here with Me. All else can wait. I have much to speak to your heart. You are under attack from all

sides. Yes My child, do not make any decisions without My guidance. Try to make Mary's Fiat your fiat now. It will be difficult at times. Remember, We are with you always to protect and care for you. Rest here in My Eucharistic Presence and in the silence of spirit I will speak to your heart. Try to put aside the needs of others. I need you child."

11ᵗʰ November 1995
Before The Blessed Sacrament:

Beloved, I was afraid last night. Here all fear is gone. Thank You, thank You. Here You give me the strength for the day and renew my hope. I bring before You the Charismatic Conference being held this day in Dublin.

Holy Spirit, Spirit of truth and holiness, invade the hearts of all, specially all the priests, as all the prayer groups are in danger of being divided and broken up through the Toronto Blessing. Beloved, spare us from this evil. Jesus we trust in You. Jesus we trust in You. Jesus we trust in You. We know You will direct us about this phenomenon.

"Wait My child, be patient. All is well. I have My plan prepared. I will direct you and others. Await a further word."

Beloved, was it in order, to send the word re. referendum to O.H. yesterday?

"Yes child, much debate will follow this, to the benefit of the country and the result. Thank you My little one. Do not be afraid. I know the strain this word places upon you. Do not be afraid. I repeat again and again, I take care of your mind. Come back later little one. I will be waiting. Rest now My little one."

Reading : The temptations of the Lord. Matt. 4. 1-11. (Power. Prestige. Possessions.)

The Temptation of Jesus

Then Jesus was led by the Spirit into the desert to be tempted by the devil. He fasted for forty days and forty nights, and afterwards he was hungry. The tempter approached and said to him, "If you are the Son of God, command that these stones become loaves of bread." He said in reply, "It is written:

'One does not live by bread alone, but by every word that comes forth from the mouth of God.' "

Then the devil took him to the holy city, and made him stand on the parapet of the temple, hand said to him, "If you are the Son of God, throw yourself down. For it is written:

'He will command his angels concerning you' and "with their hands they will support you, lest you dash your foot against a stone.'"

Jesus answered him, "Again it is written, 'You shall not put the Lord, your God, to the test.'" Then the devil took him up to a very high mountain, and showed him all the kingdoms of the world in their magnificence, and he said to him, "All these I shall give to you, if you will prostrate yourself and worship me." At this, Jesus said to him, "Get away, Satan! It is written:

'The Lord, your God, shall you worship and him alone shall you serve.'

Then the devil left him and, behold, angels came and ministered to him.

12ᵗʰ November 1995
Before The Blessed Sacrament:

Beloved, another day in my walk with You in faith. Without Your promise, without Your strength, I couldn't survive. It is truly a lesson and promise in the power of the Eucharist.

"My child, I know your tiredness, I know your weakness, but I need you My little one to write."

Here I am my Beloved. I am listening now.

"Thank you My little one for your obedience to My call. You see little one the result of the word being delivered on Friday evening. (1/11/95) It has made people think and listen and it has given encouragement to all My little ones working for Me. They will now stand on My promise and it will be a lesson in faith for all who listen.

Afterwards, your main mission will begin. You will be strengthened in the wake of My promise coming to fruition. You will then speak with My authority within you and others will be prepared to listen. You are right to hold back now. Little one, do not carry this as if it were a great burden. I have given you My Spirit of Peace, joy and hope to sustain you. I will have more to speak to your heart about the situation in the North. Pray for peace to prevail in the hearts of all, but more about this later.

I will send you helpers to do all the paper work and My ministers to minister to you. Child, you have continued to fill the chalice of strength for My priests down the years - will I not send you My helpers now?"

13ᵗʰ November 1995
Before The Blessed Sacrament:

Beloved, Beloved, You know, You see how the evil one is trying to bring division and confusion between us. We call on You, we call on Your Holy Mother to protect us and direct us in the present situation. In Your direction to me in the past days, were You not warning me to hold back.

I wonder was it a mistake to issue the leaflets re. messages yesterday after the Conference?
Beloved, You told me You would direct me.
What should I do now?

Beloved, I thank You for the beautiful word of 19/6/96. You led me to in my writings - so appropriate for these times. It pains me to see how Your love is ignored.

"Child, you see now the necessity of the prayers of intercession I gave you before the rosary for priests. You see now My plans coming to fruition. It is a time of great change, a time of conversion for the individual and for the institution of the Church. It is a time of healing and purification. I must destroy to rebuild. Yes My child, My word to you, many years ago is now taking place. But child, it is not a time to be disturbed, sad. I am in control.

Child, the evil one is trying to disturb, destroy you. I ask you to remain firm in faith. He is using others to do his work. All is well child. Be firm little one."

14ᵗʰ November 1995
Before The Blessed Sacrament:

"Yes child, I call you to write.
These days are most important. Pray - there is so much at stake.

The evil one is very active. He is about trying to ensnare all My little ones in every possible way. Be aware. Pray specially for My priests. Offer all for them to persevere. under all circumstances and temptations.

Yes child, all concerned and working for My Mother of Glencree will come under attack through their own weaknesses. You already are aware of these happenings in your midst. Call a meeting of those who speak for all in the near future. Be honest and truthful with one another. Much needs to be unravelled to dispel the urgings of the evil one who is trying to bring confusion and division between you. Call on My Holy Mother to bring peace and tolerance between all, to open all hearts to Her future plans for this holy place."

15th November 1995:

Abba Father, Beloved Jesus, Most Holy Spirit.
Oh so many of my friends, Your friends are suffering much these days - specially Your priests. They suffer because of Your pain for their brethren. Oh Triune God, help them, strengthen them through this great purification of the Church. We are all challenged, because we are all sinners.

Without Your grace we would all be guilty of grievous sin. Let us not go into temptation.

Turn back our souls to Thee O Lord.

16th November 1995: *Abba, I have many questions on my mind today. Please guide me - it is the most special day in my home - my Beloved comes in the Eucharistic Presence. Should I visit where He will be also this day? Would I be putting another before Him. Is it necessary to meet the other person or not? I leave all to You. Your need is above mine. Direct me about today and tomorrow.*

"It would be a greater sacrifice to remain at home My child. See, I will not fail you. I will lead her to you."

Reading from P. Luke 10; Rev. 13.

Abba, Abba, should I ring P. ?

"Wait child, wait. Am I not in control?"

Abba, Abba, I am hopeless, so impatient, so lacking in trust. Forgive me. Oh I need You so much. Help me and all I carry in my heart.

17ᵗʰ November 1995
Before The Blessed Sacrament:
Only one week off now to the referendum. May love be the centre of our intentions. Take all self-righteousness from the hearts of those proposing a No vote and bitterness and hurt from the Yes voters. Let us look to You and Your Holy Will in the situation, and that all evil influences will be destroyed on both sides to allow the truth prevail in our hearts.

May the Spirit of truth and holiness invade all our hearts with Your love. Beloved, I believe in the word, I trust in the word You gave me on 8th October. I have delivered Your word as You have asked. Please help me now to detach myself from all the arguments and discussions. Turn back my soul in silence to You again. Holy Mother Mary, help me to live in the perfection of the present moment and know that all is well - all will be well. In one word - Wisdom.

19ᵗʰ November 1995
Before The Blessed Sacrament:
Beloved, all the discussions and arguments of the past days are a challenge to each and everyone of us. Let the healing of our land begin in me. Beloved, we have so much to be grateful for. Let us count our blessings today and everyday.
Later :
Thank You Beloved for speaking to my heart at the Eucharist. You leave me in no doubt about the word of 8th October. How wonderful You are!

You lead me to writing of 11/2/92 on marriage and celibacy of priests at the present time. Another confirmation why it should be a No vote in the coming referendum.

20ᵗʰ November 1995
<u>Before The Blessed Sacrament:</u>

Beloved, it is not surprising to be fearful at times when You leave me standing on the edge of a precipice and my greatest fear is my fear of heights. Truly Beloved, You use us in our weaknesses. Your ways are above and beyond the ways of mankind. Beloved, I unite and relate with the arrows aimed and directed at You during these days and I find consolation in the Psalms You sent me through another and specially in the version for modern times.

Beloved, I bring our country, the people of this land, before You like Jonah at Nineveh. Many, many people are praying and fasting these days and worshipping before Your Eucharistic Presence. You will not disappoint so many but accept their prayers of intercession and again Beloved, as You said in a previous writing - the cease-fire rests on a pinhead. Some side must relent. Beloved, You alone can touch the hearts of those in control to relent.

"My child, My little one, your prayers and tears touch My Heart. I try to touch the hearts of all but are they listening?"

Beloved, how often and for how long did You not call me. The seed fell on barren ground. Truly that parable was for me also. If anyone in government, in power, knew Your Love, Your unconditional love for each one, they would all surely listen and want to change.

"Child, if they would only open their hearts, I would be able to touch all with My Love. But, do they, do they want to? You know I do not force anyone to do My will.

I have given free will to all. Now dear child, I will not place a further burden on you for the present. I know you trust fully in My word for the referendum.

Sufficient for now. Come to Me - now rest in Me. I wait for you, My little one."

21ˢᵗ November 1995   -   Feast of the Presentation of Our Lady
<u>Before The Blessed Sacrament:</u>
Mary, the prayer on my heart this day is for all those addicted to

drink. We are all disturbed about the spread of drugs amongst the youth but first we must rid ourselves of the drink addiction in parents and adults, because of the example they give the young people.

Many of our youth are living in a drink culture. Wherever one or two parents are dependent on alcohol, the seed is planted in young people to find comfort and consolation and security in all forms of addiction also.

If we look into the homes of addicted parents or parent, we see the beginning, the bed of a disturbed or broken marriage.

Mary, save our land, save our people, help marriage to become a stable institution in our land again and there will be no need nor place for a divorce culture or ethos.

22ⁿᵈ November 1995
Before The Blessed Sacrament:
"My child, I know, I see the torment within you. Do not be afraid. It is My torment you experience now.

Child, the opposition are beyond themselves now. They see at last defeat facing them. I stand on My promise child. Trust Me. Trust. Remember a previous word - you stand between the arrows that are directed at Me - now.

I am in control. We will overcome the evil, the forces of evil that are trying now to destroy the institution of marriage. Child, I ask you to come away with Me and spend the next few days in prayer of intercession for My people and your country. Thank you My little one. Remember all is well - all will be well."

23ʳᵈ November 1995:
Resounding NO.

'No, let thanksgiving be your sacrifice to God.' Ps. 50.

Beloved, I thank You for the times I have no voice. All I know, You teach me.

Oh how I thank You for the stammer I grew up with. It was my saving grace. Truly You know all that is rest for each of us.

24ᵗʰ November 1995
Before The Blessed Sacrament:
Today, our country votes for divorce or no divorce. May the honour and glory be Yours and Yours alone. You show us the power of prayer. Bless all those who prayed and worked, that Your Holy Will be accomplished. May we never cease thanking You.

25ᵗʰ November 1995
Before The Blessed Sacrament:
"Rose, Rose, Rose - Do not worry. Keep hoping. Keep trusting. The last counted votes will decide.

I have My victory. I will always have the victory over evil. Much you will learn in the days ahead. You have been faithful over a little, now I will place upon your little shoulders, much, much greater.

Come back to Me later."

26ᵗʰ November 1995
Feast of Christ The King:
My Beloved, You know my thoughts this day. I know You are the Way, the Truth and my Life - my King.

Others I know are disturbed by my interpretation of the writing about the referendum. I regret causing any pain, but deep down, I carry Your peace. For me that is all that matters now - that Your will be done. It is not known yet what the final outcome will be. I know that You are in control and You can bring good out of evil. Maybe we all need a lesson. I am sorry if I mislead others with false hope. And yet I know You have Your own way of answering prayer. Always we must see the perfection of Your love and holy will in all circumstances. Here now in Your Holy Presence I surrender myself, to allow You do with me all You will. Above all else I ask for the virtue of humility - something I cannot achieve on my own.

Mary my Holy and Immaculate Mother, I ask for a spirit of loyalty, reverence and trust in my Lord and King.

Later
At home:
"Yes My child, I hide the present situation. I ask you to stand on faith now. Have faith in My word in the darkness of the present moment. All is not lost. All is well - very well. Remember these words always. I write them on your heart now. Give thanks for the peace, My peace that surrounds you. Keep out of the limelight as far as possible. It will drain all your energy and I need you My little one, My little Rose, for My plans for the future - remember."

29th November 1995 - (before meeting for Glencree)
Before The Blessed Sacrament:
Beloved and Holy One, we gather in Your name this night and in the presence of Mary, Mother of Peace and Reconciliation.

We come in love, to love and under Her powerful intercession to pray for peace in our land.

We repent, I repent of all I failed to do, my failure to answer Your call in the past and specially before the referendum. Please give us another chance and perhaps through this appeal to the High Court.

Let us support those who work so hard, so steadfastly in Your cause by our faithfulness in prayer, in loving reverence before The Eucharistic Presence.

30th November 1995 - Feast of St. Andrew
Before The Blessed Sacrament:
St. Andrew, I feel I have a special claim on Your prayer this day. My father's name was Andrew and a baby brother who died in infancy. Our land is so in need of the prayers of intercession of all who surround the Throne of the Most High. We stand on a precipice between good and evil. You keep telling us You have the victory over all evil. We believe in Your word. We ask for the same faith for all those drawn to despair, specially the parents of young people who are influenced by the evil peer pressure of these times.

Later :
Mary, my Holy Mother, clasp me to Your bosom. You know all I

carry in my heart - the pain of those I love.

Mary, how we must make You suffer - the tears we cause You when we reject Your Son, His word, His love, His love for others. Our land has sunk so low into paganism, liberalism and materialism. We are all part of the new culture. It has overtaken us unknown to ourselves. We have allowed the evil one to brain-wash us into submission.

Mary, once I learned to live in the womb of Christ. Help me now to regain my intimacy with my Beloved. Let me enter Your womb that my soul may be nurtured again, moulded and developed through Your love, to become one with Your Immaculate Heart, to become one with the Two Hearts of Love.

Tonight, the vigil of the First Friday is so precious to the Sacred and Eucharistic Heart of Your Son, Jesus. Oh Mary, help me to turn back my soul again to the place I seek to be, to where I belong.

1st December 1995 - 1st Friday
Before The Blessed Sacrament:
Beloved, oh Beloved, I regret all the wasted time last night. Please help me to change my ways. (My cold is much improved while I stay in bed. Direct me about going out to Mass this morning.)

Beloved, my one consolation is in the fact that each day I can begin again. Do not let me make the same mistakes as yesterday. As each day is another day nearer eternity, may each day bring me a step nearer to You.

Oh Beloved, today Your Sacred Heart is overburdened with love for each and everyone and so many out there are not aware of the pain of Your unrequited love. I carry in my heart one girl in particular. Please, please touch her, perhaps through another. So many young people are being drawn into the web of evil through peer pressure. But I know and believe, You have the victory over all. Nothing happens without Your permission.

Perhaps You seek to challenge all those in control in Church and state, all parents and adults with responsibility for young people, by their own example.

Does not Mary come again and again to call us back to prayer and repentance. Mary, we pray that through Your powerful intercession we, all the peoples of this land will receive a fresh outpouring of the Holy Spirit to change our hearts, our lives. Most of us are struggling, struggling, trying to fulfil the needs of Your Divine Son. May the Holy Spirit, Your Holy Spouse, the Spirit of truth and holiness, invade our hearts with His light this day and the days ahead. Mary, make me better, to be able to go to Glencree to-morrow for the Mass of the Generations.

Beloved, do not let me entertain thoughts that do not come from You. Beloved, I seek only the truth. Let me not make judgements on others. Only You know the state of a soul, specially of priests.
Tell me if I am wrong about the conclusions I come to about certain situations in the Church. We are all under attack in this day and age. May all who are struggling to follow You be protected from the spirits of division and confusion prevalent in our midsts. It would appear that on one is immune from their evil ways. St. Michael we call on you again and again, not to allow the ship of Peter to be dismantled and destroyed from within.

*Beloved, I am fearful at times, but I must never lose hope nor trust in Your promises to protect and safeguard us through the dark days ahead. Beloved, You remind me from the writings: 'Always look beyond the happenings taking place. Never lose hope. Always trust in My promises. **All is well. All will be well**.'*

Beloved, how do You have such patience with me? and surround me with such loving, holy and prayerful people. These people are a comfort and consolation to the Two Hearts of Love. And may all who come to Glencree tomorrow be abundantly blessed at the healing Mass for the Generations and specially the celebrants who give of themselves so unselfishly every month in their over loaded schedule.

Before The Blessed Sacrament:
Beloved, I unite my tears with Thine. This is the first time the tears cause me pain in my eyes. Beloved, why is this? Are they Your tears of pain? I wouldn't wonder at the pain we cause You. We have been so ungrateful for all the blessings You bestow on us always and forever.

Beloved, may I answer Your need of me now. May we forget about all the glitter and materialism of the Christmas season out there to answer the call of this Advent season.

I mustn't forget to thank You for the shield of peace surrounding me during these days since the referendum, in spite of the disappointment, hassle, pain in family etc. etc. You sustain me. I must walk in dark faith now. Bless all Your little ones - You army of little ones, Your faithful little ones, who comfort You in this faithless world where all the evil forces are hell-bent on taking all away from You. But how good to be able to rejoice with all the angels and saints in heaven in Your victory over all evil, here in Your Eucharistic Presence.

"Oh My dear, dear child, your words comfort Me. Truly you comfort Me My little one. Remember to walk steadfast in faith, in hope and in My infinite, constant and everlasting love. How I love all. How I desire all, to know My Love. Oh how I suffer when My love is rejected. Oh the 'thirst' I suffer - greater than My thirst on the Cross - for all souls, specially those who reject My Love. My child, My dear child, continue to pray specially for the Church, the division in the Church. You face dark days ahead. Child, I place a heavy burden on your little shoulders. You will be aware and sense the evil, the evil forces that seek to destroy and divide all My followers. But, I must allow you this awareness, that you will be open to write all I ask of you. You will not be frightened by these writings because I will be with you to protect you. Keep trusting dear child. Trusting is synonymous with loving, truly loving. I use your little mind now in all its weakness - loss of memory at times, lack of concentration in prayer. Always remember child to come to Me as you are. I accept you as you are. I love you as you are. I trust you as you are. I use you as you are."

Beloved, I am always making mistakes. I lack the discernment of others.

'Come Holy Spirit through the powerful intercession of the Immaculate Heart of Mary' *on Her coming feast-day on 8th December - into our families, Church, government, peoples of this land and throughout the world - Amen.*

5ᵗʰ December 1995
Before The Blessed Sacrament:
"I speak to the legislators of this land. You are not dealing now with the Church, the people but Me, your God. If you do not listen to My words, the word I speak to you through others of My choosing, you will have much to answer for in the days ahead.

I beseech you My children, each and everyone of you, I consider My children whom I love. I give you another chance. I will make it possible to have another referendum in the near future. Do not impose your will on My little ones. Let each one have a free vote in the forthcoming referendum. Do not decide for others. I give you My freedom. Give this same freedom to others. You cannot change the gospels, the word of the gospels to suit the prevailing circumstances of these days."

Beloved, I await Your directions about this further word. Beloved, You honour me to tell me these things before they come about - but You will have to lead me every step of the way. Thank You for the people of discernment and wisdom You place around me. Thank You, but how do I curb my impulsiveness at times. Help me, help me.

8ᵗʰ December 1995
Before The Blessed Sacrament:
Oh Mary of the Immaculate Conception, thank You for inviting me to Glencree to-night. I didn't expect to be able to go but with You caring for me, I know it will not make my chest any worse.

Oh Mary, You have been so good to me down the years. How I have neglected You, but now I am depending on You for everything in my life - my body, mind and spirit, my family and above all my relationship with Your Divine Son.

Mary, I want to give all in preparation for His coming this Christmas. We live in very disturbing times now in our land. We cause such pain and suffering to the Sacred Heart of Your Son and Your Immaculate Heart. The Church is in a great time of purification and our government is in great need of purification also. And we, the people of this land are truly in need of a great purification also. But, I know now that if we give ourselves to You, place ourselves under Your care and protection, You will see us through all the dark days ahead. But I believe dear Mother Mary, that living in You, You will lift us above the dangers and sustain us in the darkness and bring us into the glorious light, the light of truth and holiness.

Mary, we prepare for our visit to Glencree tonight. May our hearts be open to the graces and blessings You have prepared for us all. We bring our country specially tonight. Truly it would appear that the cease-fire is in danger. We deserve no better. We failed You in the referendum, but we look forward in hope that the legislators will be open to the word Your Son has given them. Mary, we go with expectant hearts this night. May it be a pilgrimage of love that will bring comfort and consolation to the Two Hearts of Love. We bring Kay especially and all who would wish to be there and cannot go, in our hearts and all we carry in our hearts also. You know all Holy Mother, You see us as we are. You hear our cries of petition and above all You know our needs. We give ourselves, we offer all to You this night, this special night.

Oh Jesus, help us to love Mary with Your Heart. Oh Mary, help us to love Jesus with Your Heart, to become one with the Two Hearts of Love.

"My child, My precious child, I will speak to your heart during the Holy Sacrifice of the Mass, My greatest joy, My greatest suffering. Later you will write all. Yes child, I wouldn't, couldn't disappoint My little one. Do not be anxious."

9th December 1995
Before The Blessed Sacrament:
"Yes child, I did tell you that I would disclose to you later about your consecration yesterday."

Child, I cannot reveal only step by step My need of you now, but you will join with Me in intercession for your land. I do not want it to be a heavy burden on you, but you will be conscious of your calling now as you are called to pray. I will guide you moment by moment, day by day. Yes child, you are not ready, but I do not call you because you are ready. I will be with you every step of the way. Part of your burden will be not being able to reveal all I speak to your heart to others but those whom you can depend on and who support you in prayer. Child, yes you will join Me in the rosary of tears now each day or night as I lead you. I have sent many to support you in this mission. Be not afraid. You do the will of My Divine Son Jesus in being obedient to My Immaculate Heart."

15ᵗʰ December 1995
Before The Blessed Sacrament:
Beloved, I know I shouldn't be anxious about the word of 5th December. I take another's discernment as very important. Perhaps I should see the whole question in a new light, the light of freedom of the individual and see others rendering of new relationships. I suppose I feel from a different angle, from a more possessive view that perhaps is my own weakness. I need the spirit of truth to invade my heart if I am to be open to Your word. Beloved, I call on You. I trust in You that all is well and all will be well about this.

"Child, I will speak to your heart at length about this later. You are right to a point, but I have much to teach you yet. Be patient little one. All is well, do not be anxious. I will speak clearly to you when I need you to move about the word and how I want it made public."

16ᵗʰ December 1995
(I was wondering whether I should stay in bed with my cold)
Mary :
"Child, I am waiting for you as usual. Do not fail Me. I take care of you. My Son awaits you also. We miss you. Spend some time with Us also. It is most important now. We look forward. My Son is waiting to give all of Himself."

16ᵗʰ December 1995
Before The Blessed Sacrament:
Beloved,

"My child, come closer, I wait for you in the depths of your heart and soul. Come deeper, find Me in the depths of your being where I dwell at oneness with you My child. How I seek all and so few are listening to My call, My invitation these days - so much preparing for the material and commercial side of Christmas, a way of life now. But My little ones give hope, My hope for My future Church which is in the making now. The time is fast approaching when the needs and wants of future generations will be more easily pleased and satisfied.

Yes children, future Christmases will be different, must be different for the sake of all. Yes child, My little ones are becoming aware of the changes that must come about for change. Something must happen to allow My people make this change, to seek this change within themselves. This is the great conversion that will be offered to all in the days ahead.

Be not afraid dear, dear children, all who seek Me have nothing to fear. They will welcome all that must happen to bring new life, new hope to all those whom are now downcast.

Oh dear child, how I wait with a longing and thirsting Heart to welcome all My children, I mean all into My Eucharistic Presence where I will lift all burdens from their hearts and where they will find comfort and consolation for the days ahead.

Dear, dear child, I do not want to burden you with the heaviness I carry in My Heart, shared with the Immaculate Heart of your Holy Mother, so close to you now.

Child, dear child, all I ask of you is to sit here with Me. Do I not know the state of your mind at times. Yes child, all I ask is that you sit with Me. Have I not been your comfort and consolation down all the years. Give Me again the burden of your weaknesses. This was the most beautiful, one of the most profound lessons I have taught you over the years. Why not share these with others now. All I taught you was to be shared with others My little one. You will recall all as I desire and the opportunities will be given you. You have always been open to the urgings of the Holy Spirit in the past. Child, do not fail Me now.

The two I will send you, I prepare them also. They have much work ahead of them. They walk in My footsteps, they bring hope and consolation to My people, My little ones who hunger and thirst for Me in a materialistic world.

Yes child, put all your trust in the Two Hearts of Love and all will be well. All is well. Rest in Me now My little one. Prepare for My coming in the Eucharist later. Thank you. Thank you, My little one.

I ask all T.D.'s, Senators, people in government to claim freedom of conscience in the next referendum. You mustn't allow power to dominate your choice. I give you freedom of choice. Take it."

21ˢᵗ December 1995
Before The Blessed Sacrament:
I write a letter to my Beloved about my cold.

"My child, My child, your chest needs attention now. Ask P.... Be guided by her. T.... will pray with you. I will make a doctor available to you. Go home now My little one. Rest."

Mary:
"...... dear, do you not know that I answer all your prayers. Do not be afraid of the darkness. It is your protection. I am working in secret, though. I keep all hidden from you. My plan is unfolding in the way that is best for all, according to the Will of My Divine Son. Child of My Heart, do not fear. Do not be anxious, all your waiting is not in vain. Do I not know all the pain of darkness. Did I not suffer much darkness and anxiety during the days on My journey to Bethlehem. And oh the joy of that first Christmas. You will share in this same joy with Us. The star and the cross were in that first Christmas."

21ˢᵗ December 1995
Before The Blessed Sacrament:
"Do rest now with Us. We wait for you. Put all other matters aside now. Bring all those We place on your heart before The Two Hearts of Love in the Blessed Sacrament. Yes child, We await your attention now. You have had many interruptions that cannot be helped. Spend the next hour here with Us. My child, My little one, now that We are together, I can speak to your heart.

Oh child, how many of Our dear, dear children remember Us this night. The city is teaming with people rushing everywhere to find happiness and peace outside of Us. Politicians talk and talk. How many pray beforehand for wisdom. They have many advisors. Do they consult Us in prayer. Do they call on Us for direction? Child, We blessed this land down the years, preserved it from many disasters. You were an island, detached from the continent but now totally under the influence of the rest of Europe. We tried to preserve you from the evil forces of materialism and pluralism but now many feel you are losing the battle against evil forces from outside.

People, My people, the time has come when I ask you to stand up and be counted. Many do, but you must have leadership. You must unite. Do not let the spirit of division and confusion keep you apart."

22ⁿᵈ December 1995
Before The Blessed Sacrament:

"Oh My people, My dear people, oh to have this place of refuge, this home to receive Me on these busy days approaching the Christmas. We find rest here. The Holy Family has found a home to rest our weary wearying Hearts in a busy world of little holy peace, the peace We came to give, to share with all. Thank you Our dear children, all who come to visit Us. So few visit in the churches now, except where We are exposed. At least We are not alone. Oh children, We have so much to give, to share in a world, your

> *So few visit in the churches now, except where We are exposed.*

country of full and plenty this Christmas time, but not for all. We come to all seeking all, but all hearts are not open to welcome and receive Us. All are so busy, a little business and preparation is good. It was always meant to be a time for rejoicing, families coming together, lost ones returning. How We invite all back to the fold at Christmas time. Truly it is a time for children, but some spoil it by being over generous. Children can accept very little and find joy and contentment in the little things of life but, commercialism has taken over to replace the simple way of rejoicing, with it's own power and greed.

Children, I lament with you in your suffering with the burden society has placed upon you at this season. It is now beyond the power of mankind to change this, and it will pain Me more than you to make the changes that I have prepared for your own good and happiness for the future. It will be, as it were, a reversal of progress, worldly progress has to be terminated for it's own sake. This new technological age hasn't brought happiness.

Take nuclear power - such progress and now mankind has seen for itself the possibility of it's own self-destruction.

My people, My people, My children, My children everywhere ... and because of My Love, great changes must take place.

Pray dear children, that your hearts will be open and ready and the transition will be painless like a loving parent correcting a loving child, protecting a loving child from dangers of which they are unaware.

Oh children, all heaven awaits you all this Christmas with Hearts burdened with the excessiveness of Our Love for one and all."

23rd December 1995:
(Early morning - 12.30 a.m.):

"My child, My little one, I call you now to give Me your attention. I seek to speak to your heart. At this time you will have no interruptions. All is quiet and We will not be disturbed.

Yes child, I seek to speak to your heart. My Heart is heavy now. Much is taking place now that is not to My liking. Oh child, you understand My pain at Christmas time. How I suffer for souls, innocent souls, so easily lured into evil by evil. So much, so many evil forces are at large to draw My little ones into their net of evil. They make this holy season an excuse for their evil ways.
Oh child, My Heart bleeds for the innocents and this time was meant to be a celebration of joy, holy joy. The evil now abounding is greater by far than the rejection of My Holy Mother and St. Joseph at Bethlehem.

Yes child, do pray the rosary of tears now in honour of My Holy Mother. She suffers much to see My rejection by so many, but oh the comfort and solace We receive from all Our little ones. Thank you all for this night. You can never know nor understand now, the joy that filled Our Hearts in your home this day and this night. We thank you both for your generosity. Your goodness will not go un-rewarded and your blessings will be manifold."

28ᵗʰ December 1995
Before The Blessed Sacrament:

Beloved, thank You for the joyous days spent with the family over the Christmas. You were there also - and blessed all, though some were ignorant of Your Advent. Beloved, Your goodness is beyond our understanding and realisation - and You do not blame us, me especially for my lack of appreciation. I would like to feel as You once gifted me, but now I must remember to give You all You take from me. Spiritual fasting is good for us all, and as You say - the darkness is our protection if we accept it for Your sake.

Beloved, I was deeply impressed by the video I saw last night of a late, late show, shown some months ago. My Beloved, I see the events all coming to pass as You foretold - painful but also full of hope. Although we are only at the beginning of our purification (Church in a wider sense) surely it is a challenging time for all, but full of hope for the future.

28ᵗʰ December 1995
Before The Blessed Sacrament:

"Child, dear child, I take care of the child who causes much pain within her family. She suffers much herself. Yes My child, she needs much patience and understanding to cope with now. She needs much love within the family in her present state. This will repay the most in the end - for the child and the family. This is not unusual in adopted children specially in the present times, when everything is brought out in the open and causes confusion, specially during the teenage years.

My child, My dear children, trust Me and My Holy Mother. She has a special love for these children. She understands their difficulties and the pain they cause their adoptive parents who choose to rear them out of their love and generosity. Let them keep remembering - they are Ours, Our children, on loan. Give them to Us. It may be a heavy cross to carry now, but you will be rewarded in time by them and a hundred-fold by Us."

Thank You Beloved for Your word of comfort and consolation for another. Oh Beloved, the joy it gives me to share Your words of comfort with others. You know of another who awaits such a word also, a word of direction and guidance in his present work for Your

Holy Mother. I know You will not fail him but he wants the direction by way of a writing. He hopes and believes that You will give it through me.

Beloved, the year 1995 is drawing to a close. Many feared that terrible things would happen to us in this year and You preserved our land and people and the cease-fire lasted, though You said on one occasion that it rests on a pinhead. We continue to pray that it will not be broken by the evil forces that seek to destroy us. Beloved, we fail to give thanks for all the graces and blessings You pour out on us moment by moment, day by day. We do not deserve Your loving kindness today and everyday, and yet when I look around me now and see the wonderful people of prayer about me, I know why You are loathe to punish us for all the evil in our midst.

29ᵗʰ December 1995
<u>Before The Blessed Sacrament:</u>
'We are making progress when we do not understand.'

"I am love
I am a great God
Nothing impedes My Will
My Heart is open to you
My arms outstretched
The power of LOVE
Will out,
Will act tremendously
Let your fears abate
As the great tide of LOVE approaches."
(from Sr. K.)

29ᵗʰ December 1995:   *Beloved, time and time again I seek You and Your Holy Mother in other places, and You have to remind me that here in the Eucharistic Presence You are more present to me than anywhere else. Truly I understand and know that the Holy Mass is the ultimate and yet there are times and occasions we seek You in the extraordinary. I know Mary comes at times to confirm, increase our faith and bring back those of little faith and of no faith.*

I also realise now that I cannot help others by my planning of events and situations, that might help. My greatest weapon is in prayer and trusting in Your Holy Will, and then I know, all is well and all will be well.

It is very difficult dear Lord for parents of teenagers, particularly in the present climate of peer-pressure, our educational system, and our culture generally of materialism and pluralism, to stand up and be counted and yet there are those who have chosen the better path. I know we mustn't despair nor lose hope in the power of God, the goodness of God in the world of this day and times. Yes Lord, may the year of 1995 end, the year 1996 begin on a note of hope, buoyant hope in the word received this day through Your loving daughter, Kathleen. I praise and thank You, the Two Hearts of Love, for all Your goodness and loving kindness to me in the past, present and future, for the 'five', their families, relatives and friends and Fr. Cathal, Fr. Dan, that we will be open to Mary's plan for Glencree and Ireland in the year ahead.

31ˢᵗ December 1995
Before The Blessed Sacrament:
Beloved, many are preparing to celebrate the passing of 1995 and to welcome in the new year of 1996.

Beloved, we are sorry for all the pain we caused You in the past year and we pray that the coming year will be more fruitful, more of a comfort and consolation to The Two Hearts of Love. Our poor land is in dire straits - so in need of a fresh outpouring of the Holy Spirit to bring about a change of heart, from the youngest to the oldest.

Beloved, You give us Yourself in the most Blessed Sacrament, the Ultimate Presence and a living image of Yourself to strengthen, encourage us, to comfort and console us in our daily struggles, on our pilgrimage here on earth. And Beloved, so many do not know this, do not want to hear this. Their hearts are closed. You have gifted some with this knowing over the years, and yet I do not appreciate nor use this knowledge as I should. Oh Beloved, through the Immaculate Heart of Your Holy Mother, I pray for a greater reverence, understanding and appreciation of this great gift that You come to my home in Your great Sacrament of Love.

Beloved, I thank You for all the people who have visited You in our home down the years. Now many who visited You here have and can visit You in their own parishes now, to be touched by the same Power and Love that emanated here in Your Eucharistic Presence.

You blessed us by choosing us at the time for this great honour. We never did enough, could never do enough in praise and thanksgiving and loving, in response. But, others responded in such a way that it continued over the years and was extended to It's present. Over the years I saw the wonderful healings of body, mind and spirit that were effected in people - the comfort and consolation people received in Your Eucharistic Presence and now, others all over the country are receiving and knowing the love that emanates when they spend time with You before Your Eucharistic Presence. We are all a part of the renewed Church You are preparing with others throughout this land and throughout the world. Some of us are not responding as we should and yet You do not reject us but sustain us as we try each day to begin again. Now that we are on the edge of a new year, we call on You, we call on Mary to be with us as we try to be responsive and faithful to our calling.

Thank You Beloved Jesus and Holy Mother Mary, for the grace to enter 1996 with a renewed hope in our hearts. You know dear, dear Holy One, all I carry in my heart. Bless them all, they are all Yours.

MARY

"You have been truly blessed by being allowed
to have Eucharistic Adoration in your home.

This is a singular blessing from My Divine Son.
Treasure it My little one.

I am with you at all times,
specially when My Son is in residence in your home.

He is also accompanied by all the angels and saints.
Remember this always My dear little one.

It will help you dear child in your commitment.
We wouldn't have given you this honour unless We
knew you were capable of responding.

We bless you both for your generosity.
Much and many are the blessings We bestow on
you, your home, your marriage,
your offspring, your endeavours."

MY FLESH IS REAL FOOD
AND MY BLOOD IS REAL DRINK

THE PINNACLE OF MY HUMILITY

Learning to be We(e)

List of Publications:

Volume I
Extracts from writings 1976-1988

Volume II
Extracts from writings 1989-1995

Volume III
Extracts from writings 1996-1999

Kolbe Publishing
November 1999

.